SALVATION
AND THE SAVAGE

An Analysis of Protestant Missions and
American Indian Response, 1787-1862

ROBERT F. BERKHOFER, JR.

ATHENEUM 1976 NEW YORK

Dr. Robert Berkhofer, Jr., is currently a professor of history at the University of Wisconsin. He has served as an advisor of doctoral fellowships for American Indians to the Ford Foundation and is now on the Board of Planners of the forthcoming 18 volume *Handbook of North American Indians*, which will include several of Dr. Berkhofer's articles.

ACKNOWLEDGMENTS

NOT TO include acknowledgments in a work of scholarship would deceive no one but the author. William N. Fenton of the New York State Museum, Anthony F. C. Wallace of the University of Pennsylvania, Miss Erminie Wheeler-Vogelin of Indiana University, Miss Wilma C. Martin of the Department of Justice, Evon Z. Vogt of Harvard University, Bernard G. Hoffman of the National Science Foundation, Miss Mary E. Young of Ohio State University, and Mr. and Mrs. Henry F. Dobyns of Cornell University will recognize their influence in these pages.

Anyone who uses manuscripts knows the large debt a researcher owes to the people who not only make them available but also help him find his way to the ones he needs. Although I have thanked many of these people in the following pages, I would like to express special appreciation for the aid of Miss Mary Walker of the American Board of Commissioners for Foreign Missions, Mrs. Lela Barnes of the Kansas State Historical Society, and my friends at Houghton Library, Missionary Research Library, Library of Congress, and the National Archives.

I also owe gratitude to those who read the manuscript with an eye to improving communication between the author and the readers of the book. Even though this came at the expense of the author's ego at times, I thank my wife, Paul W. Gates of Cornell University, and Rodney Loehr of the University of Minnesota for their penetrating criticism.

Acknowledgments

Parts of Chapter VII, "Christians versus Pagans," is reprinted by permission from *Ethnohistory*, X (Summer 1963).

I wish to thank the Social Science Research Council for their faith in this work as expressed by a fellowship for research and writing.

This book was the corecipient of the McKnight Foundation Humanities Prize in American History for 1963.

R.F.B.

CONTENTS

PREFACE TO THE ATHENEUM
PAPERBACK EDITION

THE GREAT challenge in writing American Indian history is to move beyond the story of a tribe to a general history of Indians in the United States (or North America). The many problems of evidence, perspective, and moral judgment in tribal histories follow the historian who essays an overall history of Indian Americans. The greater obstacle is offered, however, by the vastly increased magnitude of the dilemmas inherent in all Indian history: diversity versus uniformity, trend versus process, and persistence versus change. Unique to the writing of a general history, unlike a tribal history, is the problem of focus facing the historian when he attempts to encompass the many pasts of Indian people into one narrative. Since my book suggested one solution to these many predicaments, this new introduction affords an opportunity to present my subsequent thoughts on the problems involved in a general history of native Americans and, at the same time, to place my earlier effort in a broader intellectual context.

The problem of focus is caused by the great number of peoples comprehended under the term "Indian" and the multiplicity of their specific histories. Both before white contact and until quite recent times, Indians did not exist as such beyond the stereotype of white men following the nomenclature of Columbus in calling all native Americans, *los Indios*. In their own opinions they were divided into many peoples, not unlike how the Europeans viewed themselves. Just as the European explorers and those who followed them across the Atlantic lived in many nations and sub-regions, spoke many tongues, and practiced different customs, so the original Americans were separated into an even larger number of societies with many cultures and a multitude of languages. Scholars estimate that, prior to white contact, the population of one to two million living north of the present-day Mexican border spoke at least two hundred mutually unintelligible languages. Although it is fallacious to presume coincidence between cultural areas and language groups, anthropologists believe as many cultures as languages may have existed in the same territory. When we remember that each society possesses its own history, we see immediately the problem of combining these numerous pasts into one story.

To overcome the problem of focus as well as for other reasons, almost all writing in American Indian history concentrates on the relations of whites with native American peoples. The documentary evidence traditionally utilized by historians usually derives from white sources and reflects the attitudes and prejudices of its producers. Small wonder the resulting historical writing viewed Indian peoples' pasts through white eyes and according to white values. This tendency to white-centered Indian history was fostered by the assumption of the historical guild to explain, or at least trace, how the present developed from the past. In line with this working hypothesis, Indian histories, tribal as well as general, emphasized those forces and factors that seemed responsible for producing the plight of the Indian peoples we know today on reservations and in urban ghettoes. Since those forces appeared white-generated, Indian history became mainly the tale of white-Indian relations. The seeming consistency over space and time of white perceptions and policies provided the focus so lacking in the diversity of tribal Americans' actions and attitudes, and so only reinforced tendencies inherent in the nature of evidence and the assumptions of the profession. Thus white-produced sources, historians' assumptions, and the necessity for a unifying theme in the narrative all joined to make the history of white-Indian relations synonymous with Indian history in general. Even those historians who professed moral indignation at past whites' actions and espoused an Indian viewpoint in their preface inevitably focused, in the body of the book, on the same white-centered story of white-Indian relations as those writers they opposed.

In response to this one-sided version of the Indian past, native

American spokesmen and scholars and their white friends in and out of academe call for a new Indian history. Whether those demanding the new Indian history see it as the scholarly counterpart of the so-called red power movement or not, they all seek a more favorable evaluation in history books of the past and present accomplishments of those peoples denominated "Indians." Not only do many of these spokesmen want Indian contributions and heroes given their proper prominence in books purporting to portray accurately the history of the United States, but they also want historians to stop depicting Indians as passive objects in their own pasts. They protest the standard treatment of showing Indian actions as mere reactions to white-created situations rather than as innovative and meaningful activities in the determination of native Americans' destinies. In short, these people argue that Indian history should be a story in its own right rather than a mere by-product of the white story. What they seek is nothing less than an Indian-centered history of Indian-Indian relations to replace the older white-centered story of white-Indian relations. As its name suggests, Indian-centered history would focus on Indian actors and intratribal relations, and shift white actors and relations to the periphery of attention. In this view, white deeds are not neglected but placed in their proper perspective as just some of the factors causing Indian peoples' destinies rather than the chief or main cause.

The justice and the desirability of Indian-centered history is undeniable in these days of awareness of cultural imperialism and racial prejudice. The question remains, however, is it possible to employ this focus in the writing of general as opposed to tribal Indian history? Although few tribal pasts have been treated according to the aims of the new Indian history, at least such an achievement seems conceptually possible. This is not the case with an overall history of Indians. No book attempting to tell the story of several or more tribes, let alone of all Indian peoples, has avoided following the path of a white-centered history of white-Indian relations—no matter how diversely they portray native cultures or what moral tone they adopt. Such a failure by all authors, be they red or white, suggests that the constraints of focus and theory are matters more of conceptualization than of morality. The perplexity seems to result from the inability to resolve satisfactorily the three dilemmas of diversity versus uniformity, trend versus process, and persistence versus change. Regardless of the strategy chosen to reconcile these antimonies, all authors, including this one, veer in the end toward the history of white-Indian relations as the only theme providing a unity of narrative for general Indian history. Difficult enough on the level of tribal history, the resolution of the dilemmas appears insuperable on the level of an overall history of Indian Americans. The exact nature of the challenge becomes clear in a brief examination of the dualities involved in the dilemmas.

Certainly diversity confronts the investigator everywhere he searches in Indian histories. Not only does he find a multitude of social and political units with a startling variety of cultures, but also he soon discovers that migrations, inter-tribal trade and warfare, and normal cultural developments made Indian peoples' pasts dynamic long before Columbus or even Leif Ericson arrived on the North American continent. Religions, languages, economies, political territories, and other aspects of life had all been changing before white men came. The white invasion of the continent only increased the diversity of the original Americans' histories, for to the previous dynamics were added those created by the relations with the Europeans. When contact occurred, under what circumstances, and where as well as who met whom depended as much upon native American migrations and actions as upon the extent of inland expansion by various Euro-Americans. In brief, Indian Americans' histories varied both before and after contact, although gathering evidence in the former period may prove far harder than in the latter time.

Uniformity appears as conspicuous in Indian histories as diversity. Before white contact, for example, the investigator is struck by the similarity in political procedures prevailing among those tribes resident in what is now Canada and the United States, or by the ecological balance obtaining between those same tribes and their physical environment. After contact, the general outlines of so many histories appear even more similar. Often the initial relations were friendly and trade was sought eagerly by both sides in contact. Hostility succeeded friendship as whites over and over demanded land cessions and trade goods, and as alliances altered the internal relationships in tribes. Again and again, Indian peoples went to war with whites only to suffer defeat eventually after some victories. After loss of land and maybe removal, most Indian peoples were confined to reservations, and a long period of colonial dependency began under the tutelage of government agent, missionary, teacher, and farmer. Some Indians changed, some resisted, but all were affected by the new political, social, and cultural conditions surrounding them. Among many tribes, prophets appeared and revitalization movements broke out in opposition or accommodation to the new order. Factions arose to reflect the various opinions in the tribe and outside as to what their future should be. In the twentieth century, sundry pan-Indian movements have attempted to achieve first-class citizenship for all native Americans, to assert treaty and legal rights, or to preserve ethnic pride and "Indian" customs.

Such apparent uniformities led many anthropologists to attempt the more scientific study of the trends and processes involved in Indian history. Under the notions of culture change, diffusion, assimilation, and, especially, acculturation, anthropologists sought to delineate precisely those recurring patterns found in the pasts of all or most tribes. The "high period" of such study, to use one scholar's term, dated from the "Memorandum on the Study of Acculturation," authored in 1936 by a Social Science Research Council committee composed of Robert Redfield, Ralph Linton, and Melville Herskovitz. The intensity of the investigation after World War II found expression in 1953 in another document issued by a second SSRC committee on the topic. Its culmination appeared in 1961 as the 550-page *Perspectives in American Indian Culture Change*, which studied acculturation in six tribes by as many scholars[1]. Anthropologists had hoped through the compara-

1. My book is part of this effort to discover uniformities through process, as the original introduction reveals. In point of fact, the framework of analysis was conceived, the research completed, and the first version written as a dissertation between 1956 and 1960.

tive study of social and cultural dynamics to discover an overall process or a few processes that recurred in the histories of all or most tribes. While a general trend in the direction of white men's cultures was evident in most tribal histories, no one certain sequence of change emerged in every tribe. At best, the many studies produced a list of evolving possibilities in any given tribal history, depending on such variables as initial cultural integration and social structure, the nature of the inter-cultural roles in contact, and the relative power of the groups meeting. In brief, many processes were found but no one process or trend for all tribal histories. Both trends and processes appeared present, but neither occurred in the same manner or in the same order in each people's past. The dilemma of reconciling repetitive and wide-spread processes with the overall trends in each story remained unresolved. The anthropologists' lack of success in this endeavor means that historians are still left with the predicament of diversity and uniformity as well as that of trend and process, and thus the search for focus also remains to bedevil them.

To these quandaries must be added the dilemma of persistence and change. This dilemma revolves around two equally obvious facts about the histories of Indian peoples: attitudes, behaviors, and life-styles change drastically over the years at the same time as cultural patterns and personality traits persist into the present and social relationships and ethnic identities survive from the past. In spite of the enormous pressures by white nations to eliminate Indian peoples or force their incorporation and assimilation into the dominant societies, native American social relationships and self-identification endure into the present, and earlier attitudes and beliefs outlast conquest and reservation confinement. At the same time, Indian Americans no more live like their aboriginal ancestors than Euro-Americans live today as their predecessors did in 1500. In this way, the lives of the original Americans have been as dynamic as those who conquered them. In other ways, however, as with white Americans, some customs, behaviors, and beliefs remain the same or similar to what they were in older times. In either case, different Indian peoples manifest various degrees of persistence and change in the same and different things.[2]

The perplexity of this dilemma stems not so much from things both persisting and changing but from how to measure the two phenomena. The analyst can sort out more easily in theory than in practice what changed and what continued. For example, anthropologists frequently differ about the aboriginality of certain customs and patterns. Much that was once thought pre-contact in a tribe's experience is now believed to have originated after that time or was influenced heavily by white practices. Conversely, other things hitherto presumed the result of white contact have been proven part of the original life style of the particular people. The more complex or evanescent the behavior or pattern, the more difficult to get agreement on its modification or continuance over long periods of time. So perplexing is the problem that historians and anthropologists disagree generally on the degree of persistence and change in Indian histories. Anthropologists stress the persistence of earlier social and cultural patterns and even basic personality into the present, while historians emphasize the drastic changes wrought by white practices, government policies, and military might. Such varying perspectives result partly from disciplinary viewpoint, different sources of evidence, and from examining different aspects of life, but the divergence also comes from the difficulty in measuring persistence and change. Until scholars agree upon the definition of what is being measured and how it is measured, this dilemma will continue to confound those in quest of Indian history.

As can be seen from this brief discussion, the three dilemmas are as entwined with each other as they are connected to the problem of focus in the writing of a general Indian history. The problem of focus exists because of the number of native peoples and

2. The dilemma of persistence and change also accounts for the ambiguity in the use of the term "Indian." Descendants of aboriginal Americans are called Indians at the same time as they are judged as having lost the "Indianess" of their ancestors. Since we do not consider an Englishman less English although he is far removed from Anglo-Saxon culture, why should we accuse a native American of being less Indian because he does not exhibit an aboriginal culture?

the diversity of their specific histories. The less uniformity among the various histories, the harder it is to combine them into one history. The uniformities present in the various histories result from the similarity of trends and processes, and point to a possible focus, but such hope is shattered because no overall trend or process can be discerned in all the pasts. Even if such trends or processes existed, the historian of the general story would still be faced with reconciling the differing rates of change and persistence with the chronology of his overall story. Thus diversity is linked with lack of overall trend and process, and this in turn causes the difficulty of finding a focus or unifying theme for an overall history of Indian Americans. Looked at another way, the predicament of general Indian history arises from the lack of coincidence between chronological time in the separate histories and even those processes and trends that do occur in so many of them.

Because of these problems, the historian of general Indian history, regardless of moral suasion, must choose the best strategy available to accomplish his ends. Each strategy will have its advantages and disadvantages. A strategy stressing white perceptions and policies possesses the benefit of more unity and focus than one emphasizing the diversity of Indian histories. Conversely, such a choice must neglect the rich diversity of multiple Indian pasts to gain its focus. If the strategy of seeking uniformities is chosen, then at its best it uncovers cycles, sequences, or something akin to these. The advantage of unity is retained but it is usually achieved at a high level of abstraction far removed from the record of concrete historical time. In my own case, such a strategy meant developing at great length the determinants presumed responsible for these uniformities. Therefore my book is both abstract in its discussion of sequences and white-centered in its treatment of causation. On the other hand, an Indian-centered approach works well for the story of one tribe but fails or serves poorly at best for the story of all Indians, because it is so difficult to combine all of native American diversity conceptually into one narrative and still remain loyal to the guiding spirit of the perspective. As a result of these many difficulties, the goal of a good general history of Indian Americans remains unattained.[3] Whether it is impossible only future experiments will tell.

Perhaps general Indian history will come about through native Americans' actions instead of historians' research and conceptualization. Successful pan-Indianism would provide a basis for tracing the growth of such a movement from aboriginal community to tribe to national organization.[4] Such a socio-political development would provide the necessary focus for an overall history of Indian Americans by at long last giving a real meaning to the term "Indian." To that extent the stereotype created by Columbus' category *los Indios* in the fifteenth century might become a living reality in the twentieth, and thereby make possible a general Indian history. Just as whites invented Indians conceptually, then "Indians" would have invented a true Indian history.

Robert F. Berkhofer, Jr.

3. I say this in spite of Edward Spicer's valiant effort to surmount the problems of general history in his little volume, *A Short History of the Indians of the United States*. He begins his essay with the dynamics of the variety of Indian pasts before white influences, but the bulk of the book reverts to the story of white-Indian relations. His solution to the problems of an overall history is somewhat better accomplished in his earlier volume, despite its title: *Cycles of Conquest: The Impact of Spain, Mexico, and the United States on the Indians of the Southwest, 1533–1960*.

4. This point is developed at greater length in my article, "The Political Context of a New Indian History," *Pacific Historical Review*, XL (August 1971), 357–82.

INTRODUCTION

Books upon any phase of American Indian history usually contain, explicitly or implicitly, a denunciation of American policy and express sympathy for the maltreated aborigine whose culture, if not life, was destroyed. Modern scholars find a delicious irony in the disparity between classic American ideals and the actual treatment of the first Americans. Yet in terms of recent cultural theory, an even greater irony is the failure of these writers to see that earlier Americans acted as they did for the same reason that the Indians reacted as they did. Both groups behaved according to their own cultural systems. Any contradiction that the scholar finds between professed ideals and actual behavior is more a reflection of the ambivalence in past cultural assumptions than deliberate hypocrisy, unless proved otherwise, and even then the incongruity may be explained by reference to conflicting values. Thus current indictments of past American conduct are on the same plane as earlier American condemnations of savage society. The Americans of the past were victims of their cultural values just as their latter-day judges are victims of today's beliefs.

The "Century of Dishonor" approach affects the writing of Indian history on two levels: the discovery of facts from documentary evidence, and the synthesis of those facts into a history. With the concept of culture part of today's culture, the modern analyst should be able to understand the past in terms of the actors' conceptions of their situation. While the historian can judge the resulting behavior of these actors according to his own beliefs, such an evaluation frequently distorts the reading of past evidence. Only an analysis of the contact situation in terms of the participants' beliefs will meet the canons of historical accuracy. While the culture concept does aid documentary analysis, it does not provide the writer with the framework he needs for synthesis. Recent work of anthropologists upon acculturation, however, suggests a possible alternative for the historian who seeks a new approach to the organization of his materials in an attempt to avoid moral judgments.

Probably the most significant turning point in the acculturative history of an Indian tribe was the loss of political autonomy. Although this point, which was usually marked by the commencement of reservation life, may have been indefinite and varied in different cases, it was no less conclusive in each tribe. Before this point, the Indian tribal members enjoyed a traditional way of life free of outside interference; they adopted the customs and artifacts of other peoples as they chose. Anthropologists call contact under these conditions "nondirected" or "permissive." After the loss of political autonomy, such freedom no longer existed, for the Indians lacked the opportunity to put space between them and the alien culture or to destroy its representatives among them without effective reprisal. Henceforth, the members of the Indian society were under the effective control in some form of the agents of Anglo-American civilization. These representatives had an interest, and ultimately the force, to alter some of the behavior and attitudes of the Indians. Such contact has been termed "directed" or "forced."[1] In these two different circumstances, the definition of acculturation must vary. The classic defini-

[1] Edward H. Spicer *et al.*, *Perspectives in American Indian Culture Change* (Chicago, 1961), 519-21; Edward P. Dozier, "Forced and Permissive Acculturation," *American Indian*, VII (Spring 1955), 38.

tion of it—as "culture change that is initiated by the conjunction of two or more autonomous culture systems"[2]—applies only in nondirected contact where neither society has the power to coerce the other. However, under directed contact, acculturation, as E. A. Hoebel says, is "the process of interaction between two societies by which the culture of the society in subordinate position is drastically modified to conform to the culture of the dominant society."[3]

Under either definition, the study of acculturation must concern at least two sets of variables: the nature of the two cultures in contact, and the conditions under which contact takes place.[4] But the relationship between the two sets of variables depends upon whether contact was directed or not. In the period of Indian autonomy, both cultures in contact must be studied, but the item or customs "borrowed"[5] must be examined in Indian terms in the end. Once autonomy is lost, the very nature of contact is determined by the nature of the culture in the dominant position. In other words, the Americans called the tune to which the Indians danced regardless of tribal culture. This tune was composed of certain Anglo-American social and legal concepts enforced by the power of white army and red desire for treaty annuity. Since Anglo-American civilization probably possessed basic unity over long periods of time, we should expect certain recurring long-term sequences in response to the tune. Thus American civilization not only determined the white responses but also delimited the Indian responses.

[2] Social Science Research Council Summer Seminar on Acculturation, "Acculturation: An Explanatory Formulation," *American Anthropologist,* LVI (December 1954), 974-75.

[3] Edward A. Hoebel, *Man in the Primitive World* (2d ed., New York, 1958), 643.

[4] This scheme is based on Evon Z. Vogt, "The Acculturation of American Indians," *Annals of the American Academy of Political and Social Science,* CCCXI (May 1957), 139-40.

[5] The classical use of the term can only refer to the period of nondirected contact.

Introduction

This does not mean that there was one overall sequence,[6] but rather that the number of possible responses was far fewer than the number of tribes in contact.[7]

The history of Protestant missionary activity and the Indians' response to it offers a valuable opportunity to test this hypothesis. For the purposes of study, the time was confined to the period between the founding of the first missionary societies in the new nation in 1787 and the Civil War, when the turmoil of the conflict closed many mission stations. These seventy-five years, undeservedly neglected by historians,[8] seem more valuable for initial intensive study than the colonial period or the post-Civil War period for several reasons. First, the many missionaries of all denominations who worked during this time afford a far larger sample of Protestantism, hence a greater variation in white culture, than do the few famed colonial workers. In almost any year of this neglected period, more Protestant missionaries served among the Indians than during the whole colonial period, and they used more methods of approach. Secondly, the far greater geographical extent of operations provides a wider sample of Indian cultures than in colonial times.[9] After the Civil War, the federal government utilized the missionary as Indian agent in an attempt to better Indian administration;[10] thus an artificial uniformity is introduced

[6] Such as Scudder Mickeel, "A Short History of the Teton-Dakota," *North Dakota Historical Quarterly*, X (July 1943), 196-97.

[7] Cf. A. P. Elkins, "Reaction and Interaction: A Food-Gathering People and European Settlement," *American Anthropologist*, LIII (April 1951), 164-96, and my approach.

[8] In reality, the last general work of some magnitude on the Protestant missions was Joseph Tracy, ed., *History of American Missions to the Heathen, from Their Commencement to the Present Time* (Worcester, Mass., 1840).

[9] Of course, due to the time limits set by the study, most tribes were Eastern Woodland.

[10] On post-Civil War developments, consult Henry Fritz, *The Movement for Indian Assimilation, 1860-1890* (Philadelphia, 1963); and Loring B. Priest, *Uncle Sam's Stepchildren: The Reformation of United States Indian Policy, 1865-1887* (New Brunswick, N. J., 1942).

into the later period that is not found earlier. In addition, these eight decades present Indian tribes in as many stages of acculturation as any time in American history. Lastly, but most important, the missionary seemed to spearhead the drive for acculturation at this time. Hence, missionary activity during this period offers a useful focus for the study of Indian-white relations.

The true test of the sequential hypothesis demands a comparative approach to the vast quantity of historical data available in this period. All Protestant denominations that operated during this time were studied as to aims, organization, and geography of endeavor. The tribes studied ranged from the Oneidas, Tuscaroras, and Senecas of New York State and Wisconsin; the Cherokees and Choctaws of the South; the Ojibwas and Sioux of the Great Lakes area; the Ottawas in Kansas; to the Nez Percés in the Far West. Briefer examination was made of responses by the Wyandots, Shawnees, Potawatomis, Iowas, Osages, Weas, and Creeks. In each case, the story of a mission was traced through the letters of its staff, and frequently government agents' reports, from its founding to its extinction or survival in 1862. After more than a dozen sequences of this sort, comparison with each other determined certain regularities and the minimum possible number of sequences.

The chapters that follow reflect the results of this comparative approach. Rather than a presentation in traditional narrative form, the book is organized to present the determinants of the sequential patterns in analytical form. Chapters I through IV deal with the missionaries' general attitudes and assumptions and how these were exhibited in their efforts at inculcating education, religion, and farming in their charges. Chapter V covers the relationship between the missionaries and other whites in the representation of American civilization to the Indians. From these chapters, the reader will learn the exact nature of the white culture in the contact situation and the conditions under which Americans wished Indian-white relations to occur. Chapter VI turns to the Indian response as seen in the general reactions to the missionary and the plight of the Indian convert in his own tribe. The succeeding chapter looks at Indian reaction in the more general context of acculturation and cultural change theory. An epilogue views the inevitable outcome of the missionary enterprise given the participants' cultural assumptions in the contact situation.

The book does not contain the customary conclusion, for the volume's organization represents the conclusions derived from the research. It does not pretend to be the last word upon Indian history. Sequential analysis as demonstrated in this monograph offers one opportunity to avoid the usual moral fables that masquerade as Indian history. Only the research and construction of all the sequences involving Anglo-American subcultures and aboriginal cultures in contact from early settlement till today would produce a complete framework for the true history of the Indian. In this sense, this monograph points to methods, and hopefully conclusions, beyond the narrow scope of its topic. The accuracy of the methods and the validity of its conclusions can and should be tested by others.

Chapter One

THE GRAND OBJECT

EVEN the briefest outline of Protestant missionary activity during the years 1787-1862 reveals enormous changes in numbers of workers, scope of operation, and fields of labor. At the end of the American Revolution, only a dozen missionaries survived to carry the Gospel to the perishing aborigines. These earlier workers had been inspired by the Great Awakening, but the large-scale operations of the nineteenth century flowed from that wave of pietism, called the Second Great Awakening, which began in the 1790s and was responsible for so much of the organized benevolence, particularly Congregationalist and Presbyterian, throughout the next century. After the War of 1812, a nationalistic current joined the wave of pietism to alter the course of missionary history.

Inevitably the status of the new nation compelled the societies organized from the end of the Revolution to the War of 1812 to resemble the efforts of the colonial period more than the future. The triple lack of money, national outlook, and cultural independence restricted the size of the societies, the location of fields, and experimentation with new methods. Small budgets meant few missionaries who had to serve in tribes close to society headquarters. Difficulty of transportation and communications as well as the triumph of state and regional bonds over national loyalties reinforced this result. All these factors determined that the missionary work of this period be individual preaching and itineracy similar to colonial work.

The spirit of nationalism after the War of 1812 transformed the scope of missionary operations. Denominations organized churchwide societies which drew funds from members in all regions. Missionary directors envisioned stations strung across the continent, and an expanding economy and improved transportation made these dreams practical. More money meant larger stations staffed by missionaries who lived there year-round. Better transportation offered access to tribes farther away and enabled the missionary to serve the cause of Manifest Destiny.

Once part of national life, missionary operations were affected by national events. In the 1830s the federal policy of removing all the Indians to west of the Mississippi forced the relocation of most mission stations. Once relocated in the West, the missionaries directed their attention to Indians indigenous to the Indian territory as well as to regaining the confidence of their former eastern charges. At the same time, missionary societies expanded operations to the "wilder" savages of the Plains and even to the natives of the Pacific coast. In the next decade, the slavery issue began to hamper mission effort. The missionary current as part of the national tide broke upon the rocks of sectionalism. As denominations divided into northern and southern churches, missions were parceled out between the contending parties. Finally the turmoil of the Civil War compelled many mission stations to close their doors, and for that reason provides an appropriate terminal date for this study.

Yet for all these changes over time in staff, field, and size, the goal of Protestant missionaries and their patrons remained ever the same. In spite of denominational differences, there is striking similarity in the announcements of missionary aims.

Each newly founded missionary society professed as its main purpose the propagation of the Gospel. The first two societies founded after the Revolution expressed this aim in their titles—the Society for Propagating the Gospel among the Indians and Others in North America (1787) and the Society of the United Brethren for Propagating the Gospel among the Heathen (1787). The New York (1796), the Northern (1797), the Connecticut (1798), the Massachusetts (1799), and the Western Missionary Societies (1802) wrote such an aim into their constitutions—usually article two.[1] In a later period both the American Board of Commissioners for Foreign Missions (1810) and the United Foreign Missionary Society (1817) proclaimed a like goal.[2] The Baptists who drafted the preamble to the constitution of their society in 1814 hoped the organization would direct "the energies of the whole denomination in one sacred effort for sending the glad tidings of Salvation to the heathen, and to nations destitute of pure Gospel light."[3] For the same reason the Missionary and Bible Society of the Methodist Episcopal Church in America (1820) desired to send missionaries and Bibles as "messengers of peace to gather in the lost sheep of the house of Israel."[4]

This goal, as conceived by directors, missionaries, and their patrons, rested upon the basic Protestant tenet of the acceptance of the Bible as the sole standard of faith. To the Gospel was ascribed a miraculous power to produce con-

[1] The best story of these societies and their aims is in Oliver W. Elsbree, *The Rise of the Missionary Spirit in America, 1790-1815* (Williamsport, Pa., 1928).

[2] Mary Walker, "Report on Statements of the Purpose of the American Board," April 27, 1950 (mimeographed), 2-4; Constitution of United Foreign Missionary Society, Article Two, in Records of U.F.M.S. Board of Managers, ABC 24.II:5-10, American Board of Commissioners for Foreign Missions Papers, deposited at Houghton Library, Harvard University. I wish to thank Miss Mary Walker, librarian of the American Board, for permission to use these papers. I have used the notational system devised by Harvard for these materials. Henceforth, I shall only cite these papers by this notation, which always commences with ABC.

[3] Constitution appears in William Gammell, *History of American Baptist Missions in Asia, Africa, Europe and North America* (Boston, 1840), 19.

[4] Address of the Missionary and Bible Society, in Nathan Bangs, *An Authentic History of the Missions under the Care of the Missionary Society of the Methodist Episcopal Church* (New York, 1832), 29-32.

version.[5] But was no human agency necessary? In the missionary directors' opinion, all that was necessary in frontier *white* settlements destitute of religion was simply to collect funds sufficient to have Bibles printed, distributed, and expounded.[6] But what was needed for the savage? The Word could be conveyed by preaching, but in that situation the listener relied partly upon the authority of the speaker. Should not the convert be able to determine matters of salvation for himself by reference to the Supreme Source as revealed in the Holy Scriptures? Was not literacy required, and did not this necessitate the founding of schools? Furthermore, did not the Indians need an economic system that would support the requisite schools and churches? In short, was not civilization as well as religion necessary to the establishment of scriptural self-propagating Christianity? As one writer said, "the Gospel, plain and simple as it is, and fitted by its nature for what it was designed to effect, requires an intellect above that of a savage to comprehend. Nor is it at all to the dishonor of our holy faith that such men must be taught a previous lesson, and first of all be instructed in the emollient arts of life."[7]

Others replied that the miracle of the Word was enough and, in fact, only through prior acceptance of the Truth and its reforming virtues could the savages be elevated to civilization. Persons who claimed otherwise supported the atheistic doctrine that a means more powerful than the Gospel miracle was available. The Word was the means of God,

[5] Cf. Ernst Troeltsch, *Protestantism and Progress: A Historical Study of the Relation of Protestantism to the Modern World* (Beacon ed., Boston, 1958), 54, 65.

[6] For domestic missionary work, see Colin B. Goodykoontz, *Home Missions on the American Frontier, with Particular Reference to the American Home Missionary Society* (Caldwell, Idaho, 1939).

[7] Bishop Warburton, quoted in Thaddeus M. Harris, *A Discourse, Preached November 6, 1823* (Boston, 1823), 8. This pamphlet is one of the most thorough analyses of this position. Also see John Lathrop, *A Discourse before the Society for Propagating the Gospel among the Indians and Others in North America, Delivered on the 19th of January, 1804* (Boston, 1804), 17-21.

and conversion was not by human agency but by the Holy Spirit—"it is the *power of God* to salvation."[8] One minister thus advised the infant New York Missionary Society: "Instead of waiting till Civilization fit our Indian neighbors for the gospel, let us try whether the gospel will not be the most successful means of civilizing them. . . . One Christian institution alone, the holy sabbath, will go farther to civilize them in a year, than all human expedients in a century."[9]

Thus the issue was joined, and the debate over whether first to civilize or to Christianize the savage raged throughout the pre-Civil War period. Denominations, on the whole, took different sides of the question,[10] but regardless of

[8] John M. Mason, *Hope for the Heathen: A Sermon, Preached in the Old Presbyterian Church, before the New York Missionary Society at Their Annual Meeting, November 7, 1797* (New York, 1797), 41-44.

[9] *Ibid.,* 43. A scorching refutation of Harris' discourse favoring civilization first is Benjamin B. Wisner, *A Discourse, Delivered on November 5, 1829* (Boston, 1829), 5-14.

[10] On the Christianity-first side were the Moravians, e.g., August G. Spangenberg, *An Account of the Manner in Which the Protestant Church of the Unitas Fratrum, or United Brethren Preach the Gospel, and Carry On Their Missions among the Heathen* (London, 1788), 103-104; Edward Rondthaler, *Life of John Heckewelder* (Philadelphia, 1847), 79. The strongest advocates of the civilization-first side were the Quakers: *Summary Account of the Measures Pursued by the Yearly Meetings of Friends of New York, for the Welfare and Civilization of the Indians Residing on the Frontiers of That State, with Extracts from Two Letters Relating to the Subject* (London, 1813), 9; "Summary of the Proceedings of the Committee on Indian Civilization, Appointed by the Yearly Meeting Held at Baltimore, in Maryland," in *Sketch of Further Proceedings of the Committees Appointed by the Yearly Meetings of the Friends of Pennsylvania and Maryland, for Promoting the Improvement and Gradual Civilization of the Indian Natives in Some Parts of North America* (London, 1812), 29-35; Report of Committee of Forty-five, October 2, 1795, in Indian Committee Minutes Book, I:1-22, MS volume deposited at Department of Records of Philadelphia Yearly Meeting of the Religious Society of Friends, Third and Arch Street, Philadelphia, Pa. I wish to thank Howard H. Brinton, custodian, and Miss Mary Olgilvie, secretary, of the Department of Records, for permission to use the records under their care.

Almost as ardent on this side were the Congregationalists and Presbyterians: "Instructions from the Directors of the New York Missionary Society to Their Missionaries among the Indians," March 19, 1799, in Minutes of the Directors of the New York Missionary Society, ABC 23.III; "Additional Instructions to the Missionary to the Northwestern Indians,"

position, neither side ever precluded either the spread of Christianity or civilization to the exclusion of the other. Rather the argument over the method of propagating the Gospel was reduced to a simple precedence of procedure in the dissemination of two desirable objects. Furthermore, in the actual operations of various societies, civilization and Christianity were inextricably combined. Thus the problem was really more one of semantics than of actual difference, and the real question becomes: What meaning did the words "civilization" and "Christianity" possess in the minds of missionaries and their supporters in the seventy-five years under review that inevitably made them link the two concepts together?

Civilization as conceived by Americans in this period meant an upward unilinear development of human society with the United States near the pinnacle. Comprising civilization was a cluster of institutional arrangements that

June 11, 1801, *ibid.;* Records of the U.F.M.S. Board of Managers, November 2, 1819, ABC 24.II:95-97 (cf. Annual Report of U.F.M.S. for 1819; Zechariah Lewis, *Letter to a Member of Congress, in Relation to Indian Civilization* [New York, 1822]); Western Foreign Missionary Society, Instructions, quoted in Clifford M. Drury, *Presbyterian Panorama—One Hundred and Fifty Years of National Missions History* (Philadelphia, 1952), 47-48; *Annual Report of the American Board of Commissioners for Foreign Missions,* 1817, 154; *ibid.,* 1823, 101-102; *ibid.,* 1824, 49-50; *ibid.,* 1833, 136-38; *ibid.,* 1842, 69-73 (henceforth cited as A.B.C.F.M., *Report*).

The Baptists and the Methodists took varying positions. Baptist civilization-first arguments were: Annual Report of Baptist Board, 1821, in *Latter Day Luminary,* II (May 1821), 389; "General Circular to the Baptist Associations throughout the Union," *ibid.,* I (May 1818), 40; Annual Report of American Baptist Missionary Union, 1849, in *Baptist Missionary Magazine,* XXIX (July 1849), 206-12. Baptist Christianity-first arguments are: Annual Report, 1844, *ibid.,* XXIV (July 1844), 161-62; Annual Report, 1854, *ibid.,* XXXIV (July 1854), 201-202. Methodist statements favoring the religious side are "Removal of the Indians beyond the Mississippi," *Christian Advocate,* III (December 19, 1828), 62 (cf. "Methodist Missionaries among the Indians," *ibid.,* II [July 18, 1828], 181); *Annual Report of the Missionary Society of the Methodist Episcopal Church,* 1839, 4. Methodists advocating the other side are: James B. Finley to J. Soule, November 4, 1821, in *Methodist Magazine,* III (January 1822), 29-31; *Annual Report of the Missionary Society of the Methodist Episcopal Church,* 1850, 64-65; *ibid.,* 1851, 70-72; *ibid.,* 1854, 77; *ibid.,* 1856, 63.

Americans sought to achieve between the Revolution and the Civil War. Economically, they moved toward allowing economic individualism free rein under the liberal state. Politically, they first realized republicanism, then democracy. Lastly, the liberty of the individual was foremost in their minds; hence all social institutions were assumed to exist solely for the benefit of the individual (white) members of society. Ethnocentric Americans believed that the idea of progress pointed toward a future modeled upon their way of life; thus their manifest destiny, if not mission, was to spread their superior institutions into the western wilderness and even beyond their country's boundaries.[11]

To the missionaries as to most Americans, Protestantism was an inextricable component of the whole idea of civilization.[12] Quite explicit was the thinking of Stephen Riggs, the famous Sioux missionary, who wrote in 1846: *"As tribes and nations the Indians must perish and live only as men!* With this impression of the tendency of God's purposes as they are being developed year after year, I would labor to prepare them to fall in with *Christian civilization* that is destined to cover the earth."[13] In another instance, a committee on Indian missions reported to the Baptist Board director in

[11] Tracing the concept of civilization is Charles A. and Mary R. Beard, *The American Spirit: A Study of the Idea of Civilization in the United States* (New York, 1942). Also important are Arthur A. Ekirch, *The Idea of Progress, 1815-1860* (New York, 1944); Ralph Gabriel, *The Course of American Democratic Thought* (2d ed., New York, 1956), 3-104; Albert K. Weinberg, *Manifest Destiny: A Study of Nationalist Expansionism in American History* (Baltimore, 1935); Stow Persons, *American Minds: A History of Ideas* (New York, 1958), 71-213.

[12] See Gabriel, *Course of American Democratic Thought*, ch. III, "Christianity and the Democratic Faith"; Troeltsch, *Protestantism and Progress*. A popular book on the relationship is Will Herberg, *Protestant, Catholic, Jew: An Essay in American Religious Sociology* (new ed., Garden City, N.Y., 1960). For an example that government officials could not think of civilization without Christianity, see T. Harvey to W. Medill, October 8, 1844, in *Senate Doc.* no. 1, 28 Cong., 2 Sess. (1844-1845), 433-37.

[13] S. R. Riggs to D. Greene, April 29, 1846, ABC 18.3.7.III:223 (his italics). For an earlier view, see Samuel Blatchford, *An Address Delivered to the Oneida Indians, September 23, 1810* (Albany, 1810).

1822 that it "anticipated a period not far distant when the Indian shall be brought not merely to unite with the white men in the worship of God, but cooperate with them in the business of Agriculture and Trade." Therefore, it advised the board to work toward self-sustaining Indian settlements "where the refinements of civilized society shall be enjoyed" and to work among red men yet savage so as "to carry the gospel and the blessings of civilized life to the dark and distant regions of the west, until the rocky mountains shall resound with harmony and praise and the shores of the Pacific shall be the only boundary of this wide sweep of human civilization and Christian benevolence."[14]

Perhaps the best illustration of the fusing of civilization and Christianity was an article entitled "Influence of Missions on the Temporal Condition of the Heathen." The author felt "the office of the gospel is to bring the heathen nations to be, in these respects, such as Christian nations are; to put every people under heaven on the highest platform of civilization and religion, of art and science, of learning, prosperity, and usefulness, of happiness and social advancement." In fact, the author maintained, "We cannot too highly prize the influence of Christianity in promoting true civilization. We contend that a true Civilization cannot exist apart from Christianity." On this basis, he could assert:

In general, the unevangelized nations are deficient in intellectual and moral culture. If they have any inventive genius, it is not called into action. They do not furnish their share to the advancement of society, and the prosperity and wealth of the world. They make no valuable contributions to the discoveries of science or the arts of life. Most of them add no important productions to the literature of the nations, nor even have a literature of their own. Generally, they have no idea of the

[14] Minutes of the Baptist Board, April 26, 1822, deposited at Treasury Department, American Baptist Foreign Mission Society, 152 Madison Avenue, New York City. I wish to thank Forrest Smith, treasurer, for allowing me to look at typewritten extracts from these records pertaining to Indian work.

diffusion of education among the masses, both male and female; their priests are ignorant and overbearing; their rulers are narrow and prejudiced; they have no properly instructed physicians, no schools for the benefit of the deaf, dumb and blind, no hospitals for the sick, no institutions of benevolence, nor mutual aid associations. There is nothing in their books, if they have any, nor in their religious rites, elevating, purifying and expanding; but on the contrary, that which is degrading and polluting.

The heathen possessed "no chambers of commerce, no insurance companies, no banks, no joint stock associations," because, the author pointed out, "The complete development of the tender affections, and the institution of those associations by which men express their interest in one another, and aid one another depends almost entirely upon the diffusion of Christianity."[15]

Thus the missionary held the basic values of his culture in common with other Americans. He dressed in a certain style, possessed but one wife, believed in abstract justice, ate certain foods in certain ways, and favored the specific economic and political system of his fellow countrymen. At the same time missionaries represented a subculture within American life, for they emphasized theology and morals more than other people. They adhered more vigorously to the sexual code, were more honest (or were supposed to be), propounded the theological system more seriously, and were more concerned with the minor taboos of drink and the verbal prohibitions against obscenity, profanity, and blasphemy. As one anthropologist has pointed out, "A missionary is thus a member of his society, characterized by the culture of his society, and differing only from other members of his society by emphasis in particular aspects of his culture."[16]

Because missionaries and their patrons dealt with alien

[15] "Influence of Missions on the Temporal Condition of the Heathen," *Baptist Missionary Magazine*, XXIX (April 1849), 101-105.

[16] G. Gordon Brown, "Missionaries and Cultural Diffusion," *American Journal of Sociology*, L (November 1944), 214.

cultures, many of them saw what few people generally see —the functional interrelationship of the various institutions in a society. Thus they saw, in a sense, that they spread what is called today an integrated cultural system, an entire blueprint for living which structured institutions and the roles individuals played in them. In the most sophisticated statement of missionary purpose written during the period, the American Board of Commissioners for Foreign Missions recognized this situation: "Missions are instituted for the spread of scriptural self-propagating Christianity. This is their only aim. Civilization, as an end, they never attempt; still they are the most successful of all civilizing agencies, because (1.) a certain degree of general improvement is in a self-propagating Christianity, and must be fathered as a *means* thereto; and (2.) a rapid change in the intellectual and social life is a sure out-growth therefrom."[17] It was for this reason that missionaries found themselves, as one confessed, "entirely unable to separate religion and civilization,"[18] and the version of their culture which they propagated may be called, as some of them termed it, "Christian civilization." Therefore, the only good Indian was a carbon copy of a *good* white man, or as a Methodist missionary wrote, "In the school and in the field, as well as in the kitchen, our aim was to teach the Indians to live like white people."[19]

Hence the Indian utopia envisaged by the directors of the various societies was the same—a mirror of their ideal world. Such was the goal of the United Foreign Missionary Society's Board of Managers:

Let then, missionary Institutions, established to convey to them the benefits of civilization and the blessings of Christianity, be

[17] "Outline of Missionary Policy," A.B.C.F.M., *Report*, 1856, 51.

[18] J. Potter to S. B. Treat, July 14, 1849, ABC 18.6.3.III:28.

[19] John H. Pitezel, *Lights and Shades of Missionary Life: Containing Travels, Sketches, Incidents, and Missionary Efforts, during Nine Years Spent in the Region of Lake Superior* (Cincinnati, 1857), 57.

efficiently supported; and, with cheering hope, you may look forward to the period when the savage shall be converted into the citizen; when the hunter shall be transformed into the mechanic; when the farm, the work shop, the School-House, and the Church shall adorn every Indian village; when the fruits of Industry, good order, and sound morals, shall bless every Indian dwelling; and when throughout the vast range of country from the Mississippi to the Pacific, the red man and the white man shall everywhere be found, mingling in the same benevolent and friendly feelings, fellow citizens of the same civil and religious community, and fellow-heirs to a glorious inheritance in the kingdom of Immanuel.[20]

Not only did the missionaries' concept of civilization set their goals, but it also explained the object of their benevolence. That the early nineteenth-century Americans could not observe the Indian without measuring him against their own society has been amply demonstrated by Roy Harvey Pearce in his book, *The Savages of America*.[21] A certain type of cultural relativity and moral absolutism combined in this view to show that though white and red man were of the same biological mold, the Indian possessed customs that fitted him perfectly to his level of development in the history of man, but the level was far inferior to that of the white European. The savage was the zero point of human society. As Pearce remarks, "Savage life and civilized life are realms apart, separated by centuries of cultural history, or by entirely different environmental situations, most likely by both."[22] Thus even seemingly superior savage traits were products of an inferior society and, though excellent for this level, were backward in a more advanced society. Men of the period evaluated not so much the qualities of individual Indians but those of a society by placing it in relation to their own in such a way that the idea of progress solved the

[20] Records of U.F.M.S. Board of Managers, May 5, 1823, ABC 24.III:209 ff.
[21] *The Savages of America: A Study of the Indian and the Idea of Civilization* (Baltimore, 1953). This paragraph is based upon this book.
[22] *Ibid.*, 103.

problem of evaluation. The idea of history as progress made it possible for them to comprehend the other culture as earlier, hence morally inferior. Therefore, seemingly objective observations on Indian character were always normative analyses of what the Indian should be in terms of nineteenth-century American society. Thus were the aborigines accounted uncivilized.

Persons engaged in the missionary movement particularly viewed the objects of their benevolence in this manner, because moral evaluation was their stock in trade. Pearce uses the Moravian missionary John Heckewelder[23] and Jedidiah Morse, who not only was influential in missionary circles but shaped many Americans' views of the Indians by his writings,[24] as illustrations of his thesis. Even missionaries sympathetic to the Indian described him as if he were a negative prototype of all that was civilized. For instance, in the middle of the nineteenth century, a Baptist missionary could write after years of contact with his flock:

Very indefinite, not to say erroneous, ideas prevail respecting the character and condition of the Indians. . . . The milder affections are active, especially in their domestic relations, and their hospitality to strangers is proverbial. Parental love is strong to a fault, and the death of a child is not infrequently the occasion of extreme agony, though proportionally brief. . . . Their cruelty to persons of war results more from errors in their moral code than from a cultural thirst for blood.

They have some marked peculiarities:—they are naturally, or from habit, indisposed to regular industry, impatient of restraint, fickle, prodigal, and reckless. The fiercer passions, envy, jealousy, anger, malice, by no means lack occasions of development; and without the restraint of higher principles than their reason and the light of nature afford, sometimes rage to a fearful degree. In the conjugal relation they have special need of the gospel to strengthen and hallow the marriage bond.[25]

[23] *Ibid.*, 115-17.   [24] *Ibid.*, 96-97.
[25] Francis Barker to ——, October 2, 1851, in *Baptist Missionary Magazine*, XXXII (February 1852), 59.

The directors of the missionary societies may not have held such enlightened views. An article in one religious magazine noted, "the condition of the heathen is truly deplorable. Their minds are in gross darkness. They know not the True God nor the only Savior of lost sinners; and are strangers to that blessed gospel which 'has brought life and immortality to light.' They are exceedingly depraved, and enslaved to sin, Satan, and the world."[26]

In light of these attitudes, missionaries and their supporters believed both Indian institutions and Indian "character" had to be transformed. The necessary institutions were those already possessed by Americans. As a Presbyterian missionary remarked, "It is to make these [savage] abodes of ignorance and degradation, as happy, as gladsome, as the happiest and most gladsome village in our peaceful land."[27] The arrogant savage was to be turned into a man of humility who implicitly believed, "Industry is good, honesty is essential, punctuality is important, sobriety essential."[28] This new man also abhorred idleness and considered labor good for the body and "not unprofitable to the spirit."[29] The Christian Indian was to manifest "tenderness of conscience, a docility, and a desire for further instruction" in the great mysteries.[30] Yet many missionaries wanted him also to show "Yankee enterprise—go ahead determination."[31]

What was the method required to achieve these goals of character transformation and civilized institutions? Fieldwork was to be a simple matter of instruction to be accom-

[26] "Condition of the Heathen," *Foreign Missionary Chronicle*, V (March 1837), 45. Although this paragraph refers to all heathen, the Indian was not exempted from the generalization.

[27] W. O. Smith to Kerr and Cloud, July 22, 1833, AIC 3:1:4. AIC stands for American Indian Correspondence deposited in Presbyterian Historical Society, Philadelphia.

[28] Joseph Elkinton Diary, February 11, 1828, transcript in Friends Historical Library, Swarthmore College.

[29] *Ibid.*, April 23, 1827.

[30] A.B.C.F.M., *Report*, 1824, 70-71.

[31] L. H. Wheeler to S. B. Treat, February 17, 1854, ABC 18.4.1.I:235.

plished quickly—if all men were rational. Not thinking in terms of cultures as is done today, but in terms of "human nature," the missionaries and their patrons assumed the same system of basic values was held by savage and civilized alike.[32] If a savage merely lacked knowledge of the more advanced condition to which human society had evolved, then a missionary had but to point out the way and the savage would adopt it. Any right-thinking savage should be able to recognize the superiority of Christian civilization when shown him. Thus in regard to secular knowledge, the New York Missionary Society directors instructed their missionary among the Tuscaroras to "persuade" the Indians "by every rational motive to the practice of civilization, and to relish the enjoyments of domestic society" by pointing out to them that the whites increased in population because they farmed. "This argument will operate on the feelings of the patriotic Indian, and will serve to establish with convictive energy the arguments adduced from self interest, so clearly evinced in the diminution of bodily fatigue, in the alleviation of mental anxiety, & improvements of domestic comforts; [and] will strengthen [and] confirm the more powerful [and] weighty motives derived from the obligations of Religion."[33] Likewise with Christianity, since Protestantism embraced the highest evolution of morals, the missionary had only to mention its superiority over savage degradation to secure mass conversion. Thus, not only were the goals of mission societies prescribed by the sponsoring civilization, which was only to be expected, but even the method used to achieve

[32] E.g., "Methodist-Mission among the Indians," *Christian Advocate*, II (July 18, 1828), 181. The author states, "Human nature is the same whether observed in the savages of the forest, or among the higher walks of civilized life; and whoever conforms to the apostolic mode of preaching may expect . . . success."

[33] "Additional Instructions to the Missionary to the Northwestern Indians," June 11, 1801, in Minutes of the New York Missionary Society Directors, ABC 23.III.

these aims developed in line with a preconceived image of the Indian rather than through field experience.

Since conversion to Christ and civilization was conceived as an instructional problem, mission stations were educational establishments in the broadest sense. There the Indians would be persuaded by "right reason" and rationally calculated self-interest to adopt the white religion and ways, and would learn how to pray, farm, and behave. Whether the stations were large model communities in the form of manual labor boarding schools or small model families as represented by a missionary couple, all stations served three functions—piety, learning, and industry—and were to model school, church, home, and farm. Only a detailed examination of these efforts in terms of the missionary mentality will persuade the reader how no custom was too picayune for censure and change, and no demand too sweeping and drastic in the missionaries' attempts to revamp aboriginal life in conformity with American ideals.

Chapter Two

NURSERIES OF MORALITY

A PRIMARY aim of American education in the nineteenth century was the conscious development of personal character through moral training. The inculcation of the virtues assumed to be based on the Christian religion constituted such instruction. Since missionaries were active participants in their culture with a particular emphasis on this phase, their approach to Indian education was dominated by this training. Their adherence to their culture also determined their use of contemporary pedagogical methods and curricula no matter how poorly suited to their immediate goals—let alone to the entire transmutation of Indian life. Their blind acceptance of their own culture also meant the translation of minor habits and even ridiculous practices into the Indian schools, as well as the more secular qualities generally known as the middle class virtues.[1]

Missionary belief in the inferiority of aboriginal customs and morality only emphasized the necessity for the character training of the youth, for they aimed to revamp Indian life by raising a godly generation. The missionary hoped to snatch the children before their "habits of life" were formed and teach them to become "fluent readers, write a good hand," and see them "well instructed in the arts and customs of civilization, refined and docile in their manners, [and] have their minds stored with considerable knowledge of Christianity."[2] By thus instructing the untrained children the missionaries would, as Gideon Blackburn said, "not only rescue the rising race from savage manners, but also to light up beacons, by which the parents might gradually be conducted into the same field of improvement."[3]

Such a child-training theory demanded close attention to every detail of an Indian youth's life. Minor habits in this view were as important as primary habits. Of all habits, punctual and regular attendance was the most essential, for if there were no children in school, there could be no education. Besides, the missionaries considered a well-ordered life an intrinsic good.

Irregular attendance and tardiness were particularly the bane of the day school. In a detailed statement of Sioux attendance for three terms in an American Board school, Stephen Riggs presented the pattern in vivid statistics:

TERM	*AVERAGE ATTENDANCE*[4]
First	10-15 3/5 per week for 6 weeks.
Second	12 1/5-33 1/2 per week for 12 weeks in morning.
	4 2/5-8 1/4 per week for 3 weeks in afternoon.
Third	10-34 per week for 11 weeks in morning.
	4 1/5-11 1/5 per week for 11 weeks in afternoon.

Not only were the scholars irregular in their day-to-day attendance but also in their attendance during the day.

---

[1] For the moral element in American education of that period, see R. Freeman Butts and Lawrence A. Cremin, *A History of Education in American Culture* (New York, 1953), 214-17; Richard D. Mosier, *Making the American Mind: Social and Moral Ideas in the McGuffey Readers* (New York, 1947); Merle Curti, *The Social Ideas of American Educators* (New York, 1935), 60-61; William K. Dunn, *What Happened to Religious Education? The Decline of Religious Teaching in the Public Elementary School, 1776-1861* (Baltimore, 1958).

[2] A. Finney *et al.* to J. Evarts, August 27, 1823, ABC 18.3.1.I:42-43.

[3] G. Blackburn to J. Morse, November 10, 1807, in *Panoplist*, III (December 1807), 322-23.

[4] "Report of Average Attendance of the Lacquiparle Mission School Commencing in the Quarter July 15th, 1839," ABC 18.3.7.II:58. For an even more detailed statement, see *Senate Doc.* no. 1, 26 Cong., 2 Sess. (1840-1841), 378.

They cared little for punctuality or endurance. Thus the Quaker teacher on a Seneca reservation recorded how a child might drift in about ten o'clock and then more children would arrive until the greatest attendance occurred about noon. They would gradually leave until the last scholar departed about four o'clock.[5] Even in boarding schools, turnover was high. In the first year of the Iowa school, only one boy of the twenty students admitted at the beginning remained after a year. The remainder spent nearly half the time at home.[6] Letter after letter to missionary headquarters complained about attendance, regardless of the tribe or time. The parents in semiagricultural tribes claimed, just as rural white parents did and still do, that their offspring were needed at home.[7] In the tribes of migratory habits, attendance was even more irregular.[8]

In addition to the economic reasons, disappointments and jealousies caused irregular attendance. Many parents and children expected much more concrete results from the "magic" of reading than mere literacy after attainment of such an arduous mystery. Some Sioux, for example, thought the mere writing of a request for a gift and the presentation of the slip of paper to the missionary would make him grant their wish. When the missionary paid no attention to the magic paper, they angrily denounced the school: "the book lies—the book is not WAKAN."[9] Many natives feared the missionaries would demand compensation for their teaching in the future. They preferred to retain their land and kept their children at home. If the teachers demanded no compensation, then reasoned the Indians, the schools must bene-

[5] See Joseph Elkinton Diary for the years 1818 and 1819, transcript in Friends Historical Library, Swarthmore College.

[6] W. Hamilton to W. Lowrie, February 3, 1848, AIC 4:3:103.

[7] E.g., see Jacob Taylor *et al.* to Philadelphia Indian Committee, July 6, 1797, in Dept. of Records, Philadelphia Yearly Meeting, Box 1.

[8] E.g., L. Compere to Corresponding Secretary, September 21, 1826, in *Baptist Missionary Magazine*, VII (March 1827), 85-88.

[9] S. R. Riggs to S. Treat, March 24, 1849, ABC 18.3.7.III:245, is a good analysis of this and the problem to be discussed.

fit the missionaries. Therefore, they asked payment for their children who attended school. Since the missionaries refused to pay, the parents withheld their children. Few Indian attitudes vexed the teachers more.[10]

The real cause of poor attendance at school was what the missionaries termed a lack of "family government." The tribal cultures encountered by the teachers placed no value on prompt and steady attendance. In fact, little value was placed upon the schools introduced by the alien culture. Even the patient Quakers bemoaned the "unhappy" upbringing of the children, because the prospective scholars were "for the most part intirely [sic] left to act as the rude propensities of nature dictates, and accustomed to this unsubjected condition makes it very trying on them to be confined to learning."[11] In this permissive environment the child left school after the novelty wore off. Children preferred to play rather than attend school.[12] The child-training theories of the Indians thus notably conflicted with those of the missionaries. For example, one Iowa Presbyterian missionary asked a hunting party to leave the children behind for schooling. The parents left the decision up to the children, and the missionary lamented that "the children would much rather travel over the prairies than up the hill of science."[13]

[10] For example, see Minutes of a Joint Missionary Meeting, November 4-6, 1823, in A. Finney to J. Evarts, November 10, 1823, ABC 18.3.1.I:51.

[11] — to —, February 28, 1801, in Dept. of Records, Philadelphia Yearly Meeting, Box 1, copy. Similar complaints are P. Dougherty to R. Stuart, August 27, 1841, AIC 1:3:63; S. Hall to S. Treat, August 12, 1848, ABC 18.4.1.I:72; A. Hamill to Corresponding Secretary, July 12, 1827, in *Christian Advocate*, I (August 10, 1827), 194.

[12] L. Compere to Corresponding Secretary, September 21, 1826, in *Baptist Missionary Magazine*, VII (March 1827), 85-88; S. W. Pond to D. Greene, September 18, 1844, ABC 18.3.7.III:186.

[13] S. Irvin to W. Lowrie, November 2, 1843, AIC 8:1:114. Similar actions occurred in more acculturated tribes: see R. Powell to President, February 13, 1822, in *Western New York Baptist Magazine*, III (May 1822), 296-97; Philadelphia Indian Committee to Allegheny Senecas, September 20, 1854, in Indian Committee Minutes, IV:14-16, Dept. of Records, Philadelphia Yearly Meeting.

Aside from prayers for change or toleration of bad attendance, several avenues were open to the missionaries to
secure the desired punctuality and regularity. The simplest
method to bring order from aboriginal chaos was the declaration of vacations at times of sickness, feasts, or hunting
expeditions.[14] Inducements were also offered. During times
of famine or severe cold, a little food and a heated house
were sufficient to fill the school.[15] One young woman visited
from hut to hut in a Wea village with a few picture books
and dried fruit in an attempt to gather scholars for a school.
To encourage attendance, she offered dinner. Eight children
came for this bait. Corn planting intervened and other
children demanded three meals; so she abandoned her
efforts.[16] Others distributed clothing.[17] Many missionaries
opposed such lures. They did not believe in catering to the
Indians' demand for compensation for the services for which
the beneficiaries really should feel obligated.[18] To secure
greater control over pupil attendance, the missionaries frequently resorted to the boarding school.[19] In some ways
this was the largest bribe of all, since the children received
gratuitous clothing, board, and lodging.

Even boarding schools suffered from the parents' arbitrary
removal of their children, and so the missionaries resorted
to contractual obligation backed by legal force to secure
steady attendance. Gideon Blackburn, who established the

[14] J. Finley to J. C. Calhoun, September 28, 1824, in National Archives,
Bureau of Indian Affairs, Letters Received, School File (henceforth cited as
NABIA, L.R., School Files); Mrs. William Potter to J. Evarts, May 14, 1827,
ABC 18.3.1.IV:103.

[15] S. W. Pond to D. Greene, September 18, 1844, ABC 18.3.7.III:186.

[16] N. Henderson to E. P. Swift, October 28, 1835, AIC 3:1:47.

[17] T. S. Williamson to D. Greene, May 10, 1842, ABC 18.3.7.II:21.

[18] S. R. Riggs to D. Greene, September 23, 1845, ABC 18.3.7.III:216.

[19] D. Greene, "Visit to the Missions among the New York Indians,"
October, 1842, ABC 18.5.8.I:36; Report of the Subcommittee on Education,
in Indian Committee Minutes, III:225-27. For the evolution of the manual
labor boarding school, see Robert F. Berkhofer, Jr., "Model Zions for the
American Indian," *American Quarterly*, XV (Summer 1963), pt. 1, 176-90.

first boarding school in an Indian tribe in 1803, set one pattern. He persuaded the Cherokee chiefs to rule that any child leaving school without permission or remaining home beyond ten days after vacations forfeited any clothing given him by the station. Furthermore, the chief of the child's district bound himself to return the delinquent's clothing to the school, or Blackburn had the privilege of deducting the clothing's value from such chief's share of the annuities.[20] At the later insistence of the American Board missionaries, the Cherokee Council enacted a law in the fall of 1820 requiring all parents to return their children to school promptly after vacations or pay all the expenses incurred for their education,[21] and Choctaw missionaries of that society persuaded the tribe's chiefs to enact a set of rules governing attendance.[22] The superintendent of the board's Mackinaw Mission relied upon an act of the Michigan Legislative Council which provided for binding the children to him by legal indenture so that they could not be removed before coming of age or their education completed.[23]

Essentially, regular attendance was not a matter of legal indenture or inducement but of educating the parents as to the value of schooling. Thus the children most prompt in attendance were those of parents who attended church most regularly.[24] For the same reason, children of halfbreed parents or mixed marriages had better attendance records than those of fullblooded parents. In fact, the early schools

[20] G. Blackburn to J. Morse, —— 1807, in *Panoplist,* III (July 1807), 84-86.

[21] Law passed October 26, 1820, in *Laws of the Cherokee Nation: Adopted by the Council at Various Periods* (Tahlequah, Cherokee Nation, 1852), 13-14.

[22] Rules for the Schools at Mayhew, October 25, 1825, ABC 18.3.4.IV: 288; C. Kingsbury to J. Evarts, December 11, 1825, ABC 18.3.4.III:158. Cf. J. P. Shaw to Corresponding Secretary, n.d., in *Christian Advocate,* XI (January 6, 1837), 78.

[23] Act approved April 12, 1827, in *Laws of the Territory of Michigan* (Detroit, 1827), 454-55; A.B.C.F.M., *Report,* 1827, 140.

[24] L. H. Wheeler to S. Treat, July 14, 1852, ABC 18.3.4.I:229.

in each tribe were almost entirely composed of halfbreed scholars. Frequency of attendance increased as the Indians' values changed due to acculturation. Thus in the Civilized Tribes of the South, schools were established from the beginning of the mission. In 1827 the Cherokee chiefs incorporated a provision into their constitution which showed the value transformation: "Religion, morality, and knowledge being necessary to good government, the preservation of liberty, and the happiness of mankind, schools and the means of education shall forever be encouraged in this nation."[25] Yet even in these tribes attendance never was as regular as the missionaries desired.

Luring the Indian youth into the schoolrooms was a far greater problem for the missionaries than developing a curriculum for their would-be scholars. Bound by their culture, the missionaries assumed that the subjects taught white children were best for red children too. While the emphasis and level were altered to fit the particular circumstances of "savage life and mentality," the curriculum for day or boarding school was much the same as for schools among the whites. As textbooks changed and newer methods were invented, the missionaries attempted to introduce them into their classrooms.

The few records that do exist as to the texts and practices used in the missionary schools in the years immediately following the Revolution indicate that the teaching was probably similar to the white common schools of the time. In these small schools a teacher heard each pupil individually say his lesson, and knowledge was chiefly acquired by rote. Scholars ranged from "A-B-C-darians" to the more advanced. All busily memorized, often without comprehension, their few books in morning and afternoon sessions each day. The path of learning led from the alphabet to a primer (perhaps

[25] Article VI, Sec. 10, Constitution of 1827, in *Laws of the Cherokee Nation*, 129.

the famous *New England Primer*) to a spelling book to psalter and then to the New Testament followed by the Old Testament.[26]

With customary thoroughness, Gideon Blackburn described the operations of his Cherokee schools in 1807. The order of the schoolday opened with reading the Scriptures and public prayers, and then the children engaged in lessons until breakfast. After an hour of recreation, they returned to lessons till noon. Dinner and play for two hours was followed by school till evening. Between sundown and dark in the winter and between dark and 9 o'clock in summer the children had spelling lessons. The day closed as it had begun, with hymn singing and prayers.[27] The curriculum and organization of the school were revealed in the annual examination. Of twenty scholars, thirteen spelled with accuracy from the "universal Spelling Book"; the same number read the scriptures well; twelve repeated the Shorter Catechism in its entirety, and ten missed not a word; twelve wrote a "tolerable" hand, and three had learned some arithmetic. The remaining students were learning to read and

[26] That this was probably the case may be seen in the list of supplies sent an Indian school in 1792 by the Boston S.P.G.: 2 Bibles, 6 psalters, 6 spelling books, 6 Testaments, 6 primers, 6 inkhorns, and 6 pairs of spectacles. Records of the Select Committee of the Society for Propagating the Gospel among the Indians and Others in North America, May 23, 1792, I:17-18, deposited at Massachusetts Historical Society. Also see *ibid.*, June 7, 1792, I:20. The New York Missionary Society instructed its missionaries to teach the common education of the time. "Instructions from Directors of the New York Missionary Society to Their Missionaries among the Indians," March 19, 1799, in Minutes of the New York Missionary Society Directors, ABC 23.III. For information of the white schools of the time, see Edward H. Reisner, *The Evolution of the Common School* (New York, 1930), 311-13; Walter H. Small, *Early New England Schools* (Boston, 1914), 365-66; Warren Burton, *The District School As It Was, by One Who Went to It*, ed. Clifton Johnson (New York, 1928); James P. Wickersham, *A History of Education in Pennsylvania, Private and Public, Elementary and Higher, from the Time the Swedes Settled on the Delaware to the Present Day* (Lancaster, Pa., 1886), 178-209.

[27] G. Blackburn to J. Morse, November 10, 1807, in *Panoplist*, III (December 1807), 322-23.

spell. The majority had memorized some hymns.[28] Blackburn assured the readers of an influential religious periodical
that he designed to introduce as much Christianity into the
school as the young mind was capable of understanding.
The Presbyterian Shorter Catechism and religious questions
of a similar nature were taught early. The young scholars
were required to memorize hymns and singing was an
important exercise. An alternation of singing and instruction
kept the students' "minds open to the truth," according to
Blackburn. This innovation in the common school curriculum was justified, he felt, because "I will not say music
can *transform,* but sure I am, it has a remarkable tendency
to *soften,* the savage mind."[29]

By the time of the renewed surge of missionary expansion
after the War of 1812, the common school curriculum had
broadened to include geography, arithmetic, and grammar
as well as the use of a wider variety of texts, and so a parallel
development occurred in the missionary schools.[30] In 1824,
Cyrus Kingsbury reported to the Secretary of War on the
progress of the male scholars in a Choctaw boarding school.
Two scholars read and spelled in two syllables, and another
group of five spelled in three syllables. The next class read
easy reading lessons. The fourth class read the New Testament poorly. The fifth and largest class read and spelled
well in the New Testament, wrote English sentences, and
gave translations into Choctaw. The highest class read with

[28] I. Anderson and M. Donald to Presbytery of [Union?], n.d., in *Panopolist,* IV (April 1809), 520. Also see G. Blackburn to T. Jefferson, September 11, 1807, in National Archives, War Records, Secretary of War, L.R.,
Unregistered Series; Letter of Children of Sale Creek School, October 30,
1807, in *Evangelical Intelligencer,* II (January 1808), 43-44.

[29] G. Blackburn to J. Morse, —— 1807, in *Panopolist,* III (July 1807),
84-86.

[30] For white schooling, see Clifton Johnson, *Old-Time Schools and School-
Books* (2d ed., New York, 1935), 133; Butts and Cremin, *History of Education,* 269-74; Wickersham, *History of Education in Pennsylvania,* 191-207;
Henry R. Warfel, *Noah Webster, Schoolmaster to America* (New York,
1936), 5-21, 51-94, 378-400.

"fluency and propriety," spelled well, wrote compositions, and studied geography and arithmetic. For the female school he reported similar accomplishments, except the highest class was the fifth, which read an English reader and the Bible, recited the most interesting historical parts of Genesis and Exodus and most of the history of Christ in the New Testament, and answered map questions in geography.[31] This was the basic pattern for lower school education till after the Civil War. Female education was similar to that offered the boys except for the more advanced subjects. Both sexes received an education of better quality than white boys and girls in many rural areas.[32]

At the same time as the federal government began subsidizing Indian schools from the civilization fund created in 1819, a new teaching method became popular in the larger northeastern cities. The Britishers, Andrew Bell and Joseph Lancaster, originated a system for teaching the common branches of spelling, writing, and arithmetic in an amazingly cheaper way: one trained teacher could instruct hundreds. To achieve this, Lancaster, after whom the system was named, carefully graded the children according to their stage of progress to correspond with a systematic arrangement of subject matter. These classes were put through their lessons by monitors, who were older children trained by the master. Rather than spend money on expensive books, large cards were printed, and a class of children learned under the monitor from a card suited to its advancement. To save paper, the children wrote in sand or on slate. As an organizational genius, Lancaster stipulated classroom arrangements, desk sizes, and even student movements. He utilized a system of tickets and small rewards to recognize merit in

[31] C. Kingsbury to J. Calhoun, October, 1824, NABIA, L.R., School File. His use of "classes" meant merely groupings for the purpose of recitations.

[32] A reading of the School Files referred to in the preceding note will reveal the subjects for the four decades under discussion. Cf. Wickersham, *History of Education in Pennsylvania*, 191-207.

behavior and learning, and employed other methods to excite emulation.[33] In 1806 the Lancastrian System was first introduced into New York City and five years later into Washington.[34] By the latter date the New York Missionary Society had already attempted unsuccessfully to institute the system in its Tuscarora school.[35]

The leader in successfully adopting the Lancastrian System for missionary operations as in so many things was Cyrus Kingsbury. At a Cherokee manual labor boarding school, the children progressed through the alphabet, to spelling one, two, three syllables, to reading, then writing in sand, on slates, and finally on paper in the prescribed Lancastrian pattern under monitors. To excite effort, little cards bearing the initial letters of the words "Punctual attendance," "Behavior," and "Diligence" were awarded twice each day to the small red practitioners of those virtues. Besides the honor attached to their possession, the tickets were valued at a half cent, one cent, and three and a half cents respectively in exchange for knives, books, and other purchases. Damaged slates, lost pencils, and misbehavior cost fines in tickets. Under this plan a teacher at Brainerd taught fifty-three scholars.[36] After his inspection of the

[33] [Joseph Lancaster], *The British System of Education: Being a Complete Epitome of the Improvements and Inventions Practiced by Joseph Lancaster: To Which Is Added a Report of the Trustees of the Lancaster School at Georgetown, Col.* (Georgetown, D.C., 1812); David Salmon, ed., *The Practical Parts of Lancaster's Improvements and Bell's Experiment* (Cambridge, England, 1932), especially the introduction. For a brief view of the system, see Reisner, *Evolution of the Common School,* 250-57.

[34] John C. Proctor, "Joseph Lancaster and the Lancastrian Schools in the District of Columbia with Incidental School Notes," *Records of the Columbia Historical Society,* XXV (1923), 1-35.

[35] Annual Report, in Minutes of N.Y.M.S. Directors, March 22, 1810, ABC 23.III.

[36] Calvin Jones, "Account of the Cherokee Schools," *Niles Register,* XVI (1819), supp., 98. Also see Evart's account in A.B.C.F.M., *Report,* 1818, 193. At Elliot, the other boarding school, the missionary family resolved that the tickets be worth twelve and a half, six and a quarter, and three and an eighth cents. Elliot Journal, December 14, 1819, ABC 18.3.4.I:10.

school, the American Board's treasurer considered the scholars equal in proficiency for their ages to children in the northern schools.[37]

Kingsbury's success with the system called it to the Secretary of War's attention. At the same time the inventor personally promoted the plan before the War Department.[38] In mid-1821 the War Department sent out a specially written pamphlet by Lancaster to all missionary societies with the suggestion that all adopt the system.[39] With promises of governmental funds to back the suggestion, a flurry of adoptions followed.[40]

Prior to the War of 1812, few Indian students completed the rigorous routine of higher education with its sole aim of preparation for college. For this reason the missionaries of the early 1800s disapproved of educating Indians beyond

[37] A.B.C.F.M., *Report*, 1818, 193.

[38] J. Lancaster to J. Monroe, January 22, 1820, in Joseph Lancaster, *Letters on National Subjects, Auxiliary to Universal Education, and Scientific Knowledge; Addressed to Barwell Bassett, Late a Member of the House of Representatives; Henry Clay, Speaker of the House of Representatives and James Monroe, President of the United States of America* (Washington, 1820), 34-44; J. C. Calhoun to J. Lancaster, March 13, May 16, 1820, in Edgar W. Knight and Clifton L. Hall, *Readings in American Educational History* (New York, 1951), 141-42.

[39] War Dept. Circular to Lewis de Schweinitz *et al.*, August 29, 1821, NABIA, L.S., D:151. The pamphlet was probably Joseph Lancaster, *The Lancastrian System of Education, with Improvements* (Baltimore, 1821).

[40] The Baptists were especially eager for funds. At Fort Wayne, Isaac McCoy favored the plan. Isaac McCoy Journal, December 30, 1820. The Isaac McCoy Papers and Journal are deposited at the Kansas State Historical Society, Topeka, Kansas. I would like to thank Mrs. Lela Barnes for aid in using this collection. Among the Cherokees, another school was established on the Lancastrian system. T. Roberts to J. Carelton, February 18, 1824, in *Baptist Missionary Magazine*, IV (May 1824), 336-38. Abel Bingham established a school on the plan at Sault Ste. Marie. A. Bingham to Mrs. E. A. Sheldon, October 21, 1852, in *Michigan Pioneer and Historical Collections*, XXVIII (1900), 520-24. At the specific recommendation of the Secretary of War, the Choctaw Academy adopted the system for all but its advanced classes. T. Henderson to Secretary of War, May 1, 1829, NABIA, L.R., School File; Shelly D. Rouse, "Colonel Dick Johnson's Choctaw Academy: A Forgotten Educational Experiment," *Ohio Archaeological and Historical Quarterly*, XXV (January 1916), 99.

the common branches of knowledge.[41] After the war a new plan for white education arose which also seemed to fit Indian needs. In response to the democratic pressures of the nineteenth century, the academy gained popularity as a school of advanced studies for students not contemplating college. To meet these needs it expanded the curriculum beyond the subjects taught in the traditional Latin schools and adopted a more flexible arrangement of courses. Academies offered combinations of both classical and English courses as well as such practical subjects as science, mathematics, bookkeeping, and surveying.[42] With the greater success of southern Indian education and the availability of the new plan after 1815, academies to train future Indian teachers, physicians, and politicians were demanded.

The Foreign Missionary School established by the American Board at Cornwall, Connecticut, in 1817 was the first to meet this new demand.[43] The school's constitution proclaimed its goal: "the education in our country, of Heathen Youths, in such a manner, as, with subsequent professional instruction, will qualify them to become useful Missionaries, Physicians, Surgeons, School-masters, or Interpreters; and to communicate to the Heathen nations such knowledge in agriculture and the arts, as may prove the means of promoting Christianity and civilization."[44] Students from all the American Board mission schools around the world came to Connecticut. Indians from Asia and America completed their lessons in the lower branches of knowledge before

[41] E.g., J. Sergeant to P. Thacher, January 10, 1794, in Samuel Kirkland Papers, Hamilton College; Meeting, June 29, 1812, in Minutes of N.Y.M.S. Directors, ABC 23.IV.

[42] Butts and Cremin, *History of Education*, 275-83.

[43] Actually, such a school was projected by Samuel Kirkland at Oneida, New York, and the institution formed the nucleus for Hamilton College. Joseph D. Ibbotson and Simon N. D. North, *Documentary History of Hamilton College* (Clinton, N.Y., 1922), 49-56.

[44] Quoted in Jedidiah Morse, *Report to the Secretary of War of the United States, on Indian Affairs* (New Haven, 1822), app., 264.

pursuing Latin, Greek, Hebrew, geography, rhetoric, composition, natural philosophy, as well as astronomy, navigation, surveying, and theology.[45] Cherokees, Choctaws, and New York State Indians studied at the school until it closed in 1827.[46]

The next academy resulted from the scramble for the Choctaw educational annuities in 1825 in which the ardent Baptist senator from Kentucky, Richard M. Johnson, was the victor. In the Choctaw Academy, which educated more Indian youths in one year than the Cornwall school did in its entire existence, the students studied surveying, natural and moral philosophy, bookkeeping, history, algebra, and astronomy in addition to subjects pursued in the lower schools.[47] Later at the request of a student and the Secretary of War, instruction in mechanical trades was introduced into the curriculum. Under the impact of congressional investigation and withdrawal of the southern Indian annuities in the early 1840s, the school closed its doors.[48]

After removal westward, the southern Indians founded their own academies from their treaty annuities. None of these institutions obtained the level of the better academies in the Northeast but seemed to equal their sisters in the rural areas. Few Indian academies could demand real competence in lower school learning as an entrance requirement and were under the necessity of teaching these subjects. The most advanced school of this character was Spencer Academy in the Choctaw Nation under control of the Presbyterian

[45] H. Daggett to S. Worcester, February 6, 1819, ABC 12.1.II:102 (pt.2); Edward C. Starr, *A History of Cornwall, Connecticut, a Typical New England Town* (New Haven, Conn., 1926), 141.

[46] In addition to Starr, see Carolyn T. Foreman, "The Foreign Mission School at Cornwall, Connecticut," *Chronicles of Oklahoma*, VII (September 1929), 242-59.

[47] T. Henderson to Secretary of War, May 1, 1829, NABIA, L.R., School File; "Report Showing in Detail the Condition of the Choctaw Academy in Scott County, Kentucky on the 30th September, 1838," *ibid.*

[48] Rouse, "Colonel Dick Johnson's Choctaw Academy," 100-105.

Foreign Board. Under the directorship of James Ramsey, it was the first Indian school to adopt a division of pupils by grades in which students of about the same age and "literary attainments" were confined to the same room under a teacher instead of having, say, three schoolrooms with all levels of learning mixed indiscriminately throughout the rooms.[49] The highest grade in the school studied Scripture and advanced reading, translations of Choctaw and English, arithmetic, English grammar, astronomy, geography, algebra, English composition, and vocal music. Occasionally, brighter students learned surveying and Latin. Yet even in this school the lowest grade was composed of A-B-C-darians and spellers.[50] Other southern Indian academies taught the same subjects as Spencer except Latin and surveying, but they did not adopt the system of grades, which was only coming in among the more progressive white schools of the day. Girls learned all except the more advanced subjects.[51]

No institution with the specific name of academy was founded in the northern tribes, but some of the mission schools taught the advanced studies. Though little Iowa scholars at the Presbyterian mission recited Latin lessons,[52] most northern Indian schools concentrated on the education usual in the common school.[53] The bright Indian boys and

[49] J. Ramsey to W. Lowrie, June 10, 1846, AIC 9:2:41.

[50] For a description of the grades and their studies, see A. Reid to D. H. Cooper, in *Senate Exec. Doc.* no. 1, pt. 1, 33 Cong., 1 Sess. (1853-1854), 414-18. Also see O. P. Stark to W. Lowrie, June 21, 1847, AIC 9:2:100; Report of Rev. A. Reid for year ending July 11, 1855, in *Home and Foreign Record,* VI (December 1855), 368-69. Manual labor was also required of the students. "Report of Spencer Academy. Its Condition for the Year Ending July 12, 1850," *ibid.,* V (February 1851), 54-55.

[51] See reports of southern Indian academy superintendents in Indian Commissioner's Reports in congressional document series. On grading in white schools, see Butts and Cremin, *History of Education,* 275. For comparison with white academies, see Charles L. Coon, ed., *North Carolina Schools and Academies, 1790-1840: A Documentary History* (Raleigh, 1915), *passim.*

[52] S. Irvin to W. Lowrie, February 20, 1855, AIC 3:2:91.

[53] See letters in Commissioner of Indian Affairs' Reports and NABIA, L.R., School Files.

girls in these tribes received their advanced education outside the tribe in a white academy or, in exceptional cases, a
college.[54] Even in the more acculturated tribes, a missionary
doubted, as others had a half century earlier, whether
college classical courses prepared Indian minds for "public
stations," but rather separated the learned from the mass of
people and instilled feelings of superiority to their unedu-
cated tribesmen.[55]

Religion, as the survey of curriculums suggests, was an
integral part of Indian education. For the greater part of
the period under study, Bible and catechism were reading
textbooks as in white schools. In both day and boarding
schools, prayer and hymn singing were frequent, and attendance was required at Sabbath services.[56] Even the
Quakers taught Bible history and used the Bible as a text.[57]
At the Presbyterian Iowa school, the children memorized
Scripture verse. During one quarter the "best" girl recited
359 verses from memory and the "worst" girl said a mere 39.
For the boys the figures were 241 and 30 respectively.[58]
James Finley even organized his Wyandot scholars into a
Methodist Society class.[59]

When the Bible was superseded in educational practice by
textbooks, the new readers stressed moral themes. The
regular texts adopted by the missionaries bolstered char-

[54] For an example of such a youth and a brochure describing the academy
he attended, see William Jemerson to T. H. Crawford, August 30, 1839,
NABIA, L.R., School Files. Members of the southern Indian tribes also
were educated outside the tribe. See J. P. Wilson to [O. Brown], n.d., in
House Exec. Doc. no. 5, pt. 2, 31 Cong., 1 Sess. (1849-1850), 1174-75; A.
Bond to O. Brown, November 26, 1849, *ibid.*, 1175-76.

[55] A. Bliss to S. Treat, January 19, 1855, ABC 18.6.3.II:131.

[56] E.g., M. Hall to S. Worcester, June 30, 1820, ABC 18.3.1.III:189; D. S.
Butrick to Greene, November 10, 1842, ABC 18.3.1.X:28.

[57] Joseph Elkinton Diary, December 9, 1819; Report to Yearly Meeting,
April 12, 1855, in Indian Committee Minutes, IV:23-25.

[58] S. Irvin to W. Lowrie, March 30, 1854, AIC 3:2:63.

[59] James Finley, *History of the Wyandott Mission at Upper Sandusky,
Ohio, under the Direction of the Methodist Episcopal Church* (Cincinnati,
1840), 243-44.

acter training—the fad of the age. The texts enjoined
kindness, truthfulness, temperance, modesty, and goodwill;
condemned profanity, gambling, intemperance, and vice;
and exalted thrift, industry, hard labor, and economic individualism in addition to praising regular religious habits.[60]
Frequently the missionaries translated these types of text
into the native language, or if they compiled new spellers
and readers in an Indian language, they merely pointed up
those lessons particularly applicable to aboriginal life. Most
of the little volumes contained Bible stories and moral
tales.[61] *The Osage First Book*, compiled by American Board
missionaries, is an example of a text specifically written
with its red audience in mind. The little volume is divided
into four sections—"Familiar Sentences," "Moral Lessons for
Children," selections from the Scriptures, and the Ten Commandments—besides the alphabet and spelling lessons. Among
the first complete familiar sentences are strictures on the use
of tools, the proper female role, the importance of a log
cabin with a stone chimney, the significance of agriculture,
the concept of private property, and the general benefits of
civilization. The second section admonished the young
scholars to love their parents, never to lie, and to think of
God; it contained such sentences as: "It is bad not to know
the talk which God hath sent us," and "People without the
scripture are in darkness."[62]

[60] For the lists of texts used by the missionary schools, see NABIA, L.R.,
School Files, and appendixes to Indian Commissioner's Reports. Cf. Johnson,
Old-Time Schools and School-Books; Mosier, *Making the American Mind;*
Warfel, *Noah Webster,* 51-94, 378-400; Dunn, *What Happened to Religious
Education,* 79-89. A general analysis of school texts is Ruth M. Elson,
"American Schoolbooks and 'Culture' in the Nineteenth Century," *Mis-
sissippi Valley Historical Review,* XLVI (December 1959), 411-34.

[61] E.g., Stephen Riggs and Gideon H. Pond, *The Dakota First Reading
Book* (Cincinnati, 1839), was mainly Bible translations; Samuel W. Pond,
Wowapi Inopa . . . The Second Dakota Reading Book (Boston, 1842), con-
tained Old Testament stories; Stephen R. Riggs, *Wowapi Mitawa Tamakoce
Kage. My Own Book* (Boston, 1842), had both Biblical and moral stories.

[62] William B. Montgomery and W. C. Requa, *Wabashe Wageressa
Pahogreh Tse. The Osage First Book* (Boston, 1834).

Even the choice of subjects at times served a religious purpose. A Quaker schoolmaster taught geography to force the older scholars "to reflect on a sistom [*sic*] that we believe to be more correct in its nature than the one they hold."[63] Another teacher requested some science apparatus from his society in order to demonstrate that the earth was neither flat nor borne on the back of a turtle and that two benevolent forefathers did not create and carry the sun and the moon.[64] The instructors hoped geography and natural history would batter down the bulwarks of savage cosmology preparatory to the invasion of Christian sentiments.[65]

Just as obvious to the missionary mind was the moral implication of the language in which the young students were taught. Many missionaries agreed with the conclusion expressed in the Northern Methodist Annual Report for 1851: "With the English language, the Indian will acquire the elements of English literature, and the forms of thought, and the feelings which it represents, both social and religious. We doubt whether the Indians will ever be raised to a good state of civilization and religion, without the use of the English language. The influence of a language upon the principles, feelings, and habits of a people, is not appreciated as it ought to be."[66] The government also assumed this attitude and requested English to be taught in the manual labor boarding schools it aided.[67]

Acting upon both principle and recommendation, many missionaries instructed their charges solely in the English language. The stress on memorization in schools of that

[63] J. Thomas to T. Wistar, May 20, 1820, in Dept. of Records, Philadelphia Yearly Meeting, Box 3.

[64] W. Hall to D. Greene, August 17, 1843, ABC 18.5.8.I:177.

[65] E.g., P. Dougherty to W. Lowrie, July 6, 1843, AIC 7:3:96.

[66] *Annual Report of the Missionary Society of the Methodist Episcopal Church*, 1856, 71. Cf. the thinking of an old Moravian missionary, J. Gambold to T. L. McKenney, August 30, 1824, NABIA, L.R., School Files.

[67] T. L. McKenney to C. Kingsbury, April 10, 1826, NABIA, L.S., III:19-22; Alfred Brunson, *The Western Pioneer; or, Incidents of the Life and Times of Rev. Alfred Brunson* (Cincinnati, 1879), II, 95-96.

era inevitably meant that most students never acquired more than a mechanical reading ability without any comprehension of the material, for the teachers never thought to translate the text.[68] A Choctaw missionary reported after seven years of this type of teaching that only ten of the many students who completed the missionary schools' course really understood English.[69] In an attempt to remedy this wasteful result, some missionaries followed the method of the Seneca schoolteacher who overcame the lack of interpreters by referring the scholars to the object as he pronounced the word and by learning the native language in order to translate moral and other abstract concepts.[70] Others concluded, as did the government officials, that only removal of the scholars from the native language environment into an all-English-speaking boarding school was the solution.[71]

As in so many missionary efforts, the teachers encountered the stubborn cultural reality that the children preferred their own language. Since attendance depended upon the scholar's interest rather than parents' discipline, many teachers soon discovered that the tedium of spelling and reading in a foreign language did not retain the students' allegiance long. Many of these teachers also believed that if the children learned to read in their native language, they would acquire English reading more quickly.[72] For these reasons, many missionaries, especially those of the American Board, instructed in the native language.[73]

[68] Meeting, September 7, 1812, in Minutes of N.Y.M.S. Directors, ABC 23.IV.

[69] C. Byington to J. Evarts, November 28, 1825, ABC 18.3.4.III:73.

[70] Meeting, September 7, 1812, January 4, 1813, in Minutes of N.Y.M.S. Directors, ABC 23.IV.

[71] D. Kingsley to Corresponding Secretary, March 28, 1837, in *Christian Advocate*, XI (April 21, 1837), 138; W. Hamilton to W. Lowrie, March 26, 1840, AIC 8:1:56.

[72] E.g., E. Jones to Corresponding Secretary, August 17, 1822, in *Latter Day Luminary*, III (October 1822), 310-13.

[73] For arguments in favor of this course, see Stephen R. Riggs, *Tah-koo Wah-kan; or, the Gospel among the Dakotas* (Boston, 1869), ch. xxiv, "Education."

Interested as the missionaries and their directors were in pedagogical methods and curriculums, they never forgot that the whole purpose of the Indian school system was to inculcate the social and moral virtues deemed essential to a civilized Christian life. A remarkable consensus existed on what constituted these virtues in the abstract. In 1822 an American Board missionary stated these qualities to be "those habits of sobriety, cleanliness, economy, and industry, so essential to civilized life."[74] Twenty-eight years later, a Quaker committee listed almost the same traits: "Those habits of order, industry, and economy, on which depend in so great a degree, the success of individuals in life, and the comfort and happiness of the domestic circle."[75]

The instructional programs for the inculcation of these virtues were uniform, except for the divisions between day and boarding schools. Here the essential difference was not so much in the program as in the control the teachers possessed over their charges. The day school teacher could only persuade parents at best to correct their children according to certain rules he laid down. In at least one case, such a list of rules is preserved in the archives of the American Board. A Cherokee missionary required parents to see that (1) no scholar used profane language or broke Sabbath by laboring, hunting, fishing, or amusement, but rather attended Sabbath school and public worship;[76] (2) no scholar attended ball games, gambled on cards or horses, or assembled with those who did; (3) no scholar danced at any rites or feasts; (4) no scholar drank intoxicating liquors; (5) no scholar fought, wrestled, or employed provocative language.[77] Another missionary of that society wrote a short pamphlet for Choctaw parents on *Family Education and*

---

[74] D. S. Butrick to J. Evarts, May 10, 1822, ABC 18.3.1.II:172.

[75] Report of Subcommittee on Education, December 18, 1850, in Indian Committee Minutes, III:225-27.

[76] In fact, if he did not come to his station on the Sabbath, the child must present evidence of hearing services at another station.

[77] D. S. Butrick to D. Greene, November 10, 1842, ABC 18.3.1.X:28.

Government. It advised the parents to instill early obedience, self-discipline, industry, book learning, and a knowledge of God. In a long section the missionary told the parents how to discipline their children to achieve the desired goals, and he warned them not to be fooled by loud crying in doing their Biblical duty of using the rod.[78]

In the boarding school, character training reached its highest development. Only in these institutions could the whole environment be controlled for this result. Moral and social training preceded academic studies in these institutions. From the very moment of entering, the student had to be prepared. As one Quaker teacher described it: "The service to a new pupil was to trim his hair closely; then with soap and water, to give him or her the first lesson in godliness, which was a good scrubbing, and a little red precipitate on the scalp to supplement the use of a fine-toothed comb; and then he was furnished with a suit of new clothes, and taught how to put them on and off. They all emerged from this ordeal as shy as a peacock, just plucked. A new English name finished the preparation for the alphabet and the English language."[79] Even in the day school, cleanliness was emphasized, and the use of combs, washbasins, and towels formed a part of the school exercises in the Oneida Methodist school.[80] All schools demanded the scholars be clothed, for the most part in white man's garments.[81] In all the manual labor schools, the laundering and making of the clothing devolved upon the girls as part of their work training. Day school teachers occasionally distributed soap to

[78] Loring S. Williams, *Family Education and Government: A Discourse in the Choctaw Language* (Boston, 1835), 48, "Synopsis of Preceding Discourse."

[79] Wilson Hobbs, "The Friends' Establishment in Kansas Territory. Personal Recollections of Wilson Hobbs, M.D., among the Shawnee Indians, from November, 1850, to November, 1852," *Kansas Historical Collections,* VIII (1903-1904), 253.

[80] "Indian Mission," *Christian Advocate,* XI (May 1855), 13.

[81] E.g., Mayhew Journal, May 1, 1822, ABC 18.3.4.I:82.

the parents of children residing at home for cleaning young faces and small shirts.[82] Young scholars also learned to sit on benches and chairs and to hold a knife and fork.[83]

Among the usual acquisitions of the new scholar was an English name. From the viewpoint of the mission societies' directors, beneficiary naming was a method of obtaining contributions, for upon the donation of a stipulated sum per year, the donor had an Indian child named after him or for someone else. The donor received a brief letter annually from the teacher or directly from his namesake.[84] Probably more than pecuniary reasons recommended such a system. Surely the missionaries felt "more pronounceable" names removed some of the superficial vestiges of barbarism from their charges.[85]

Since idleness was regarded as sinful and the helpmate to temptation, manual labor performed by the scholars combined the highest goals of Christianity and civilization. Work developed those virtues of labor, industry, and economy deemed essential to good character at the same time as it taught the children civilized customs. This felicitous combination of moral worth and practical affairs underlay the work ethic as seen in the educational phase of missionary operations. Not only did manual labor boarding schools provide such experience for their charges, but even some day schools furnished that form of recreation.[86] Manual labor as part of the curriculum commenced before and continued to flourish long after it was a fad in white acad-

[82] J. Kerr to E. Swift, April 1, 1836, AIC 3:1:59.

[83] S. Irvin to W. Lowrie, January 29, 1852, AIC 3:2:29.

[84] For such a letter, see T. S. Harris to J. Sandford, September 4, 1826, ABC 18.3.1.VI:4½.

[85] Another example of the process is G. Blackburn to the Standing Committee, March 8, 1805, in *General Assembly's Missionary Magazine*, I (May 1805), 259-62.

[86] R. Scotton *et al.*, to Philadelphia Indian Committee, July 7, 1825, in Indian Committee Minutes, II:187-88; "Amount Manufactured by the Girls in the School at Tunesass [*sic*] since Last Account," March, 1828, in Dept. of Records, Philadelphia Yearly Meeting, Box 3.

emies, because of the necessity of training Indian youth to white work values.[87]

The activities and the order of the day for the work varied little from school to school. Each sex worked at those tasks considered appropriate to it from the white standpoint. Older boys cut wood, made fires, fed cattle, cared for the cows, and worked in the fields at planting, hoeing, and harvesting. Little boys carried water and assisted in feeding the cattle. Girls cooked, baked, washed, and ironed clothes, swept the buildings, made beds, spun, knitted and wove, made candles, and processed meats. The Iowa school hours were typical. The children awakened at five o'clock, washed, and dressed. At six all reported to the chapel except the larger girls, who prepared breakfast. All dined together, and then all the girls except the dishwashers went to the schoolroom to knit and sew, and the boys worked on the farm or in the fields till nine. At that hour all assembled for lessons, which lasted till dinner at noon. After a period of recreation, lessons were continued till 4:15 p.m. The girls resumed sewing or prepared supper for 5:30, and the boys returned to the fields and farmwork. After supper a brief worship service was held, and then all exercised for a short period. Between seven and eight the children returned to their classrooms, where they prayed and sang before turning in for the night.[88]

Usually the scholars were divided into "classes" or groups to promote emulation somewhat on the principle of the

[87] For both a history of the movement and a comparison of programs among whites, see Carl B. Wilson, "The Baptist Manual Labor School Movement in the United States: Its Origin, Development and Significance," *Baylor Bulletin*, XL (December 1937).

[88] S. Irvin to W. Lowrie, August 18, 1853, AIC 3:2:52. For another Presbyterian plan, see "Choctaw Indians—Spencer Academy," *Foreign Missionary Chronicle*, XII (September 1844), 273-76; P. Dougherty to W. Lowrie, January 16, 1854, AIC 7:1:108. For a Methodist plan, see William Goode, *Outposts of Zion, with Limnings of Mission Life* (Cincinnati, 1864), 130-31; Finley, *History of the Wyandott Mission*, 184. For A.B.C.F.M. efforts, see *Report*, 1818, 191-93. For Baptists, see T. Roberts to J. Calhoun, February 18, 1824, in *Baptist Missionary Magazine*, IV (May 1824), 336-38.

Lancastrian System, and these groups accomplished surprising amounts of labor. At the Wyandot school, Finley organized the eighteen oldest boys into six classes so that each boy worked one day a week on the farm in addition to the usual woodcutting and other farm tasks. The girls were also classed so that all knew in the morning without specific instructions what the day's task was.[89] At the Shawnee Quaker school, thirty-six girls during one year made four hundred articles of clothing for the scholars and fifty pieces, such as sheets and towels, for home use, knitted eighty pairs of socks and stockings, spun one hundred pounds of wool and wove it into linsey for girls' dresses and blankets, wove forty yards of rag carpet, churned eight hundred pounds of butter and six hundred pounds of cheese, made two and one-half barrels of soap, and dipped about one hundred pounds of candles in addition to the usual washing, cooking, and cleaning. To accomplish this labor the girls were divided into work gangs of four to milk and attend the dairy, four to wash and iron, two to cook, and two to attend the dining room. The jobs rotated every two weeks so that all the girls practiced every branch of housekeeping.[90] At Brainerd, a Cherokee school, about ten of the boys planted six or seven bushels of potatoes one morning before breakfast and an acre of corn another morning before breakfast.[91] At some of the schools the boys learned in addition to farming such trades as shoemaking, saddlemaking, blacksmithing, and tanning.[92]

As Cyrus Kingsbury pointed out in his proposals for such an institution, the manual labor boarding school was supposed to become self-sustaining by farmwork, and student

[89] Finley, *History of the Wyandott Mission*, 184.

[90] T. Wells to T. Mosely, Jr., August 14, 1851, in *Senate Exec. Doc.* no. 1, pt. 3, 32 Cong., 1 Sess. (1851-1852), 345-48.

[91] C. Byington *et al.* to J. Evarts, January 3, 1822, ABC 18.3.4.I:69.

[92] Mayhew Journal, April 5, 1827, ABC 18.3.4.I:99. For Baptist work schedules, see I. McCoy to W. Staughton, November 18, 1820, in Isaac McCoy Papers, II, draft.

labor contributed to this goal of thrift and independence.[93] At times stations abused the student labor idea by exploiting the students at the expense of their education. Records, of course, seldom reveal this case, but the Presbyterian Iowa school during the 1850s was a clear instance of such exploitation. Already by 1852 a missionary admitted that the larger girls worked almost full time in the kitchen and dairy because of the scarcity of kitchen help. He also wrote, "the little girls are great help, indeed we could not get along without them."[94] The boys worked at least half time on the farm during the summer, and some of the larger boys even more.[95] Three years later a teacher at that school resigned because the larger boys worked so much that their attendance at learning was too irregular for proper teaching.[96] In another instance at a Baptist station among the Potawatomis, when workhands dwindled, the boys supplied their places.[97]

Many Indian parents objected to their children doing any manual labor. From the very commencement of Dwight, a manual labor boarding school, the Arkansas Cherokee parents accused the missionaries of making "negroes," that is, slaves, of their children.[98] Not only did the southern Indian tribes complain of their children's peonage, but so did the Shawnees, for example, in the North.[99]

[93] "K.C.," "Sketch of a Plan for Instructing the Indians," *Panopolist*, XII (April 1816), 150-51. I believe the initials "K.C." signed to this article are the inverted initials of Cyrus Kingsbury. Also see C. Kingsbury to C. Worcester, November 28, 1816, ABC 18.3.1.III:6. A more complete history and analysis of the manual labor boarding school for Indian missionization can be found in Berkhofer, "Model Zions for the American Indian."

[94] W. Hamilton to W. Lowrie, August 7, 1852, AIC 3:2:34.

[95] W. Hamilton to W. Lowrie, October 31, 1852, AIC 3:2:38.

[96] C. McCain to W. Lowrie, September 6, 1855, AIC 3:2:104.

[97] Robert Simerwell Journal, January 7, 1828, in Kansas State Historical Society.

[98] A. Finney *et al.* to J. Evarts, July 27, 1822, ABC 18.3.1.I:33-36.

[99] Hobbs, "The Friends' Establishment in Kansas Territory," 252. This may well be due to the southern slavery influence of Thomas Johnson and the Shawnee Methodist mission, for which see Martha B. Caldwell, comp., *Annals of Shawnee Methodist Mission and Indian Manual Labor School* (Topeka, 1939).

As the tasks assigned to Indian boys and girls would indicate, the moral training of the sexes was not neglected by the missionary schools. To prevent any trouble from the intermingling of sexes at the school, missionaries attempted whenever practical to separate the sexes by classrooms if they could not have separate schools. The most "heart-sickening, heart breaking circumstance" to the teachers was that involving improper relations between the sexes. Isaac McCoy reported such a scandal in 1826. One of his most "sensible, diffident, obedient, and decent" female scholars, who was a first-rate seamstress, was delivered of a child prematurely. The guilty father had been sent east to college before the mother gave birth. The young people had desired to marry, but the teachers in good white fashion advised postponement until after his education. McCoy and the other missionaries decided to dismiss the girl, but she pleaded so fervently against the action that they declared the "crime" had been committed really by the boy and advised the trustees of the Hamilton Theological Institute to punish him.[100] One night in the Presbyterian school at Mackinaw some of the girls obtained the keys to the boys' apartment and lured the boys to their quarters. A missionary discovered two boys among the girls. The girl chiefly responsible for the affair was dismissed, and the boys and other girls involved were whipped.[101]

Dismissal was the punishment for sex and other gross offenses against school authority, but a variety of chastisements was meted out for lesser breaches of prescribed conduct. While whipping was common in white schools, Indian parents would not tolerate such harsh treatment of their offspring, particularly if they considered the teacher under obligation to them for sending the children to school. Only education of the parents to a new value system made

[100] I. McCoy to L. Bolles, July 14, 1826, in Isaac McCoy Papers, XII, draft.
[101] P. Dougherty to W. Lowrie, January 1, 1855, AIC 7:1:145.

the parents acquiesce in what they considered cruel punishment.[102] In cases in which corporal punishment was impossible because of the parents' attitude, the teachers employed rewards and forfeits or devised unusual punishments, such as imprisonment, long periods of standing in odd positions, or sitting with a hood over the head.[103]

The results of this educational program are illustrated in three English compositions written by advanced female scholars in Presbyterian schools. A short composition on "Indian Customs" discussed the changed concept of sex roles: "The Indian man never works. His wife always does the work. . . . The Indian woman has hard times when she has to do all this work. Her husband hardly ever works any; he takes care of the horses and goes to see other Indians and have a chat with them; when he is at home he sleeps and sometimes some other Indians come to see him." Another little girl discussed "Indian Burials" during which the Indians sometimes hired women to wail over the dead body. A sentence reveals her alienation from her culture: "On one occasion when a woman had died, two of these mourning women came and commenced wailing so mournfully that the children were very much annoyed, and as they had been at the mission they were ashamed of this heathen practice." A third composition reflected the new-found Christianity.

There are here about forty of us Indian boys and girls, who were once perfect heathen. But God in his merciful kindness sent out good missionaries to this heathen land twenty-two years ago. [She continued,] We ought to be very thankful to God for all his mercies; but there are a great many wicked men and women that use God's name in vain and do use such wicked expressions of his holy name! God is angry with the wicked every day. It is a

---

102 E.g., Mayhew Journal, December 8, 1822, June 6, 1823, ABC 18.3.4.I: 95, 106; M. Palmer to Greene, May 24, 1832, ABC 18.3.1.IX:39.

103 E.g., Clara Gowing, "Life among the Delaware Indians," *Kansas Historical Collections*, XIII (1911-1912), 186; Isaac McCoy Journal, December 22, 1820, April 16, 1821. Cf. punishments among whites in Wickersham, *History of Education in Pennsylvania*, 207-209.

wonder God has not struck us down dead before this time for our wickedness. But he has been merciful to us in sparing our lives.[104]

In accordance with the missionaries' plans and hopes, the schools frequently converted the young scholars. To the missionaries and their patrons, in fact, the criterion for measuring the success of the schools in transforming savage attitudes was the number of conversions among the students. As a result of their schooling, many children did become anxious to join the church.[105] Some of the conspicuous converts who became the heroes and heroines of Sabbath school missionary pamphlets, like Catherine Brown and John Arch, were converted through the school. An example of the school's usefulness in this regard is provided by Isaac McCoy's experience. In the few years following his establishment of Carey, eleven of the seventeen Potawatomis he baptized had been students.[106] In these instances and others, missionaries could be happy that the schools had served their basic function as doors to the sanctuary.

[104] "Indian School Papers," *Foreign Missionary*, XVIII (September 1859), 122-24.

[105] E.g., S. Irvin to W. Lowrie, October 17, 1855, AIC 3:2:109; T. S. Harris to R. Anderson, February 17, 1827, ABC 18.3.1.VI:13.

[106] I. McCoy to D. Hascall, November 24, 1825, in Isaac McCoy Papers, X, draft.

Chapter Three

TEMPLES IN THE FOREST

THE propagation of the Gospel was the professed goal of all missionary societies, and the creation of self-sustaining native churches was the abiding hope of all missionaries. Although each denomination in theory furthered the same Church and preached the same Gospel, each considered its presentation the superior view and hoped its meetinghouse would be the abode of the Indian convert. To the people of the period, considerable differences existed between denominations and their work. Yet in observing their efforts in the Indian tribes, little variety is seen because of the uniform extrareligious assumptions previously discussed. For this reason, this chapter will stress the similarity of the missionaries' religious approach rather than the specific theological doctrines and practices, believed so vital at the time, which separated Protestants.

Two means existed for the spread of the Gospel—oral and printed. The oral method was more widely used, particularly at the beginning of a mission. Missionaries were instructed to preach and talk at every opportunity,[1] and they heeded their orders. When a Sioux requested from Stephen Riggs a piece of cloth to make a sacrifice to the great spirit, the missionary lectured the Indian on Christ's sacrifice and refused the favor. Another time this missionary occupied the place just vacated by the medicine man to tell a dying girl about Heaven.[2] One missionary's wife resorted to an interesting stratagem to gain access to the pagan town upon the Cattaraugus Reservation of Senecas. She loaded a harmonium on a wagon and played at the edge of the town, knowing the Indians could not resist music of any kind. After many weeks of playing and singing, she gained their confidence sufficiently to meet her in their schoolhouse. After the usual instrumental and vocal music, she knelt to pray. Fear gripped her listeners. The frightened pagans rushed for the door and leaped from the windows in panic.[3]

In a less dramatic manner the missionaries usually itinerated from house to house and grove to grove at the commencement of missions. Rarely was the opposition to preaching so great that the missionary was compelled to talk only to people at scattered huts or on the edge of crowds as happened among the Creeks during one period.[4] Occasionally a missionary preached with amazing success upon entering a tribe, because the Indians were curious and knew nothing about missionaries. Samuel Parker met such enthusiasm among the Nez Percés in 1837. He explained to a few chiefs the significance of the Sabbath and asked them to construct a shaded place to preach. Lured by the novelty of the occasion, an audience of four or five hundred men, women, and children knelt before the blackcoat dressed in their best clothing.[5] In a more usual circumstance, the missionary gradually assembled a small Sabbath audience after much visiting, without the secrecy of the Creek efforts or the extraordinary numbers of Nez Percé labors.[6]

[1] E.g., [D. Greene], Instructions to Henry R. Wilson, November 23, 1832, ABC 8.1.I:12.

[2] S. R. Riggs' Anecdotes, ABC 18.3.7.III:220.

[3] Harriet S. Caswell, *Our Life among the Iroquois Indians* (Boston, 1892), 157-58.

[4] L. Compere to Corresponding Secretary, September 21, 1826, in *Baptist Missionary Magazine,* VII (March 1827), 85-88; Report of Baptist Board for 1829, *ibid.,* IX (June 1829), 198; Report for 1830, *ibid.,* X (June 1833), 176.

[5] Report of Exploring Tour beyond the Rocky Mountains, June 21, 1837, ABC 18.3.1.IX:195.

[6] Itinerancy was an integral part of Methodist Church structure and so it was extended to Indian work. Wade C. Barclay, *History of Methodist*

When the missionaries first arrived in a new field, they optimistically wrote their home boards describing in glowing terms how ripe the field was for a harvest of converts; they soon discovered Indians attended the Sabbath services as infrequently as they did school. When the Indians did attend the meetings, apathy at best and hostility at worst prevailed. At an Iowa missionary's meeting, the women continued their work in the tent without paying any attention to the preaching and made so much noise that no one else could hear the preacher. The women in typical Indian fashion, the missionary noted, "seem to view it as a council into which the principal men only are necessary."[7] An Indian advised this missionary to offer the traditional feast if he wished their attendance,[8] and one of his fellow laborers offered each attendant at Sabbath meeting a slice of bread with molasses. Although his board disapproved of his bribery, his audience increased.[9] During cold weather a warm, snug meetinghouse lured more listeners than the cheering Word, but spring dispelled such a congregation.[10] Even if the audience was attentive and assented to all said, it was mere Indian courtesy at most times.[11]

Even after long contact with missionaries, Indian congregations were not regular. Among the Cherokees in 1855

Missions, Part One, Early American Methodism, 1769-1844 (New York, 1950), II, 287-301. Other denominations utilized itinerancy in addition to their permanent stations, and most missionaries made short preaching trips around their quarters. E.g., Baptists: Evan Jones to ——, June 28, 1837, in *Baptist Missionary Magazine*, XVIII (January 1838), 17-18; Extracts of Journal of Abel Bingham, *ibid.*, XVII (August 1837), 205-208; Congregationalists: D. S. Butrick's Journals, ABC 18.3.3.IV and V.

7 W. Hamilton to W. Lowrie, April 29, 1839, AIC 8:1:40. Cf. J. Pratt to L. Bolles, June 24, 1837, in John Pratt Correspondence, Kansas State Historical Society.

8 W. Hamilton to W. Lowrie, April 29, 1839, AIC 8:1:40.

9 A. Porter to W. Lowrie, January 25, 1853, AIC 7:1:54; A. Porter to W. Lowrie, May 11, 1853, AIC 7:1:74.

10 J. Potter to S. Treat, August 4, 1855, ABC 18.6.3.III:88.

11 Extracts of Lee Compere's Journal, October 15, 1826, in *Baptist Missionary Magazine*, VII (May 1827), 143-47; I. McCoy to J. Loring, October 5, 1824, in Isaac McCoy Papers, VIII, draft, Kansas State Historical Society.

a missionary noted attendance as variable after a half century's mission work. Attendance figures at the popular communion seasons varied from a high of 200 to a low of 145. With such extraordinary occasions deducted, the maximum figure equaled only 140 and the minimum figure totaled only fourteen one cold winter's day.[12] As in the schools, the missionaries could not secure punctual attendance at a given time, and so Sabbath services were often repeated three or four times a day.[13] Other missionaries discovered Sabbath attendance depended directly on the number of house visits made during the week.[14] In some cases religious instruction could only be accomplished by visits to the Indian lodges.[15]

Attendance at church as at school was a result of transformed values. Halfbreeds early attended church and were converted.[16] The longer a tribe was in contact with whites and missionaries, the larger the congregation. This slow process embittered many a missionary to think as one missionary's wife complained: "But should an angel, or the Lord of glory himself come and preach to them, I see no reason to believe they would regard the message."[17] In spite of disappointment, most missionaries doggedly remained in the field and hoped and prayed. At times their prayers seemed answered when a revival swept through a tribe. To aid the revival spirit, the Methodists and American Board missionaries held protracted meetings and camp meetings, especially among the southern Indians.[18]

[12] S. A. Worcester to S. Treat, June 21, 1855, ABC 18.3.1.XIII:317.
[13] E.g., S. R. Riggs to D. Greene, May 1, 1845, ABC 18.3.7.III:214.
[14] L. H. Wheeler to D. Greene, February 8, 1848, ABC 18.4.1.I:206.
[15] W. Hamilton to W. Lowrie, December 31, 1851, AIC 3:2:28.
[16] E.g., S. Hall to D. Greene, June 14, 1832, ABC 18.3.7.I:38.
[17] Mrs. E. Walker to D. Greene, April 20, 1848, ABC 18.6.3.IV:165.
[18] A. Talley to B. M. Drake, August 23, 1828, in *Christian Advocate*, III (October 24, 1828), 30; L. Williams to J. Evarts, February 2, 1829, ABC 18.3.4.III:60; C. Byington to J. Evarts, June 25, 1829, ABC 18.3.4.III:91; W. Thayer to D. Greene, July 12, 1831, ABC 18.6.3.I:148; H. H. Spalding to Greene, enclosure with September 11, 1838, to D. Greene, ABC 18.5.3.I: 25; O. Stark to S. B. Treat, August 10, 1858, ABC 18.3.4.VIII:280.

Even with an audience gathered, the missionaries found preaching the Word difficult in an alien language. At the mission's commencement, interpreters were employed. Frequently it was next to impossible to obtain such help, for these essential intermediaries were already hired by traders or demanded high wages.[19] The missionaries considered most of these hirelings immoral or infidels and wondered whether such a "cracked vessel," should carry the precious Gospel tidings. Trans-Mississippi American Board and United Foreign Missionary Society missionaries at a joint meeting decided the Lord's Word could work its miracles even if interpreted by these people.[20] Many other workers recognized the simple necessity of having interpreters regardless of their purity.

Because the missionaries believed a "simple" people must possess a "simple" language, they considered the Indian languages deficient in abstractions suitable for theology.[21] From this conception flowed two complaints. Missionaries found the language barren of concepts to express God's relation to man in terms of king, government, and court, which were alien to Indian thinking.[22] In addition many thought an interpreter must be converted in order to enrich his vocabulary through his own pious experience.[23] The missionaries only realized their assumption unfounded after long study revealed an Indian language rich in abstraction sufficient for all religious purposes.[24]

19 E.g., C. Sheppard to E. Swift, May 17, 1836, AIC 3:1:64; F. Ely to D. Greene, August 30, 1834, ABC 18.3.7.I:108.

20 Minutes of a Joint Meeting, November 4-6, 1823, in A. Finney to J. Evans, November 10, 1823, ABC 18.3.1.I:51.

21 E.g., T. S. Williamson to D. Greene, August 4, 1837, ABC 18.3.7.II:2.

22 S. R. Riggs, *Tah-koo Wah-kan; or, the Gospel among the Dakotas* (Boston, 1869), 10.

23 Alfred Brunson, *The Western Pioneer; or, Incidents of the Life and Times of Rev. Alfred Brunson* (Cincinnati, 1879), II, 63.

24 E. Jones to Corresponding Secretary, August 17, 1822, in *Latter Day Luminary,* III (October 1822), 310-13. Cf. Paul Radin, *Primitive Man as Philosopher* (Dover ed., New York, 1957), xxi-xl, on the ability of primitive languages to express abstractions.

For the most effective preaching, the missionary had to learn the native language. He approached the task with confidence, for he assumed that the language was so simple that he would master it in a short time. After a year or so, he realized the language was far more complex than he at first thought and extraordinarily difficult to learn. After much study he sometimes concluded he would never fully learn the language. Cyrus Kingsbury admitted he had not mastered the Choctaw language after twenty years of residence in the tribe.[25] In 1851 none of the Cherokee missionaries of the American Board preached in Cherokee, though the mission had been founded thirty-six years earlier. Some missionaries did compile dictionaries and even preached in the aboriginal languages, but these were few.[26]

Even with the words at hand, the missionaries differed over what the Word should be. Some ministers and the Quakers believed it best merely to advance a system of morality—the "simple and intelligible moral precepts of Gospel, which have a reforming and purifying influence on the temper and conduct."[27] Most Protestants preferred urging

[25] Kingsbury to D. Greene, June 26, 1838, ABC 18.5.1.I:44.

[26] Auxiliary to the religious and academic efforts of the missions were their publishing activities in English and the native languages. The most prominent society for this phase of missionary work was the American Board. An incomplete list of their publications in Indian languages may be found in Thomas Laurie, *The Ely Volume; or the Contributions of Our Foreign Missions to Science and Human Well-Being* (2d ed., Boston, 1885), 522-24. A more complete list is in manuscript, "Printing Done at Mission Presses during the 1st Half Century—1810-60," ABC 8.6.1, last nine pages. Two other societies maintained presses in the field. For Baptist efforts, see two publications by Douglas C. McMurtrie, "The Shawnee Sun: The First Periodical Publication in the United States to Be Printed Wholly in an Indian Language," *Kansas Historical Quarterly,* II (November 1933), 339-42, and *Jotham Meeker, Pioneer Printer of Kansas, with a Bibliography of the Known Issues of the Baptist Mission Press at Shawanoe, Stockbridge, and Ottawa* (Chicago, 1930). For the Presbyterian Iowa mission press, see D. C. McMurtrie and A. H. Allen, *A Forgotten Pioneer Press of Kansas* (Chicago, 1930).

[27] Thaddeus M. Harris, *A Discourse, Preached November 6, 1823* (Boston, 1823), 11; Indian Committee to Allegheny Senecas, August 14, 1806, in Indian Committee Minutes, I:232-34, Dept. of Records, Philadelphia Yearly Meeting.

their religions' "most sublime and distinctive truths" on the natives from the very commencement of the mission.[28] After adopting the latter view, most missionaries and their patrons argued to what extent subtle and complex doctrines should be propagated. All agreed that man's fall, his subsequent depravity, the redemption of man through Christ's atonement, and his future happiness or misery after death dependent upon his life on earth were doctrines of primary importance. But should predestination and the details of sacred history, for instance, be taught the natives? Should sectarianism be propagated?

Debate on these questions continued throughout the seventy-five years under study. Moravians felt only Christ's suffering and death affected heathen hearts and eschewed all discussion of God's majesty as tending to alienate the Indians and all talk of denominational differences as confusing to their hearers.[29] Similarly the New York Missionary Society in 1799 instructed its missionaries to stress only the great doctrines of divine revelation.[30] In the 1790s John Sergeant did not instruct his Stockbridge charges in the "high points, such as predestination, and the origin of evil," but preached "faith, repentance, and morality," while his neighboring colleague, Samuel Kirkland, discoursed to the Oneidas on all the intricate points of Calvinism.[31] In 1821

28 Benjamin B. Wisner, *A Discourse, Delivered November 5, 1829* (Boston, 1829), 14, points up the argument.

29 August G. Spangenberg, *An Account of the Manner in Which the Protestant Church of the Unitas Fratrum, or United Brethren, Preach the Gospel, and Carry on Their Missions among the Heathen* (London, 1788), 60-76, gives a summary of their teaching; J. Heckewelder to C. Chapman [1820], in Edward Rondthaler, *Life of John Heckewelder* (Philadelphia, 1847), 78-79.

30 "Instructions from the Directors of the New York Missionary Society to Their Missionaries among the Indians," March 19, 1799, in Minutes of N.Y.M.S. Directors, ABC 23.III.

31 Jeremy Belknap and Jedidiah Morse, "The Report of a Committee of the Board of Correspondents of the Scots Society for Propagating Christian Knowledge, Who Visited the Oneida and Mohekunuh Indians in 1796," *Massachusetts Historical Society Collections*, First Series, V (1798), 19.

the United Foreign Missionary Society directed its men to adapt their preaching to the capacity of their hearers by employing simple terms, short sentences, and plain language as well as dwelling only on the more prominent doctrines of the divine truth.[32] On the other hand, the American Board desired its agents to preach the law of God in all its holy strictness as well as the fullness of the Saviour's mercy and love.[33] Many of the board's missionaries lectured on subjects bound to confuse the Indian. A Nez Percé missionary presented a detailed chronological view of the Bible and prepared maps showing the Israelites' journey to Canaan.[34] This missionary also orated at length on Protestant church history with its many denominational differences.[35]

Regardless of the missionaries' position in this debate, they had to teach the Indians the conception of sin before they could save them. To this mighty task of value transformation, the missionaries bent their every effort. A sincere belief in the depravity of human nature divided the Christian Indian from his pagan brother just as it did among the whites. Only after an acceptance of human depravity was hope on Christ's atonement meaningful. In fact, only prior acceptance of man's fall made Christ's sacrifice sensible. So important was the concept of sin that the Bishop of Mann in his book, *The Knowledge and Practice of Christianity Made Easy to the Meanest Capacities; or, an Essay towards an Instruction for the Indians*[36] made his dialogue, "Of the Corruption of Our Nature," second only to the explanation of God.

[32] U.F.M.S. Board of Managers to T. S. Harris, October 18, 1821, in Records of U.F.M.S. Board of Managers, October, 1821, ABC 24.II:317-20.
[33] [D. Greene], Instructions to Henry R. Wilson, November 23, 1832, ABC 8.1.I:12.
[34] H. H. Spalding to D. Greene, February 15, 1842, ABC 18.5.3.I:38. Also see C. Washburn to J. Evarts, July 18, 1826, ABC 18.3.1.VI:20.
[35] H. H. Spalding to D. Greene, January 24, 1846, ABC 18.6.3.IV:132.
[36] Several London editions commencing in 1742 and reprinted by the Boston S.P.G. in 1815.

For this reason missionaries of all denominations endeavored to convince the Indians of their sinfulness. The first missionary sent out by the New York Missionary Society directors was charged to impress on the "rude minds" of the Cherokees "that all have sinned and come short of the glory of God—*that by the works of the law no flesh living can be justified—that sinners are justified, freely by God's grace, through the redemption that is in Christ Jesus*—and that his blood cleanseth from all sin."[37] One of Kingsbury's first sermons to this tribe nearly two decades later endeavored to "explain and enforce the doctrine of total depravity."[38] In his first sermon to the Nez Percés, Samuel Parker explained man's fall, the transgressor's deserts, and Christ's atonement.[39] Later, Marcus Whitman pressed this tribe with "their lost ruined and condemned state in a particular manner, in order to remove the hope that worshiping will save them. It has stired [*sic*] up no little opposition of heart to the truth," he wrote, "but I trust it may result in striping [*sic*] them from a reliance which I think was given them [by Catholic missionaries], before we came into the country; that worshiping will aid them."[40] Baptists and Methodists also emphasized this sinfulness. A Methodist missionary to Choctaws explained clearly his successful approach to Indian conversion: "Our plan of preaching to them was, to convince them of their guilt, misery, and helplessness by reason and experience: not appealing to the Scriptures as the law by which they were condemned, but to their own knowledge of right and wrong; and the misery felt from the consciousness that they have done wrong. The gospel profferring to them

[37] Charge to Joseph Bullen by John Rodgers, March 21, 1799, in *Two Sermons, Delivered before the New York Missionary Society* (New York, 1799), 75-84, italics in the original.

[38] Brainerd Journal, March 2, 1817, ABC 18.3.1.II:1.

[39] Report of Exploring Tour beyond the Rocky Mountains, September 6, 1835, ABC 18.3.1.IX:195.

[40] M. Whitman to D. Greene, October 15, 1840, ABC 18.5.3.I:91.

an immediate change of heart, was seized by them as Heavens best blessing of ruined man."[41]

At the heart of the conversion experience was a deep emotional conviction of one's depravity. A vivid example of such an emotional foundation was Jason Lee's letter about Sampson, a scholar who was a backslider.

While one after another of his former associates had humbled themselves under the mighty hand of God, and came out rejoicing in God their saviour, Sampson had remained unmoved, and seemed to stand aloof, as if he had neither part nor lot in this matter. One of the boys commenced praying for Sampson, and *such* a prayer—oh! Who could hear it without having his sympathies moved for the poor culprit, on the brink of ruin? The Lord seemed, in a moment, to roll a burden of soul upon all his children present for poor Sampson. Their faith seemed to seize, instinctively, upon the promises of God with a death-like grasp, and claim them in his behalf. I heard the deep groan—the impassioned sigh. I gazed around upon the sight with astonishment, and it seemed to me that I was left alone in the plains of unbelief. I knew indeed, the Lord had power to save; I hoped he would save; but I doubted whether he would save *now*. Not so with the children, not so with the brethren present. Feeling deepened. Intensity increased to agony. Each, as if a host in himself and bent on victory, offered supplications; and these commingling with many sighs and tears, borne on the wings of faith, came up before the eternal throne. I looked again, and behold, Sampson was in the midst of a group, who, in their agony, had gathered about him to wrestle in his behalf; and behold, he trembled like a leaf in the wind. He sprung up on his feet, and with a faltering voice, a tremulous tongue, and quivering lips, which almost refused to give utterance to his words, he stammered out, "My friends, I have been a great sinner. I fraid I go to hell. Pray for me, my friends, I pray for myself." Down he went on his knees, and with strong cries and tears confessed his sins, and cried out in agony for mercy. The emotions within were too big for utterance, and he could only groan (I was about

[41] Alexander Talley to Mississippi Annual Conference, n.d., in *Christian Advocate*, III (March 13, 1829), 110. For Baptists, see extracts of Abel Bingham's Journal, August 25, 1836, in *Baptist Missionary Magazine*, XVII (July 1837), 179.

to say) unutterable groans. . . . The enemy seemed determined not to give up his victim. The conflict was severe, but the united prayer of faith prevailed. The struggle ceased, bless the Lord. "Praise the Lord" was heard in soft accents throughout the room. Soon Sampson arose, with a smile on countenance, and said, "My friends, I happy now, the Lord has blest my Soul."[42]

Without such emotional conviction full acceptance of certain Christian practices was not possible. Unless the supposed convert accepted his sinfulness, he confused repentance with oral confession, failed to appreciate Christ's atonement, considered goodness to be mere external good behavior, and believed Heaven was the just reward for following mere external forms of religion. Yet for a missionary to determine whether the convert genuinely practiced religion or merely masqueraded under a set of practices and words, he had to judge the genuineness of the conversion experience. The Baptists and Methodists found their converts fully aware of their sinfulness. Isaac McCoy reported his converts' evidence of "their discovery of the depravity of their natures and of their entire inability to contribute in any degree to their own salvation is remarkable."[43] Missionary after missionary of the American Board, on the other hand, complained in much the same words as a Chippewa missionary, that even the church members "have never manifested such pungent convictions of sin, as I have desired to see, though I have taken much pains to instruct them correctly with regard to the nature of sin."[44] If the missionary believed the Indians lacked a strong sense of sin,

[42] Jason Lee to ——, March 30, 1842, in *Monthly Missionary Notice,* II (September 1843), 65-67.

[43] I. McCoy to J. Loring, January 18, 1825, in Isaac McCoy Papers, IX, draft. Cf. E. Jones to Corresponding Secretary, August 17, 1829, in *Baptist Missionary Magazine,* IX (November 1829), 389-90.

[44] S. Hall to D. Greene, February 10, 1847, ABC 18.4.1.I:66. Cf. E. Walker to D. Greene, September 18, 1840, ABC 18.5.3.I:77; C. Eells to D. Greene, March 3, 1846, ABC 18.6.3.IV:100; S. A. Worcester to S. Treat, June 23, 1852, ABC 18.3.1.XIII:254; J. Potter to S. Treat, July 5, 1854, ABC 18.6.3.III:65.

then he judged their religion to be mere outward display.[45]

In light of such experience, the missionaries who were pessimistic about the Indians' convictions questioned whether the proofs of conversion should be as strict for red as for white Christians.[46] Acculturation probably had much to do with the evidences given, for the red convert was more familiar with white expectations and practices after increased contact. Two American Board missionaries averred that proofs of piety among the Tuscaroras and Cherokees were the same as among whites.[47] A factor equally powerful in judging the conversion experience was the missionary's and denomination's strictness in questioning the conversion narrative and observing the fruits of the conversion.

The only objective test of true conversion was its effect on the convert's life. Redemption from depravity made a difference in the conduct and psychology of the newborn Christian observable both to his fellow Christians and unredeemed tribesmen. His Christian brethren theoretically expected "fear, disquiet, anxiety, disharmony in personal relations, anger, malice, jealousy, hatred, cruelty, selfishness, give place to faith, confidence, joy, sympathy, peace, love, gentleness, meekness, unselfishness, and a purpose to live a life of service." They further looked for profound changes in the "very self" which were not "wrought by the subject but upon him by a power greater than himself; . . . the subjects' whole world acquired new meaning; . . . the change included a new sense of freedom and power, an enlargement of self, and attainment of a higher level of life both in a spiritual sense (relation to God) and in relations to others."[48]

But church membership depended not solely on conver-

[45] Samuel Kirkland Journal, March 9, 1773, in Hamilton College Library; C. Eells to D. Greene, March 8, 1841, ABC 18.5.3.I:43; J. Potter to S. Treat, July 5, 1854, ABC 18.6.3.III:65.

[46] E.g., P. Dougherty to D. Wells, June 27, 1842, AIC 7:3:74.

[47] S. A. Worcester to S. Treat, June 23, 1852, ABC 18.3.1.XIII:254; G. Rockwood to S. Treat, July 23, 1852, ABC 18.6.3.III:165.

[48] Barclay, *History of Methodist Missions*, II, 313.

sion and pious experience but also on doctrinal knowledge. The extent to which even the most Christian Indian comprehended the doctrines of his church was open to inquiry. The New York Missionary Society dispatched a special agent to investigate just this question among the Tuscaroras in 1806. He discovered all the candidates for church membership gave "a pretty satisfactory account of their sense of & sorrow for sin: of their dependence on the mercy of God through Christ for pardon & acceptance. But their knowledge and views of the person of Christ, of the way of salvation, through him, and of the exercises of the soul in believing appeared to me considerably imperfect." They could not, for example, distinguish between God and Christ.[49] But a Methodist bishop was surprised the Wyandots understood the doctrine of "trinity in unity" so well.[50] The Brothertown Indians understood the subtleties of doctrine sufficiently to divide into parties in favor of election versus free salvation.[51] Yet a Seneca Quaker saw no difference between the Presbyterians and the Friends other than that the former sang at their services.[52] After several years of missionary activity two Weas thought Methodism and Presbyterianism exactly alike.[53] Such ignorance resulted not only from the deliberate obscuring of denominational differences at times but also from the Indians' lack of comprehension. Though an extensive knowledge of Scriptural history and appreciation of complex doctrinal views were infrequently found in even the most acculturated tribes, the fundamental

[49] Report of Dr. McKnight, August 4, 1806, in Records of N.Y.M.S. Directors, ABC 23.III.

[50] J. Soule to ——, November 13, 1824, in *Methodist Magazine,* VIII (January 1825), 32-38.

[51] Dorothy Ripley, *The Bank of Faith and Works United* (Philadelphia, 1819), n.p. (July 16, 1805).

[52] J. Elkinton and R. Scotton to Philadelphia Indian Committee, September 14, 1823, in Dept. of Records, Philadelphia Yearly Meeting, Box 3.

[53] Bool and Gó ta tra poòh to Presbyterian Board of Missions, May 13, 1838, AIC 8:1:18.

"Truths" were understood by many in the farthest outposts of missionary expansion after a few years of Gospel propagation. Failure to convert was not from lack of knowledge, a missionary pointed out, but from "Human depravity, fortified by degrading superstition." The missionaries did not know, as anthropologists do today, that basic values change very slowly.[54]

The extent of doctrinal knowledge and pious experience necessary for admittance to church membership varied among denominations. Almost every denomination possessed a standard procedure of examination into these two subjects and observation of the candidates' "walk and conversation" before a convert gained formal church membership. Moravian requirements were strictest. A converted person seeking entrance into the church of this denomination first enrolled for instruction as a candidate for baptism after learning some of the basic doctrines. Upon passing an examination, he was baptized and he became a candidate for communion, during which period he received further instruction. Finally after another examination he was admitted to communion and therefore church membership.[55] These requirements proved so arduous to Cherokees that the Moravian Church in the tribe contained only eight members after twenty years of missionary effort. Membership in the Methodists

[54] E.g., C. Eells to D. Greene, March 3, 1846, ABC 18.6.3.IV:100; L. H. Wheeler to S. Treat, December 29, 1847, ABC 18.4.1.I:205. For what a church member should have known and believed, see Articles of Faith and Covenant for Brainerd Mission, in Robert S. Walker, *Torchlights to the Cherokees: The Brainerd Mission* (New York, 1931), 119-22; for Baptists, see *The Christian Professor's Assistant, to Which Is Added Declaration of Faith and Covenant, of the Baptist Mission Church, Delaware, Indian Territory* (Stockbridge, Indian Territory, 1848); for Pottawatomie Baptist Church, see Isaac McCoy Journal, August 3, 1822; for Presbyterians, see *The Shorter Catechism, Composed by the Assembly of Divines at Westminster; Containing the Principles of the Christian Religion,* many editions; for Methodists, see *The Doctrines and Discipline of the Methodist Church* (New York, 1836), 8-19.

[55] Spangenberg, *An Account of the Manner,* 89-90.

and Baptists appeared easiest. A prospective Methodist member met with the leader of a society for a trial of six months or more, after which time he was recommended for membership, examined by a minister before the church members for correctness of faith and willingness to observe the church rules, and admitted to the denomination.[56] Privileges of Baptist membership were accorded in a similar manner. After satisfying all the church members of his real piety, a person was baptized and received in full membership.[57] Between these positions lay Congregationalist and Presbyterian practice. Usually a person was examined as to his belief in sin and the atonement of Christ before he was admitted as a candidate for baptism by these denominations. After suitable instruction in the Shorter Catechism or by other methods, he was again examined by the church members if Congregational or by the minister and church elders if Presbyterian, baptized, and admitted to communion, that is, church membership.[58] For baptism in the Episcopalian Church, some basic doctrinal knowledge was necessary; after receiving that sacrament, the candidate was catechised until confirmed by the bishop and admitted to communion.[59] The Quakers did not encourage Indians to form First Day

[56] See *Doctrines and Discipline of the Methodist Church,* 76-77, 81; James Finley, *History of the Wyandott Mission at Upper Sandusky, Ohio, under the Direction of the Methodist Episcopal Church* (Cincinnati, 1840), 119-21.

[57] William Crowell, *The Church Member's Hand-Book: A Guide to the Doctrines and Practice of Baptist Churches* (Boston, 1850), 44-46; *Christian Professor's Assistant,* 3-5, 11-12; Jesse Bushyhead to Treasurer, September 17, 1833, in *Baptist Missionary Magazine,* XIII (November 1833), 438-39.

[58] Meeting, June 5, 1806, in Minutes of N.Y.M.S. Directors, ABC 23.III; Report of Dr. McKnight, August 4, 1806, *ibid.;* D. S. Butrick to J. Evarts, September 3, 1824, ABC 18.3.1.IV:1; P. Dougherty to D. Wells, May 14, 1841, June 15, 1844, AIC 7:3:54, 107; S. Irvin to W. Lowrie, November 2, 1843, AIC 8:1:114. At times the American Board missionaries adopted the extended instructional period of the Moravians. Rufus Anderson, *Memoir of Catherine Brown, a Christian Indian of the Cherokee Nation* (3d ed., Boston, 1832), 23-24.

[59] Eleazar Williams, *The Salvation of Sinners through the Riches of Divine Grace* (Green Bay, Wisconsin Territory, 1842), 20; S. Davis to ——, April 22, 1843, in *Spirit of Missions,* VIII (June 1843), 188-89.

Meetings until sufficiently under the exercise of the spirit, and membership was long in coming and difficult to determine.[60]

Every missionary society warned its workers to maintain the purity of the church by cautious admittance of members.[61] Fears were expressed constantly that incomplete conversion led to apostasy which hurt not only the specific denomination but the entire cause of Christ in the eyes of the heathen. For this reason various denominations accused each other of lax membership requirements by admitting persons without sufficient faith or knowledge. All Protestants attacked Catholicism as mere "baptized heathenism," and the Catholics reciprocated the epithet with venom.[62] Both the American Board and Baptist missionaries complained that Methodists allowed all persons who merely signified their intentions to join a society.[63] Presbyterian and Congregationalist missionaries thought the Baptists fostered unsound doctrine and "ignorant fanaticism" as much as the Methodists.[64] Yet a strict American Board laborer found the

[60] E. Joey and others to Friends' wives, June 23, 1797, in Dept. of Records, Philadelphia Yearly Meeting, Box 1; Philadelphia Indian Committee to Senecas, August 14, 1806, in Indian Committee Minutes, I:232-34; Joseph Elkinton Diary, August 20, October 8, 1821, April 22, 1827, transcript in Friends Historical Library, Swarthmore College.

[61] E.g., "Instructions from Directors of the New York Missionary Society to Their Missionaries among the Indians," March 19, 1799, in Minutes of N.Y.M.S. Directors, ABC 23.III; U.F.M.S. Managers to T. S. Harris, October 19, 1821, in Records of U.F.M.S. Board of Managers, ABC 24.II: 317-20.

[62] Samuel Kirkland Journal, November 26, 1788, Hamilton College Library; P. Dougherty to D. Wells, September 27, 1845, AIC 7:3:124; E. Arnold to Corresponding Secretary, November 24, 1847, in *Missionary Advocate*, III (February 1848), 85. For an example of the Catholic view, see Samuel C. Mazzuchelli, *Memoirs, Historical and Edifying of a Missionary Apostolic of the Order of Saint Dominic among the Various Indian Tribes and among the Catholics and Protestants in the United States of America* (Chicago, 1915), 123-25.

[63] W. Chamberlain to J. Evarts, July 8, 1824, ABC 18.3.1.III:24; Isaac McCoy Journal, September 9, 1832. This did not mean membership, however.

[64] E. McKinney to W. Lowrie, September 11, 1845, AIC 9:2:16; E. Butler to S. Treat, July 7, 1851, ABC 18.3.1.XI:185.

Baptist missionaries and their native assistants among the Cherokee fully orthodox and knowledgeable.[65] Requirements varied from missionary to missionary as from denomination to denomination, but no society allowed a person into the church without proof of conversion and doctrinal knowledge. Many of the bickering letters to society headquarters reveal more about interdenominational jealousy than actual facts.

In many ways the process leading to and the reaction after church membership resemble the "rites of passage," which ease a transformation of social relations.[66] The instruction and examinations guided the new convert on the path to his new life. As such, these rites marked a change from heathen aboriginal life to Indian Christianity, or as the *Christian Professor's Assistant,* a Baptist handbook for Delaware Indians, noted, "to become a church member is to leave the ranks of Satan, and join the friends of Christ; it is to give to the public a pledge to live as a Christian and an heir of heaven ought to live."[67] Membership was an institutional approval upon the new way of life pursued by the Indian after conversion and introduced him to several organizational arrangements which remodeled his old view of social relations.

As a result of conversion the church member was expected by the missionaries to practice a new standard of behavior. Fundamental to this new life was the decalogue. In the eyes of the missionaries some of the commandments needed special emphasis in relation to Indian life. Sabbath observance was strictly enjoined upon the red churchmen. A new concept of time was thus introduced to the Indians, for the missionaries had to instruct them in the concept of the week and invent various devices to help the Indians keep

[65] D. S. Butrick to S. Treat, February 6, May 29, 1850, ABC 18.3.1.XI: 238, 241.
[66] See Eliot D. Chapple and Carleton S. Coon, *Principles of Anthropology* (New York, 1942), ch. xx.
[67] p. 8.

track of the passage of days until Sunday.[68] Missionaries repeatedly lectured on the seventh commandment against adultery, because they felt the aborigines too promiscuous and too quick to part from their spouses. Under the sixth commandment the missionaries condemned the warfare which in many Indian societies was a fundamental part of the whole male role. Though the Indians did not violate the dicta against false gods and images, the missionaries harangued against attendance at "heathenish" dances and witchcraft as well as the use of medicine men.

Missionaries urged certain practices upon their charges as essential to continued church membership. More words probably were devoted to the evils of intemperance than to any other subject. Liquor was evil not only because drinking wasted time but also because intoxication led to quarrels and murder. Idleness was condemned, as was gossip. Native dances, ball games, and "frolics" violated the dicta against intemperance and idleness. All church members had to pay their debts promptly or face expulsion. Church members were expected to attend Sabbath services regularly and support the cause of Christ among the heathen. Minor bickering, grudges, and other examples of selfishness were supposed to be erased from the new life.[69]

For failure to practice these virtues a church member was subject to the discipline of his church. The church's reason for judging the lives of its members was stated succinctly by the *Christian Professor's Assistant*, "Its purity, its reputation, its efficiency, and its existence, all depend on the

[68] P. Dougherty to W. Lowrie, June, 1839, AIC 7:3:28; Robert Simerwell Journal, July 4, 1824, in Kansas State Historical Society; Lawrence Gipson, *The Moravian Indian Mission on the White River. Diaries and Letters, May 5, 1799 to November 12, 1806* (Indianapolis, 1938), 181.

[69] The best list of duties is "Statutes and Rules Agreed upon by the Christian Indians at Lagunto Utensink and Welkek Tuppek, August, 1772," in Kenneth G. Hamilton, "Cultural Contributions of Moravian Missions among the Indians," *Pennsylvania History*, XVIII (January 1951), 12-13; *Christian Professor's Assistant*, 15.

conduct, public and private, of its members. It has, therefore, the right to investigate and judge of their belief and
conduct, so far as these affect their religious or moral characters and standing."[70] The backslider could only retain his
membership by confessing his faults to the minister and
other responsible church members when his errors were
called to his attention. Upon his failure to appear for trial
or examination or to confess his fault, he was suspended or
excluded from communion.[71]

The missionaries found it difficult to maintain the strict
discipline they thought desirable. Violations of Christian
practices were so frequent that one missionary admitted
that if all the immoral members were excommunicated, his
church would have ceased to exist.[72] An American Board
agent reported in 1828 that half of one Cherokee church's
members had been suspended and twenty out of fifty in
another church since their founding.[73] Most exclusions
resulted from adultery and intemperance. Maintenance of
discipline proved difficult also because in most churches
fellow tribesmen participated as members or officers of the
church in judging the Indian sinner.[74] Either because the
backsliders were chiefs or relatives, or merely because of
sympathy for each other's failings, a vote of exclusion was
seldom given. Frequently when one person was disciplined,
many of his relatives left the church in umbrage.[75] Com-

[70] pp. 5-6.

[71] *Doctrines and Discipline of the Methodist Church*, 88-90; *Christian Professor's Assistant*, 12-17; T. S. Harris Journal, August 7, 1826, ABC 18.3.1.VI:7.

[72] A. Bliss to D. Greene, September 24, 1833, ABC 18.6.3.I:72. Cf. I. Proctor to J. Evarts, July 28, 1827, ABC 18.3.1.IV:187.

[73] D. Greene to J. Evarts, January 28, 1828, ABC 18.3.1.V:320.

[74] For a good demonstration of discipline proceedings in Indian Baptist churches, see Kirke Mechem and Lela Barnes, ed., "Two Minute Books of Kansas Missions in the Forties," *Kansas Historical Quarterly*, II (August 1933), 227-50.

[75] D. Greene to J. Evarts, January 28, 1828, ABC 18.3.1.V:320; W. Hall to D. Greene, January 21, 1845, ABC 18.6.3.II:249; W. Boutwell to D. Greene, May 10, 1846, ABC 18.4.1.I:42; Finley, *History of the Wyandott Mission*, 168-70.

promise with Indian custom and fallibility varied according to the missionary. Such compromise prompted interdenominational accusations of hurting Christ's cause by lax discipline. A Presbyterian missionary accused the Catholics of permitting intemperance.[76] American Board missionaries complained that members under censure or even exclusion in their churches were received into Methodist and Baptist churches.[77] Yet all denominations possessed institutional procedures for insuring a certain standard of conduct for its members in an attempt to preserve a difference between Christians and pagans.

As much as church membership was assumed to transform an individual's conduct, so it was supposed to change his relations to other persons. Sometimes a spouse left a mate after conversion[78] or dropped a second wife.[79] At all times the mission church was a new association inserted into the customary social organization of the tribe. The church hoped to supplant the indigenous rituals and religious societies as the new religious and social gathering place and entertainment center.

Even more significant were the new organizational techniques introduced into the tribe. Indians learned to conduct meetings in a new manner, elect officers, and organize campaigns. Churches in the congregational mode such as the Baptists and Congregationalists allowed their members to vote on new members, to discipline backsliders, and to conduct much of the business. In most of the denominations involved in Indian work, the church members elected some officers. Congregationalists and Baptists elected deacons to assist the minister to administer church rites and to look after

[76] P. Dougherty to D. Wells, September 27, 1845, AIC 7:3:124.

[77] C. Washburn to D. Greene, November 9, 1837, ABC 18.3.1.X:46; S. A. Worcester to S. Treat, September 19, 1849, ABC 18.3.1.XIII:217; J. Potter to S. Treat, January 22, 1858, ABC 18.6.3.III:111.

[78] T. S. Harris to J. Evarts, March 6, 1827, ABC 18.3.1.VI:14.

[79] D. S. Butrick to D. Greene, July 13, 1835, ABC 18.3.1.VII:36; S. A. Worcester to S. L. Pomeroy, April 18, 1854, ABC 18.3.1.XIII:285; T. S. Williamson to D. Greene, June 15, 1847, ABC 18.3.7.III:378.

the poor.[80] Indian Presbyterians elected elders from the church membership to form with the minister the church session, which examined candidates for membership, conducted backsliders' trials, and managed temporalities.[81] Class leaders and stewards in the Methodist Church were appointed by the minister rather than elected.[82] Similarly in the Moravian communities the "helpers" who conducted small prayer meetings, visited the sick, reported backsliding, and aided the minister in other ways were selected by the missionaries.[83]

Even greater training in organizational techniques was afforded by the many voluntary associations organized by the missionaries to supplement the church in enforcing the prescribed virtues. Almost all provided for elective officers and regular meetings as well as campaigns to bend public opinion to their causes.[84] These organizations which reflected the institutional expression of corresponding humanitarian movements among whites did not become popular in Indian work until the late 1820s.

Missionaries considered liquor the greatest obstacle to Indian improvement, and intemperance was probably the

[80] For Baptists, see *Christian Professor's Assistant,* 11; for Congregationalists, see [E. R. Tylor], *The Congregational Catechism, Containing a General Survey of the Organization, Government, and Discipline of Christian Churches* (New Haven, Conn., 1844), 87. For instances of meetings of these two denominations, see "A True Copy of the Records of the First Presbyterian Church in the Territory of Oregon," in *Minutes of the Synod of Washington,* II (1903), app., 256-80; "Two Minute Books of Kansas Missions in the Forties."

[81] Joel Parker and T. Ralston Smith, *The Presbyterian's Handbook of the Church* (New York, 1861), 117-21; C. Byington to D. Greene, August, 1831, ABC 18.3.4.V:159.

[82] *Doctrines and Discipline of the Methodist Church,* 40, 163-65; J. Gilruth to Editors, May 31, 1826, in *Methodist Magazine,* IX (August 1826), 307-309; J. Emory to Corresponding Secretary, October 16, 1832, in *Christian Advocate,* VII (November 9, 1832), 41.

[83] Spangenberg, *An Account of the Manner,* 83-88.

[84] For an example of such organization, see "Cherokee Temperance Society," *Cherokee Almanac* (Park Hill, Indian Territory, 1847), 27-31; S. A. Worcester to D. Greene, August 12, 1847, ABC 18.3.1.XIII:190; *Cherokee Messenger,* I, 15-16, 29.

largest single cause for church exclusion. Missionaries before the War of 1812 harangued against the evils of alcohol,[85] but not until the late 1820s did they commence temperance societies. Among the founders of the American Society for the Promotion of Temperance in 1826 were several members of the American Board, so that it is not surprising to find this board's missionaries following their patrons.[86] The Cattaraugus Seneca Christian Party formed a temperance society in 1829 based upon the abstention from whisky and distilled spirits for a year. Each member pledged to forfeit five dollars to the treasurer of the Indian Benevolent Society for breaking his word.[87] "The Allegheny Indian Temperance Society" was founded the following year by the Senecas living on a neighboring reservation upon the principle of total abstinence.[88] By 1832 all the church members on the Cattaraugus Reservation had joined the temperance society, and they resolved that thereafter total abstinence was a requirement for church membership.[89] The delegates to the first joint convention of Christians of the four Seneca reservations formed a general temperance society for the entire tribe in 1832.[90] In 1830 the Arkansas Cherokees organized male and female temperance societies based on total abstinence.[91] Both societies also dedicated themselves to stamping out other vices, such as gambling, horseracing, dancing, ballplaying, and other idle amusements in which liquor flowed.[92] In 1833 the Cherokees east of the Mississippi also founded a "National Temperance Society," and

[85] E.g., Samuel Kirkland Journal, February 7, 1796; Philadelphia Indian Committee to Allegheny Senecas, July 21, 1814, in Dept. of Records, Philadelphia Yearly Meeting, Box 2.

[86] John A. Krout, *The Origins of Prohibition* (New York, 1925), 108-109. The whole book deals with the movement for prohibition in this period.

[87] W. Thayer to J. Evarts, April 28, 1829, ABC 18.3.1.VI:108.

[88] W. Thayer to D. Greene, December 3, 1830, ABC 18.6.3.I:143.

[89] W. Thayer to D. Greene, February 20, 1832, ABC 18.6.3.I:152.

[90] A. Wright to D. Greene, September 28, 1832, ABC 18.6.3.I:37.

[91] C. Washburn to J. Evarts, December 22, 1830, ABC 18.3.1.IX:3.

[92] M. Palmer to J. Evarts, February 15, 1831, ABC 18.3.1.IX:35.

almost the entire tribal council signed the pledge of total abstinence.[93] Removal disrupted the societies in east and west, and so Samuel Worcester reestablished a new association in Indian Territory. He preached total abstinence at a camp meeting in 1836 and fired the cause. After two years of promotion, 550 Cherokees had signed the pledge.[94] Other missionaries commenced temperance work almost as soon as their American Board brethren.[95]

To teach charity and benevolence, the missionaries urged their charges to establish charity and missionary societies. Under such urging, the Wyandot church members formed in 1828 a missionary society which affiliated with the Ohio Conference Missionary Society. Fifty-seven Wyandots signed the constitution, elected officers and a board of managers, and paid fifty-cent dues.[96] The Christian Seneca women on the Cattaraugus Reservation organized a missionary society in the same year as the Wyandots. According to their constitution, they agreed to contribute annually a pair of mocassins worth a dollar to raise a sum to support pagan children of the tribe in school. The male Christians on that reservation organized a society for the same purpose with a constitution stipulating one dollar annual dues. No member could vote for the officers without paying his dollar.[97] Cherokee Baptists joined the American Baptist Missionary

93 E. Butler to D. Greene, November 6, 1833, ABC 18.3.1.VIII:93.

94 S. A. Worcester to D. Greene, July 10, 1837, October 31, 1838, ABC 18.3.1.X:83, 122.

95 A. Bingham to Corresponding Secretary, June 13, 1831, in *Baptist Missionary Magazine*, XI (August 1831), 248; J. Seys to Corresponding Secretary, March 8, 1834, in *Christian Advocate*, VIII (March 28, 1834), 122; J. Clark to B. Waugh, February 21, 1834, *ibid.*, VIII (April 11, 1834), 130; T. Thompson to Corresponding Secretary, May 14, 1835, *ibid.*, IX (June 12, 1835), 166; Daniel Lee and J. H. Frost, *Ten Years in Oregon* (New York, 1844), 140; J. Kerr to A. Kerr, December 9, 1834, AIC 3:1:27.

96 R. Bigelow to Corresponding Secretary, September 24, 1828, in *Christian Advocate*, III (December 5, 1828), 50.

97 W. Thayer to R. Anderson, May 14, 1828, ABC 18.3.1.XI:104. Cf. Dorcas Society of Methodist Chippewa Women, "An Address . . . by Peter Jones," *Christian Advocate*, IV (December 25, 1829), 65.

Union rather than organize their own society,[98] but the Six Nations Baptists formed an intertribal missionary society.[99] Many missionaries also encouraged their charges to donate in the monthly concert meetings for aiding missionary work held by the churches of many denominations in the United States and Europe.[100]

Not only did the Indian Christians financially support missionary efforts but they also provided native missionaries to convert their heathen brethren. Baptists and Methodists employed native assistants more than the Congregationalists and Presbyterians. The very nature of Methodist Church organization permitted an easy expansion along these lines. Part of the itineracy system was the licensing of local exhorters, and this practice was carried over to Indian work.[101] The Baptist Board considered a native ministry more effective than an alien white one to the Indians and depended upon many Indian preachers in the southern tribes.[102] The American Board agreed with the Baptist Board on the desirability of such labor, but insisted on a much higher level of education for its native preachers and

[98] E. Jones to ——, n.d., in *Baptist Missionary Magazine,* XXXIV (April 1854), 120-23.

[99] Minutes of Meeting of Baptist Churches to Tuscarora, Tonawanda, and Grand River, June 28, 1845, in Ely S. Parker Collection, American Philosophical Society.

[100] E.g., Elliot Journal, March 3, 1823, ABC 18.3.4.I:48; T. S. Harris to J. Evarts, May 21, 1829, ABC 18.3.1.II:40. The missionaries also urged their charges to form Bible and tract societies; for example, the Baptists and American Board missionaries in the Cherokee Tribe: E. Jones to Corresponding Secretary, August 17, 1829, in *Baptist Missionary Magazine,* IX (November 1829), 389-90; J. Orr to D. Greene, August 13, 1833, ABC 18.3.1.IX:98; S. A. Worcester to Greene, June 30, 1843, ABC 18.3.1.X:177; *Cherokee Almanac,* 1847, 25-27.

[101] J. Gilruth to Editors, May 31, 1826, in *Methodist Magazine,* IX (August 1826), 307-309; J. Emory to Corresponding Secretary, October 16, 1832, in *Christian Advocate,* VII (November 9, 1832), 41. For a good explanation of this system, see Barclay, *History of Methodist Missions,* II, 286-301.

[102] L. Bolles to J. Meeker, August 8, 1839, in Jotham Meeker Papers, Kansas State Historical Society.

so obtained fewer of them.[103] Because of the differing standards of licensing a native ministry, the denominations accused each other of hurting Christ's cause by employing untrained native preachers.[104]

Missionary work, Christian charity, and church membership thus brought the Indians into a new mental relationship with the world outside the tribe. They were no longer Indians alone but Christians, or at least members of a denomination stretching beyond the tribal boundaries across the United States. They and their white brethren were equal before the throne of God. The Indian Christians became aware of this enlarged horizon by the organizational apparatus of their denominations. Among the Methodists, the bishop visited the official members, exhorters, class leaders, and stewards in council.[105] Episcopalian Indians looked forward to the bishop's confirming their children and friends.[106] The presbytery provided the relation to the outside world in Presbyterian mission churches, for it was composed of the local churches which sent a minister and a church elder to the meeting.[107] And in all denominations, the connection between the missionaries and their patrons buttressed this pattern of Indian-white connection.

Thus as a result of missionary enterprise, the Indian Christians gained a different outlook on life, new social institutions, new male and female roles, and novel techniques for altering the lives of their fellow tribesmen. The spread of the true faith, according to the Protestant missionaries, could only come at the expense of traditional native life.

[103] Report of Dr. Anderson on training a Native Ministry, A.B.C.F.M., *Report*, 1841, 44-47.

[104] E.g., E. Butler to S. Treat, July 7, 1851, ABC 18.3.1.XI:185.

[105] E.g., Bishop Emory's visit to the Wyandot Mission, in J. Emory to Corresponding Secretary, October 16, 1832, in *Christian Advocate*, VII (November 9, 1832), 41.

[106] S. Davis to ——, April 22, 1843, in *Spirit of Missions*, VIII (June 1843), 188-89.

[107] E.g., A. Gleason to S. Treat, July 23, 1854, ABC 18.6.3.II:169.

Not only was the convert to abandon his old rites and priests for new ones and alter his attitudes toward the universe and his neighbors about him, but he was to change profoundly his secular ways as well. Religion in addition to being a philosophy of the unknown is a system for ranking basic values, and thus a new religion implies new behavior. With the added stress on civilization in the promulgation of the Gospel, true Indian conversion meant nothing less than a total transformation of native existence. While the missionaries may not have instituted the New Jerusalem in the forests for which they hoped, they did destroy the Gehenna, in their eyes, of integrated traditional tribal life.

Chapter Four

AN INDUSTRIOUS CITIZENRY

THE Protestant ethic enjoined work as a positive application of the doctrine of the calling. The fulfillment of each individual's worldly duties was the highest moral activity of that individual. Therefore idleness was a sin and industry was good. In the eyes of the missionaries, savage life was particularly sinful in this aspect: fighting was wrong and hunting was a mere pastime. Man must toil by the sweat of his brow to lead the godly life.[1]

Of all the occupations available in eighteenth and nineteenth century American society, the missionaries chose agriculture as the ideal employment for their charges, for above all work, farming received God's smile. It encouraged private property, which in turn spurred industry. Farming also provided a stable basis for organized society and civil government. Missionaries thus saw rural life as providing the proper social foundation for their ultimate goal of the self-sustaining church.[2]

If the tribes were migratory, then the missionaries must persuade the Indians to settle on farms, "as the roving life of a Hunter is unfavorable to the regular exercise of some duties essential to the Christian character."[3] After accomplishing this task, the missionaries assumed numerous benefits would follow automatically according to their social beliefs. This whole approach was best stated by an Episcopalian missionary in 1839:

All the history of the past shows the difficulty of applying the means of improvement to *wandering* tribes. But, induce them to become fixed and permanent, and more than all, let them be *dependent on the produce of the ground for subsistence;* then they are within our reach, and from that moment they have a special interest in the country in which they live. *Industry* then becomes *necessary* to prolong life, and *private property* is invested with an interest, which the hunter knows nothing of. *With Industry,* and *the desire of protection in individual property,* are connected some of the most important moral virtues, and there is felt, too, the *necessity of some law* for protection. In such a condition war ceases to be desirable; and then men begin to see the importance of at least so much education as may be needed in the work of legislation and administrative justice. At this stage, the work of civil improvement may simply be left, in ordinary circumstances, to take care of itself. But as surely as there is in human nature an instinctive desire to improve our condition, so surely may we, as a general rule, expect a people to improve when once brought into a condition that admits of improvement.[4]

Often the reasons urged by the missionaries in the field for settlement and farming were far less abstract. Missionaries

[1] Jeremy Belknap and Jedidiah Morse, "The Report of a Committee of the Board of Correspondents of the Scots Society for Propagating Christian Knowledge, Who Visited the Oneida and Mohekunuh Indians in 1796," *Massachusetts Historical Society Collections,* First Series, V (1798), 19; Samuel Blatchford, *An Address Delivered to the Oneida Indians, September 24, 1810, by Samuel Blatchford, D.D., Together with the Reply, by Christian, a Chief of Said Nation* (Albany, 1810), 3.

[2] Cf. the agrarian philosophy of this period, for which see Chester E. Eisinger's articles, "The Freehold Concept in Eighteenth-Century American Letters," *William and Mary Quarterly,* Third Series, IV (January 1947), 42-59, and "The Influence of Natural Rights and Physiocratic Doctrines on American Agrarian Thought during the Revolutionary Period," *Agricultural History,* XXI (January 1947), 12-23; Henry N. Smith, *Virgin Land: The American West as Symbol and Myth* (Vintage ed., New York, 1957), 138-54.

[3] "Additional Instructions to the Missionary to the Northwest Indians," June 11, 1801, in Records of the N.Y.M.S. Directors, ABC 23.III; *Records of the Synod of Pittsburgh, from Its First Organization, September 29, 1802, to October, 1832, Inclusive* (Pittsburgh, 1852), 32-33 (October 5, 1805); [David Greene], Instructions to Abel L. Barber, September 2, 1833, ABC 8.1.II:55-65.

[4] H. Gregory to ——, June 1, 1839, in *Spirit of Missions,* V (January 1840), 9-11, italics in original.

felt permanent settlement of the "wilder" tribes was necessary in order to gain simple accessibility to their minds.
Regular school and church attendance hinged upon permanent location.[5] Other missionaries urged farming as a
solution to the rapidly diminishing food supply as wild
animals receded before the advance of white civilization.[6]
The Quakers encouraged agriculture among the Oneidas to
halt the starvation customary during winter in that tribe.[7]
Probably many a missionary like his fellow whites felt the
Indians did not properly utilize the God-given land. As one
remarked, "I have been so much accustomed to farming in
my youth, that I was greatly pained to see these excellent
farms [on the reservation] growing up to briers and nettles,
while the inhabitants were starving to death. Perhaps my
feelings have carried me too far."[8]

Two types of settlement patterns were promoted. One,
which might be termed an early New England village pattern, provided for a town of houses surrounded by the fields
and pastures. Isaac McCoy planned at the commencement
of his mission to "lay off a town, not very compact, let the
houses be, say 20 poles apart, so that each family could
have room for feeding cattle, horses, hogs, sheep and poultry.
The missionaries would form one family. In this . . . town I
would invite all well disposed Indians to settle, preventing
as much as possible the introduction of ardent spirits. Our

[5] M. Whitman to D. Greene, May 8, 1838, ABC 18.5.3.I:85; F. Ayer to
D. Greene, June 1, 1844, ABC 18.3.7.II:213.

[6] C. Kingsbury to Chiefs, August 11, 1819, ABC 18.3.4.II:33; "Report of
a Subcommittee to the General Committee of Indian Concern Appointed
by the Yearly Meetings of Baltimore and Ohio," in *Accounts of Some Proceedings of Committees of the Yearly Meetings of Friends of Philadelphia,
New York, Baltimore and Ohio for the Welfare and Civilization of the
Indians of North America* (Dublin, 1817), 9-23.

[7] "Minutes of Conclusive Conferences, and Agreements, between the
Friends Settling on the Oneida Reservation, and the Indians There, Proposed
on the 25th and Agreed to on the 30th of the Sixth Month, 1796," in Dept.
of Records, Philadelphia Yearly Meeting, Indian Box 1.

[8] A. Bliss to D. Greene, [May ?], 1836, ABC 18.6.3.I:89.

fields would be a little back. At the mission house would be the place for public worship and for the school."[9] The Moravians employed this pattern in their mission work except among the Cherokees, who had their own plantation scheme already.[10] More in keeping with American experience and the agrarian ideal of the time was the location of individual families on their own farmland. Most missionaries favored this extended farm pattern. In this plan the mission was the central meeting place for the scattered families and provided the natural focus of social activity.[11]

With the idea of a farming community in mind, missionaries made arrangements at the commencement of a new station that were not strictly necessary for the mere educational and religious instruction of the Indians. The missionary carefully selected a site for the station with abundant water, good soil, and ample wood for lumber and fuel to serve not only his immediate needs but also those of prospective Indian settlers.[12] To lure the Indians to settle, the missionaries had to arrange for "something of a comfortable habitation."[13] Not only did the missionaries teach the Indians how to build log cabins, but they also financed the homes. Sometimes the aid consisted merely of hauling logs to the building site with the mission oxen. Other times the mission paid for nails and glass. Still other times the carpentry and all costs were footed by the mission treasury.[14] Methodist missionaries in Oregon formed a society to help

[9] I. McCoy to W. Staughton, September 6, 1821, in Isaac McCoy Papers, 3:154, draft, Kansas State Historical Society.

[10] "Mission among the Cherokee Indians," in *United Brethren's Missionary Intelligencer,* I (1st Quarter 1822), 15-20.

[11] For such a plan, see S. M. Irvin to W. Lowrie, May 12, 1842, AIC 8:1:89.

[12] E.g., J. Stevens to H. Hill, August 31, 1835, ABC 18.3.7.I:8; Cornelius Brosnan, *Jason Lee: Prophet of New Oregon* (New York, 1932), 71.

[13] J. Kerr to E. Swift, March 18, 1835, AIC 3:1:32.

[14] Philadelphia Indian Committee to J. Taylor *et al.,* February 18, 1801, in Dept. of Records, Philadelphia Yearly Meeting, Indian Box 1, draft; F. Ayer to D. Greene, June 12, 1837, ABC 18.3.7.I:103.

the Calapooyas to build homes,[15] and the Methodist Board
appropriated sums for such work among the Chippewas.[16]
The Baptist Board appropriated one hundred fifty dollars
for houses in the latter tribe.[17] Gristmills and sawmills were
viewed as stimulants to Indian advance in civilization as
well as providing flour and boards for the station. Gristmills
were expected to encourage Indians to raise grain, since they
could have it ground easily. Easily obtained boards were to
act as an inducement to homebuilding.[18] Further, to persuade the Indians to settle and farm, missions provided tools
and draft animals by various methods. Quakers among the
Senecas lent tools at first and finally gave them to the chiefs
to lend.[19] Some missionaries lent oxen and hoes, while others
plowed Indian land free instead of lending draft animals.[20]

With the techniques of housing and farming, the missionaries carried American society's view of the proper roles
for the sexes. Matched against most Indians' concept of the
proper work of each sex, the missionaries' view was quite
different. Thus the introduction of dwellings and agriculture
was not just a revolution in the housing and subsistence
customs of the red men but in most cases a drastic transformation of the male and female roles in aboriginal society.

[15] Daniel Lee and J. H. Frost, *Ten Years in Oregon* (New York, 1844),
150.

[16] J. Clark to Corresponding Secretary, January 23, 1834, in *Christian
Advocate*, VIII (July 18, 1834), 186; J. Clark to Corresponding Secretary,
July 8, 1835, *ibid.*, IX (July 31, 1835), 194; J. Clark to Corresponding
Secretary, July 29, 1836, *ibid.*, X (September 23, 1836), 18.

[17] Extracts, A. Bingham's Journal, October 2, 1843, in *Baptist Missionary
Magazine*, XXIV (May 1844), 108-10.

[18] —— to ——, February 28, 1801, in Dept. of Records, Philadelphia Yearly
Meeting, Indian Box 1, copy; H. H. Spalding to D. Greene, March 16, 1840,
ABC 18.5.3.I:32; S. M. Irvin to W. Lowrie, September 18, 1848, AIC
4:3:126; S. R. Riggs to S. Treat, June 16, 1855, ABC 18.3.7.III:328.

[19] Report of Committee, December 14, 1803, in Dept. of Records, Philadelphia Yearly Meeting, Indian Box 2.

[20] F. Ayer to D. Greene, May 15, 1834, ABC 18.3.7.I:95. Henry H.
Spalding developed a complex system for aiding the Indians. See his letters
to David Greene, February 16, 1837, March 5, 1839, April 1, 1840, ABC
18.5.3.I:21, 28, 33.

Hence the new life was resisted doubly, so to speak, for the missionaries demanded change on two levels rather than one. For an Indian to settle in an agricultural community meant throwing over not merely many of his customs but also many of his views of how a man and woman should act. In many tribes the erection of a house and the tilling of fields were considered woman's work. If a man were to take up an ax to fell a tree for a house, or to pick up a hoe to plant a field, or even to hold a plow in the furrow, he was ridiculed as a woman by the females as well as the males.

Yet this change in role was exactly what the missionaries demanded. The Indian males should relieve the women from heavy field tasks "altogether unsuited to their sex" so that the women could tend the house. Some Seneca chiefs in reply to such a suggestion from the Quakers said they would attempt to prevail upon the women to cease work in the fields, "But their habits have long been fixed, and it may be sometime before they will consent, yet we think in this we shall finally succeed." And this reply was after nearly a half century of missionary effort by the Friends to change Seneca values.[21] The values the missionaries esteemed, the savage despised. Two members of the Boston S.P.G. observed in 1796 the common attitude among the Oneidas around Kirkland: "They have an idea, that to labour in cultivating the earth, is degrading to the character of *man*, 'who (they say) was made for war and hunting, and holding councils, and that squaws and hedge-hogs are made to scratch the ground.' "[22] The roles envisaged by the missionaries for the members of their agricultural communities were almost as simple in their range of options as were the roles in traditional Indian society—only quite different in

[21] Meeting of May 26, 1846, in "Minutes of the Indian Committee of the Yearly Meeting of New York from 5th Month, 1828 to the 5th Month, 1863," Committee on Records, 221 East Fifteenth St., New York City.

[22] Belknap and Morse, "Report . . . 1796," 19-20.

activity. A man was to be a farmer[23] and a woman to be a housewife—the perfect base for a family under the agrarian ideal.[24]

Because of the importance attributed to the child-rearing function and the keeping of the home in developing a civilized society, the missionaries elevated the transformed female role to one of great importance in their operations. This was a reflection of the changing status of females in America. Women were coming into their own in the nineteenth century, and a great deal of financial support for missionary societies was contributed by women. So important did the female role appear to the directors of the Domestic and Foreign Missionary Society of the Protestant Episcopal Church in the United States that they stoutly asserted the "estimation of female character" constituted one of the chief dividing points between barbarism and civilization.

It is a fact too glaring to be denied, that in no country, either in ancient times or modern, where the sound of the gospel is not heard, is woman placed in a grade, which renders her a rational companion, or possessed of rights secured to her by equal law. In this single circumstance, there is a cause which has material operation on all the concerns of mankind, civil and domestic; and in the forming of the personal characters of all the individuals of a community, in their progress from infancy to manhood. It is, in a great measure, the line of discrimination between civilized society and barbarism.[25]

In the minds of the missionaries, God created woman weak for the lighter work of caring for house and children.[26]

23 Some Indian youths were encouraged to become schoolteachers, ministers, and, a few, tradesmen.

24 The effect of this scheme on social relations will be discussed in a later chapter.

25 *The Address of the Board of Directors . . . to the Members of Said Church* (Philadelphia, 1822), 8.

26 For such a statement, see Speech of Friends at Tunesassa to Cattaraugus Seneca, June 6, 1807, in Indian Committee Minutes, I:248-51, Dept. of Records, Philadelphia Yearly Meeting.

The duties taught the Indian women were typical farm-woman tasks. A decent home was a clean home, for the missionaries heartily subscribed to the old adage about the proximity of cleanliness to godliness—what one missionary called the "gospel of soap."[27] Women were taught to make soap, to wash their clothes, and to scrub their huts.[28] Instructions after "our manner" were also given the women in spinning, weaving, knitting, sewing, mending, and making clothes for the family.[29] Such instruction was provided by the mission women, who taught these tasks by example and in class. To free the women from the fields for these tasks, the missionaries expected the men to take up the fieldwork.

Accordingly as God made woman weak, He created man strong for the heavy work. First of all, the man was to do the duties vacated by his wife: housebuilding, wood-gathering, and tilling the fields. The proper accomplishment of these tasks meant erection of a decent log cabin or house and farming in the missionaries' eyes. Although the male role was divinely ordained, mere mortal means had to persuade the Indians of this decree. The most widely used method was the model farm. Sometimes this was part of the elaborate manual labor boarding school, and other times merely a small farm attached to a small station. These farms provided an example of the new male role as well as of the proper techniques, for as one missionary observed, "they need some one to show them what a man can do, and

[27] Stephen R. Riggs, "Protestant Missions in the Northwest," *Minnesota Historical Society Collections*, VI (1894), 132-33.

[28] *Ibid.;* Speech of Committee to Visit Senecas on Allegheny River, September 15, 1806, in Dept. of Records, Philadelphia Yearly Meeting, Indian Box 2, draft.

[29] Report of Subcommittee Which Visited Allegheny and Cattaraugus Reserves, October 19, 1809, in Dept. of Records, Philadelphia Yearly Meeting, Indian Box 2; F. Ayer to D. Greene, October 4, 1837, ABC 18.3.7.II:192; H. H. Spalding to D. Greene, February 26, 1843, ABC 18.5.3.I:40; L. H. Wheeler to S. Treat, March 5, 1852, ABC 18.4.1.I:223; Stephen R. Riggs, *Tah-koo Wah-kan; or, the Gospel among the Dakotas* (Boston, 1869), 388-90.

encourage them, just as so many boys, and without this, they will do little good, and perhaps go off from the means altogether."[30] Among the more acculturated tribes these model projects demonstrated crop rotation, proper pasturage, and the use and care of animals other than riding horses.[31] In the other tribes simpler devices were employed. The American Board mission among the Sioux required the men to hold the plow or drive the team if they wanted farming assistance.[32] The Quakers donated hoes, axes, plow irons, log chains, scythes, and oxen to the Senecas in 1800.[33] A Baptist missionary gave a Potawatomi chief a large number of hogs to encourage him to raise swine.[34]

Demonstration projects and gifts were not sufficient to transform Indian life as quickly as the missionaries desired. As with schooling and religion, farming and housekeeping were adopted slowly because they too involved a basic transformation of values. Many missionaries were aware of this, for as one of them noted, "to induce them to settle down, and adopt the customs of civilized life, to become industrious, and turn their attention to the useful arts would be to pull down the whole fabric of their superstitions."[35] Occasionally, conversion to Christianity instilled industry and a love of farming and housekeeping in the Indian. Once he reformed, the Indian man complained of his former idleness.[36] So most unplowed fields and dirty houses, as many missionaries discovered, resulted not from lack of

[30] A. Porter to W. Lowrie, December 17, 1853, AIC 7:1:104.
[31] A. Hoyt *et al.* to S. Worcester, March 18, 1818, ABC 18.3.1.II:104.
[32] Riggs, *Tah-koo Wah-kan*, 386-89.
[33] J. Taylor *et al.* to Philadelphia Indian Committee, September 3, 1800, in Dept. of Records, Philadelphia Yearly Meeting, Indian Box 1.
[34] Robert Simerwell Journal, June 23, 1827, in Kansas State Historical Society.
[35] S. Hall to D. Greene, October, 1838, ABC 18.3.7.II:122.
[36] See A. Talley to Corresponding Secretary, n.d., in *Christian Advocate*, III (May 15, 1829), 145; P. Dougherty to R. Stuart, August 30, 1844, AIC 7:3:109, copy; Wilson Hobbs, "The Friends' Establishment in Kansas Territory," *Kansas Historical Transactions*, VIII (1903-1904), 253.

knowledge but from lack of motivation to practice what had been learned.[37]

Casual attempts at work did not win the missionaries' favor. They demanded daily labor as the fulfillment of the work ethic. Even the converted Indians seldom felt or even understood this necessity. A Quaker lamented that the pious Senecas built houses and barns when they should have planted their crops.[38] This missionary felt discouraged because "there are no instances that I know of where a young man goes steadily to his business and works all day and every day at his own home. The Indian character is fond of roving about, upon foot or horseback, and dressed up finely, and do not regard working daily and all day as they should do."[39] And this complaint was typical.[40] The missionaries considered raising wheat more industrious than raising corn and keeping cattle and pigs more so than keeping horses, for corn was considered the crop of savages and horses were deemed conducive to idle riding.[41]

As with the church and school attendance problem, inducements were offered by the missionaries to encourage industry. By the employment of premiums or other attractions, the missionaries hoped to stimulate the Indians to apply the knowledge of farming and domestic economy they already possessed and prod their flagging industry. The most consciously evolved policy along these lines was that

[37] E.g., J. Taylor *et al.* to Philadelphia Indian Committee, December 13, 1796, in Dept. of Records, Philadelphia Yearly Meeting, Indian Box 1; A. Bliss to D. Greene, [Spring, 1836], ABC 18.6.3.I:89.

[38] Joseph Elkinton Diary, September 14, 1821, transcript in Friends Historical Library, Swarthmore College.

[39] *Ibid.*, August 28, 1827.

[40] Samuel Kirkland Journal, June 3, 1773, in Hamilton College Library; S. Kirkland to his wife, September 10, 1785, in Samuel Kirkland Papers; S. Davis to ––, April 22, 1843, in *Spirit of Missions*, VIII (June 1843), 188-89; P. Dougherty to C. Babcock, September 12, 1849, AIC 7:3:175.

[41] Copy of speech to Cornplanter *et al.*, September 14, 1799, in Dept. of Records, Philadelphia Yearly Meeting, Indian Box 1; Robert Simerwell Journal, June 3, 1827; M. Whitman to D. Greene, April 8, 1845, ABC 18.6.3.IV:180; J. G. Turner to W. Lowrie, September 25, 1857, AIC 7:1:137.

of the Philadelphia Quakers. In 1798 they proposed a set of premiums to the Allegheny Senecas. They promised two dollars to every Seneca male who raised in a given year on his own land twenty-five bushels of wheat or rye, or harvested two tons of hay and put it into a stack or barn. To each Seneca woman they offered two dollars for every twelve yards of linen spun from flax raised on her farm or twelve yards of woolen cloth or linsey spun from her own wool. The offer stood for four years, and the person applying for such an award had to present a certificate from two chiefs attesting to the veracity of the applicant's claim and his temperance for six months.[42] To further promote industry in this tribe, the Friends supplied prospective housebuilders with free boards and gratuitously ground grain raised by red farmers.[43] By 1813 the Quakers encountered the usual problem of such incentive systems among the Indians, for the Senecas considered their farming as a favor to the Quakers and the premium as their just compensation for the strenuous effort. In fact, the Friends suspected that the Indians deliberately procrastinated in improving their lands in hopes of more and better premiums. In light of this experience they discontinued all premiums.[44] Among the "wilder" Ojibwas the American Board missionary offered a bushel of potatoes for each cord of wood delivered by an Indian male to the mission. Many men of that tribe soon reconsidered the proper domain of male activity in order to collect such a premium on effort during the food scarcity in winter.[45]

The missionaries wished to develop Indian industry to the

[42] J. Sharpless *et al.* to Cornplanter and the Seneca Nation, May 22, 1798, in Dept. of Records, Philadelphia Yearly Meeting, Indian Box 1.

[43] Philadelphia Indian Committee Minutes, January 7, 1805, in Dept. of Records, Philadelphia Yearly Meeting, Indian Box 2, copy.

[44] R. Clendenon *et al.* to Philadelphia Indian Committee, March 16, 1813, in Indian Committee Minutes, I:412-15.

[45] W. Boutwell to D. Greene, February 8, 1841, ABC 18.3.7.II:186.

point where they could support their new way of life by themselves.[46] Missions were closed to throw the Indians upon their own efforts rather than continue dependence upon the whites. For this reason an American Board missionary considered it kindness "in the long run" to his charges by not tending a field they had planted and left.[47] Independence was to be achieved at the expense of traditional Indian hospitality and sharing with the needy, for such customs merely depleted the food supply of the industrious and encouraged the idle in their ways.[48]

Presumed fundamental to independence and as a spur to industry was the idea of private property. Only by possessing their land in severalty did the missionaries think that the Indians would put forth their greatest exertions to advance toward civilization. Severalty lay at the basis of the extended farming pattern advocated by most missionaries and their patrons.[49]

No religious group was more eager in promoting private property and the extended farm pattern than the Quakers. From the beginning of the Philadelphia Indian Committee's work among the Senecas, the missionaries urged their listeners to fence and farm individually.[50] After a decade of promotion, the missionaries reported Indian settlers extending along the banks of the Allegheny River rather

[46] E.g., F. Ayer to D. Greene, October 4, 1837, ABC 18.3.7.II:192.

[47] E. Walker to D. Greene, March 27, 1844, ABC 18.5.3.I:82.

[48] Riggs, *Tah-koo Wah-kan*, 247-49.

[49] Belknap and Morse, "Report . . . in 1796," 26; *Summary Account of the Measures Pursued by the Yearly Meeting of Friends of New York, for the Welfare and Civilization of the Indians Residing on the Frontiers of That State, with Extracts from Two Letters Relating to the Subject* (London, 1813), 8-9; James B. Finley, *History of the Wyandott Mission at Upper Sandusky, Ohio, under the Direction of the Methodist Episcopal Church* (Cincinnati, 1840), 274-75, 298-99, 392-94; "Outlines of a Plan for Civilizing the Dakotas," June, 1850, ABC 18.3.7.III:255; *Annual Report of the Missionary Society of the Methodist Episcopal Church*, 1856, 63.

[50] J. Thomas *et al.* to Philadelphia Indian Committee, August 29, 1804, in Dept. of Records, Philadelphia Yearly Meeting, Box 2.

than "crowding together in villages."[51] To further the movement, the Indian Committee offered small premiums to
individual Senecas to fence and plant a certain number of
acres in the new pattern.[52] After the interruption of the War
of 1812, the Quakers decided the Senecas on the Allegheny
Reservation should survey and divide their lands into lots
for individual families. Under the proposed plan no family
could have sold, leased, or transferred its lot to whites. Nor
could the tribe have sold the lot without the consent of the
family occupying it, yet all the land remained in the Seneca
tribe. Provision was made for the inheritance of lots.[53] The
pagan Indians on the reservation stopped the surveyor soon
after he entered upon the land.[54] In an attempt to overawe
this opposition to civilization's advance, the Indian Committee obtained a letter from President Monroe, who advised,
"By thus dividing your lands, each one could then say, this
is mine, and he would have an inducement to put up good
houses on it, and improve his land by cultivation."[55] Presidential prestige failed to move the pagans in their determination to prevent the survey, and the reservation was not
divided, although the Quakers continued their attempts for
decades after.[56]

As a capstone to their industrious Indian agricultural

[51] B. Cooper *et al.* to Philadelphia Indian Committee, December 28, 1808,
in Indian Committee Minutes, I:284-87; "Journal of William Allinson,
Describing Visit to Indians in New York State in 1809," September 19,
1809, in vol. II, Quaker Collection, Haverford College.

[52] B. Cooper *et al.* to Philadelphia Indian Committee, December 12,
1810, in Indian Committee Minutes, I:344-46.

[53] J. Taylor and S. Twining to Philadelphia Indian Committee, March 11,
1816, in Indian Committee Minutes, II:3-5; Plan Proposed for Dividing
Land [September 1817], in Dept. of Records, Philadelphia Yearly Meeting,
Indian Box 3.

[54] C. Fletcher to J. Taylor, August 11, 1818, in Dept. of Records,
Philadelphia Yearly Meeting, Indian Box 3.

[55] James Monroe's Speech to Senecas on Allegheny, January 15, 1819,
ibid., certified copy.

[56] Joseph Elkinton Diary, September 14, October 18, 1824; R. Scotton
et al. to Philadelphia Indian Committee, November 26, 1842, in Dept. of
Records, Philadelphia Yearly Meeting, Indian Box 5.

community, the missionaries envisaged a tribe under law. The Episcopalian missionary quoted in the beginning of this chapter felt such a development resulted inevitably from private property. Another missionary of the same denomination thought education rendered traditional tribal government inadequate in the eyes of the Indians, who then would substitute elective officers with sufficient power delegated to them "to enact and enforce wholesome laws and regulations, for the protection of the tribe."[57] Many missionaries did not possess the patience to wait for law and order to result from slow evolution. At a joint meeting of the United Foreign Missionary Society and American Board workers west of the Mississippi in 1823, they discussed the question: "Is it important in the system of means for the improvement of Indians that some degree of government be introduced, and what course would be advisable for this object?" They concluded,

Judicious laws for the punishment of men are indispensably necessary to the welfare of any community of depraved men, and but little progress can be made by the Indians in adopting civilized habits whilst the defense of property and life rests entirely on person[al] strength and courage. The establishment of some plain and important laws is desirable also as a means more readily to understand the terms and illustrations employed in religious instruction.

The measure proper for the promotion of the object should be adapted to the peculiar situation of the Indian Tribes, as under the guardianship of the United States, and to the character of the existing customs and policy of the particular tribe in view. Where the chiefs possess little or no authoraty [sic] and any business which is transacted is done in council[,] recourse should be had to that body, and endeavors use[d] to convince the principle [sic] men of the necessity and advantage of some authoratative [sic] regulations and any aid which may be necessary in their

[57] S. Davis to ——, [1841?], in *Proceedings of the Board of Missions of the Domestic and Foreign Missionary Society of the Protestant Episcopal Church in the United States of America,* 1841, Appendix Ae, 84-85.

formation, should be afforded them. But great caution will have to be observed in every case lest we incite suspicion [and] jealousy.[58]

Just how much interference these and other missionaries committed for their goal is not known, for most missionaries were cautious in writing such news.

At times only advice was offered. Some Christian Oneidas desired Samuel Kirkland in 1799 to inform them how to reform their brethren. He suggested they appoint from among the wisest young warriors eight to ten persons to act as overseers of the peace and order of the town and report to him or the Christian chief. His idea was followed.[59] The Quaker schoolteacher urged the Senecas on the Allegheny Reservation to enact laws so that the conclusions of the chiefs would be of "more consequence and power."[60] He even drafted a plan to organize a new government with elected officers who would have replaced the traditional chiefs.[61]

Some missionaries actively interfered for their governmental ideals. In 1823 James Finley proposed to the Wyandot Council to keep a journal of their acts. They agreed, and he kept a journal account of every council he attended. By this action, he wrote, "the means of introducing something like rule and law among them and of teaching them the notion of government" was effected.[62] That same year he persuaded the council to brand horses and record the earmarks of cattle and hogs to prevent disputes over ownership.[63] According to his own testimony, Gideon Blackburn was responsible for the early governmental efforts of the Cherokees, for he asserted in 1808, "the Cherokee Nation

[58] Minutes of Joint Missionary Convention, November 4-6, 1823, in A. Finney to J. Evarts, November 10, 1823, ABC 18.3.1.I:51.

[59] Samuel Kirkland Journal, February 17, 25, 1799.

[60] Joseph Elkinton Diary, September 14, 1824, October 9, 1826.

[61] *Ibid.*, October 12, 1826.

[62] Finley, *History of Wyandott Mission*, 200-203.

[63] *Ibid.*, 199-200.

has at length determined to become men and citizens. Towards this my exertions have been unremittingly directed since the commencement of my mission to them. A few days ago, in full council, they adopted a constitution, which embraces a simple principle of government."[64]

The growth of law and government in a tribe and its relationship to the missionary and his converts can be seen in Kansas Ottawa history. In August, 1843, the Christian Ottawas enacted their first laws respecting fraud, theft, and drunkenness, and requested their missionary, Jotham Meeker, to write them down for the future.[65] The principal chief and his non-Christian followers attempted to destroy these laws.[66] Five years later the Christians passed laws against drinking ardent spirits, theft, and gambling, and again had Meeker preserve these laws on paper.[67] Again the pagan opposition under the head chief demanded the dropping of the laws, especially those prohibiting gambling. After much confusion, the law against gambling was erased. In a prayer meeting during the next year Meeker worked hard to induce the brethren to adopt a rule against incurring debt beyond the means to pay from the annuity.[68] Meeker again presented this idea before the general council in early 1850 and saw it adopted as a law of the tribe.[69] At the same time the council passed three other laws and revised all the previous ones. Meeker then printed the code in the second edition of his little *Ottawa First Book*.[70]

The code of twenty-five laws represented the growth of central authority and civilization in the tribe. Fully fourteen of the laws provided protection for private property. Theft

---

[64] G. Blackburn to ——, September 16, 1808, in *Panoplist*, IV (December 1808), 325-26.

[65] Jotham Meeker Journal, August 12, 14, 15, 1843, in Kansas State Historical Society.

[66] *Ibid.*, August 19, 1843.

[67] *Ibid.*, February 4, 29, June 15, 1848.

[68] *Ibid.*, July 26, 1849.   [69] *Ibid.*, January 12, 1850.

[70] Meeker to C. N. Handy, September 3, 1850, in Jotham Meeker Papers, copy.

of animals, articles borrowed without permission of owner or not returned at the agreed time, and housebreaking were punished by paying the value of the object or the hire of it to the owner and usually a stated fine above this amount to the tribal treasury. Provision was also made for the return of strayed animals, proper fencing of fields, reexchanging of horses and other articles, and violence by a studhorse. If a person set fire to the prairie and burned another's property, he had to pay the value of whatever was destroyed. If a man suspected another of theft, he could send the lawmen to search the suspect's house. If the suspect refused to allow such a search, he was presumed guilty. To culminate the growing attachment to property was a law for inheritance. Allied with the concern for property were two laws providing for prompt payment of debts. In spite of the earlier opposition, the code prohibited gambling; any man seen at mocassin playing was fined two dollars. Whisky was not allowed on the reservation, and anyone bringing it in or sending for it paid five dollars for the first offense, forfeited his annuity for the second offense, and was delivered to the United States officials for a third violation. Injury by slander was fined. To enforce these laws, the code provided for "lawmen." Anyone who refused to serve in such an office after being selected had to pay five dollars to be excused. All lawmen were required to be present at all council meetings or pay one dollar. If any person sought revenge for a penalization under the code, the lawmen were allowed to do as they saw fit with the culprit. In addition to the fines, a tax on land and cattle provided funds for the tribal treasury. A poor tax was levied of twelve and a half cents per capita. The code specifically stated that all residents on the Ottawa Reservation were subject to the laws.[71]

[71] Jotham Meeker, *Ottawa First Book, Containing Lessons for the Learner; Portions of the Gospel by Luke, Omitted by Matthew and John; and the Ottawa Laws* (2d ed., Ottawa Baptist Mission Station [Kansas], 1850), 102-25.

Reflecting the concern for law and order was the court system and the election of officials. After this period, regular trials were held for violations of the law. The plaintiff and the defendant were both present with their lawyers and witnesses. After the evidence was rendered, two judges examined the laws and decided the case.[72] The Ottawas also held annual business councils, at which time they elected a chief, a treasurer, and two law enforcement officers.[73] The year 1850 probably marks the end of opposition to the new government.

The pinnacle of this movement for law and order was naturally American citizenship for the transformed savage. The most persistent worker in this direction was Stephen R. Riggs among the Sioux. In the summer of 1856 a civilized band of Sioux gathered under his direction, drafted a constitution that resembled a platform of behavior more than a governmental organization document, and called itself the "Hazelwood Republic."[74] Beginning with the state constitutional convention at St. Paul, Minnesota, in 1857, Riggs attempted to have his charges recognized as citizens of the new state.[75] Thereafter, he regularly attended upon the Minnesota legislature to present petitions, point out precedents in other states, secure recommendations in the governor's messages for such action, and prepare bills for the purpose. All to no avail.[76] Before the district court in 1861, Riggs advocated the case of nine fullblooded Sioux who sought the rights and privileges of state citizenship. Only one knew English, and so Riggs interpreted the judge's questions and the Indians' correct answers for the other eight. The judge claimed Sioux was a barbarous language

[72] Meeker Journal, July 6, 1852; Meeker to J. N. Chenault, October 4, 1852, in *Senate Exec. Doc.* no. 1, 32 Cong., 2 Sess. (1852-1853), 385-86.
[73] Meeker Journal, October 18, 1842, November 7, 1854.
[74] Riggs, *Tah-koo Wah-kan*, 393-94.
[75] S. R. Riggs to S. Treat, August 13, 1857, ABC 18.3.7.III:341.
[76] S. R. Riggs to S. Treat, February 22, 1861, ABC 18.3.7.IV:10.

and denied all the applications except that of the man who spoke English.[77]

Like many missionaries, the judge was unwilling to accept less than complete transformation of Indian life. Though these eight Sioux had learned to live as industrious agrarians as the missionary had demanded, they were denied the rights given to white farmers because they still spoke their native tongue. This experience was symbolic of the Christian Indian's quest for citizenship and acceptance in a white man's world. Hence it is evident that the activities and attitudes of the missionaries' fellow whites were important to the success and failure of mission work.

[77] "Applications of Sioux Indians to Become Citizens," *The Record,* June 21, 1861, clipping in ABC 18.3.1.XIV:176.

Chapter Five

OTHER WHITES

SINCE the main method of introducing civilization to the Indians was by example, the whites near the mission stations had an important effect on the success of mission programs in the eyes of the religious societies and their workers. Indian missionaries quickly classified their white neighbors. If they thought their neighbors provided a good model and aided their plans, then they were good people. On the other hand, if they considered them opposed to the mission and immoral, then they were agents of Satan out to halt the divine progress of the Gospel and moral civilization. The missionaries applied this simple yardstick to governmental representatives, other missionaries, traders, and all other whites around the tribes.[1]

The single most important white was the government agent. While this person did not convert Indians directly, he could provide the optimum conditions for the missionary to pursue his goal. For this reason the missionary expressed great concern for the agent's character. Was he an active church member? Was he sober and honest? Did he believe in Indian missionary activity? An affirmative answer to these questions rendered prospects excellent for the mission enterprise.[2] If the agent favored religious work among the Indians, he could exercise his powers to aid such endeavors greatly. His appointments of farmers, teachers, and blacksmiths from people of good character set good examples for the Indians. At times, some agents even turned these positions over to missionaries to fill.[3] By his reports to Washington, the agent could direct or withhold the tribal educational funds and the Civilization Fund appropriation from a mission. His enforcement of the liquor laws,[4] his removal of antagonistic whites,[5] and his statements about the missionaries to the Indians all affected the successful outcome of Indian religious work. The agent possessed the prestige to scotch rumors damaging to the mission and the power to prevent Indian persecution of the missionaries. His authority could even persuade the Indians to execute agreements for the maintenance of regular school attendance by the children.[6]

An agent unfavorable to mission work because of denominational, political, or other reasons commanded numerous means to bedevil the missionary and even force his departure. He could spread rumors prejudicial to the mission. He could provide an example of profanity, whoring, drinking, and dishonesty and could also appoint to the posts of teachers, farmers, and smiths relatives and hangers-on who duplicated his example. Educational funds could be diverted to schools especially established by his followers. Finally, the agent could request the removal of the missionary from the tribe.[7] In the opinion of one missionary

[1] This chapter discusses the nature of the problem and the radical solution proposed by some, rather than traces in detail all the specific conflicts by area and time. Few missionaries faced every kind of white mentioned in this analysis, for the type of contact depended upon the stage of acculturation of the Indian tribes and the advance of white settlement. For example, Indians located on reservations surrounded by dense white settlement possessed no furs to lure traders, but they were subjected to requests for leases from nearby white inhabitants. The references to specific missions illustrate the problems but do not serve as complete analyses of the situation at the stations.

[2] E.g., C. Washburn to J. Evarts, December 22, 1830, ABC 18.3.1.IX:3.

[3] E.g., Isaac McCoy Journal, July 16, 1822, in Kansas State Historical Society.

[4] E.g., W. Hamilton to W. Lowrie, September 6, 1848, AIC 4:3:125.

[5] E.g., P. Dougherty to D. Wells, June 19, 1841, AIC 7:3:59.

[6] E.g., S. M. Irvin to W. Lowrie, January 15, 1849, AIC 4:3:135.

[7] For examples of such activities, see W. Hamilton to W. Lowrie, May 26, 1840, AIC 8:1:56; P. Dougherty to W. Lowrie, May 3, 1840, AIC 7:3:53; P. Dougherty to D. Wells, June 19, 1841, AIC 7:3:59; S. Irvin to W.

a bad agent was far worse than none at all.[8] Missionary eagerness to correct such a man and set his feet upon the path of righteousness certainly did not better relations with this type of agent.

Since the agent was so important to mission enterprise, mission societies attempted to influence their appointment at times. Occasionally they petitioned a new presidential administration to retain a good agent appointed by its predecessor.[9] More frequently the missionaries sought the removal of a bad agent.[10] So significant did the Presbyterian Iowa mission consider the post that it attempted to gain an agency for one of its missionaries.[11] Not until after the Civil War were the missionaries appointed agents in an attempt to improve Indian administration.[12]

The missionaries also came in contact with the army posts in Indian country. In such cases the missionaries either approved of the garrison as an oasis of morality or preached against it as a cesspool of wickedness. The Fort Snelling commander in 1839, for example, received the accolades of the Sioux missionaries because he enforced the liquor laws among the Indians, prevented the persecution of the missionaries, and allowed church services for his men.[13]

Lowrie, December 8, 31, 1845, AIC 4:3:8, 11; S. Irvin to F. H. Harvey, January 24, 1846, AIC 4:3:23, copy.

[8] S. Irvin to W. Lowrie, September 28, 1840, AIC 8:1:63.

[9] E.g., H. Drinker to H. Dearborn, October 24, 1806, in Dept. of Records, Philadelphia Yearly Meeting, Indian Box 2; W. Hamilton to N. Ewing, November 7, 1849, AIC 4:3:153.

[10] E.g., S. Irvin to F. H. Harvey, January 24, 1846, AIC 4:3:23, copy.

[11] W. Hamilton to W. Lowrie, October 10, 1840, AIC 8:1:65. This letter analyzes at length the significance of the agent.

[12] For the story of this development, see Loring B. Priest, *Uncle Sam's Stepchildren: The Reformation of United States Indian Policy, 1865-1887* (New Brunswick, N.J., 1942), 28-41.

[13] T. S. Williamson to D. Greene, July 12, 1839, ABC 18.3.7.II:91; J. D. Stevens to D. Greene, March 23, 1839, ABC 18.3.7.II:39; Samuel W. Pond, Jr., *Two Volunteer Missionaries among the Dakotas; or, the Story of the Labors of Samuel W. and Gideon H. Pond* (Boston, 1893), 183-84; Francis Paul Prucha, *Broadax and Bayonet: The Role of the United States Army in the Development of the Northwest, 1815-1860* (Madison, 1953), 210-11.

Perhaps the choicest epithets in missionaries' letters were reserved for fellow workers in other denominations rather than the agents and the army. By tacit agreement, missionary societies did not proselyte in each other's fields in order to avoid confusing heathen minds by sectarian differences. The first society sending missionaries into a tribe staked out that tribe as its field. Yet, since some tribes were large, the societies by further tacit concurrence allowed missionary work in that tribe by a second society beyond the influence of the first.[14] The Indian Office backed this theory of exclusion to prevent interdenominational rivalry.[15] In practice, tribes seldom remained the sole fields of one denomination. Mission organizations preferred to work in fields ready for the harvest, and though all tribes were theoretically open to missionary effort, only a relatively few tribes were sufficiently acculturated (or demoralized) to offer ready access. Thus several societies would send workers to the same small tribe because it appeared ready for conversion. An interesting example of such conflict occurred among the few hundred Peorias and Weas, who lived twelve miles apart. Both remnants spoke the same language and acted together. The Western Foreign Missionary Society founded a station among the Weas in 1833 even though the Methodists had already established a mission among the Peorias. Only after several years of effort did the Presbyterians surrender the station because the Indians preferred the Methodists. Their station should never have been opened in the first place, for clearly the Methodists held the field by right.[16] Even more potent in breaking down the

---

[14] For the theory, see August G. Spangenberg, *An Account of the Manner in Which the Protestant Church of the Unitas Fratrum, or United Brethren, Preach the Gospel, and Carry on Their Missions among the Heathen* (London, 1788), 39–40; C. Kingsbury *et al.* to S. Worcester, December 20, 1819, ABC 18.3.4.I:65.

[15] P. Dougherty to W. A. Richmond, May 2, 1846, AIC 7:3:127A.

[16] J. Kerr to E. Swift, June 23, July 15, 1836, AIC 3:1:70, 73; J. Fleming to W. Lowrie, December 9, 1837, AIC 3:1:99.

theory of exclusive fields was the assumption of denominationalism. As has been mentioned, each denomination conceived of itself as part of the universal Church, but considered itself a truer version of Christianity than any other denomination. For this reason, missionary societies hastened to enter a tribe before another denomination did or had few regrets about moving into a tribe occupied by another society.

Under this belief the Protestant missionaries felt no qualms about opening stations in tribes already served by Catholic missionaries. A Presbyterian missionary who had entered the area of a Catholic missionary conceived of his fellow Christian as "one of Satans own faithful ones" and prayed for the deliverance of the tribe from the priest's machinations.[17] Protestant missionaries particularly feared that Catholicism appealed to the savage mind because "Heathenish superstitions, and idolatry produce a state of mind and heart well fitted to give credence to papal superstition and idolatry." They believed the Roman Catholic religion naught but "baptized heathenism."[18] Such thoughts spurred a Methodist missionary to race a priest to a band of Indians to save them from Catholicism.[19] Catholic missionaries entered Protestant fields for the same reasons.[20]

The Protestants also disparaged each other. A Presbyterian missionary feared the success of Baptist and Methodist efforts, for then "ignorant fanaticism will reign instead of enlightened Christianity; for these societies are not only

[17] A. Porter to W. Lowrie, December 17, 1853, AIC 7:1:104, March 17, 1858, AIC 7:2:57.

[18] See, for example, R. Simerwell to L. Bolles, November 25, 1838, in Simerwell Papers, Kansas State Historical Society, draft.

[19] John H. Pitezel, *Lights and Shades of Missionary Life: Containing Travels, Sketches, Incidents, and Missionary Efforts, during Nine Years Spent in the Region of Lake Superior* (Cincinnati, 1857), 113.

[20] E.g., Samuel Charles Mazzuchelli, *Memoirs, Historical and Edifying of a Missionary Apostolic of the Order of St. Dominic among the Various Indian Tribes and among Catholics and Protestants in the United States of America* (Chicago, 1915), 123-25.

antagonists but they are ignorant, and obtrusive to the last degree, preaching in these countries, very little sound doctrine, dogging the steps of the Presbyterians wherever they go, doing no pioneer work really, and at the same time, making no provision for the instruction of the people in *sound doctrine, letters,* or *civilization.*"[21] The American Board missionaries constantly complained about Methodists stealing their converts and even their church members.[22] Elsewhere the Baptists complained about the Methodists,[23] Quakers about Presbyterians, Presbyterians about Quakers,[24] and Methodists about Baptists.[25] So fiercely did interdenominational rivalry rage that the Quakers in the Oneida Tribe refused Samuel Kirkland, the Presbyterian missionary whose territory they had entered, any bread for his communion when he lacked some for the service.[26]

Alfred Brunson, a Methodist missionary, claimed in his book, *Western Pioneer,* that the missionaries of other denominations whom he met never raised disputed doctrines. "The Heathen to whom we ministered never knew from us the differences between denominations."[27] This claim is difficult to sustain, but a few missionaries and one society practiced the ideal of brotherly love. Daniel Butrick, an American Board missionary among the Cherokees, cooperated with all men in advancing Christ's kingdom.[28] For the Moravians'

[21] E. McKinney to W. Lowrie, September 11, 1845, AIC 9:12:16, his italics. The criticisms about doctrine, discipline, and civilization have already been discussed.

[22] E.g., S. A. Worcester to S. Treat, June 27, 1856, ABC 18.3.1.XIII:333; C. Kingsbury to S. W. Winans, January 28, 1825, ABC 18.3.4.III:5.

[23] Robert Simerwell Diary, December 10, 1837.

[24] Among Seneca and Oneida tribes.

[25] W. Johnson to Baptist Missionaries, March 12, 1842, in J. Pratt to W. Johnson, April 12, 1842, in John Pratt Correspondence, Kansas State Historical Society.

[26] W. Gregory to S. Kirkland, February 23, 1799, in Samuel Kirkland Papers, Hamilton College Library.

[27] Alfred Brunson, *The Western Pioneer; or, Incidents of the Life and Times of Rev. Alfred Brunson* (Cincinnati, 1872-1879), II, 136.

[28] Butrick Journal, September, 1832, ABC 18.3.1.VII:17; D. S. Butrick to S. Treat, June 17, 1848, May 29, 1850, ABC 18.3.1.XI:227, 241.

adherence to the exclusive field principle and its modified corollary, they were universally appreciated by other denominations.[29] If the field seemed large enough for two societies, the Protestant denominations buried their rivalries as the Methodists and Presbyterians did in Oregon, but they fought Catholic missionization together.[30]

Wielding great influence over tribal affairs were the traders, who usually preceded the missionaries in the tribe. Of all the mercantile groups the fur traders and the liquor dealers received the greatest attention in missionary letters.

Nearly all missionary societies assumed the fur trading interests opposed their activities, especially the civilization phases. Most missionaries believed fur traders thought that if the Indians were "taught agriculture they will be less needy and hunt less an[d] consequently furnish fewer skins and furs on which the trader can make a profit and if their minds are enlarged by religious instruction they will be less subject to imposition and thus the trader cannot make so large a profit on the goods which he sells them."[31] Yet there was no real agreement on this issue. In most cases the particular company under discussion was the American Fur Company. Two Quakers on a tour in the early 1840s reported the company as unfavorable to missionary work among the Osages,[32] but two years later an Episcopalian specifically refuted this charge.[33] From its records, one finds the company paid little attention to the missionaries. It supplied them with provisions and goods so long as they did

---

[29] E.g., D. S. Butrick to D. Greene, May 19, 1846, ABC 18.3.1.XI:217.

[30] H. H. Spalding to D. Greene, March 15, 1838, ABC 18.5.3.I:23.

[31] T. S. Williamson to D. Greene, May 9, 1834, ABC 18.3.7.I:15. Also see tour of Kingsbury and Byington among tribes west of Missouri in A.B.C.F.M., *Report*, 1834, 174; S. R. Riggs to S. B. Treat, November 12, 1849, ABC 18.3.7.III:249.

[32] John D. Lang and Samuel Taylor, Jr., *Report of a Visit to Some of the Tribes of Indians, Located West of the Mississippi River* (New York, 1843), 25.

[33] "Journal of a Tour in the 'Indian Territory' Performed . . . in the Spring of 1844," *Spirit of Missions* (June 1844, extra), 31.

not sell or trade them in competition with the company's agents.[34] At first the company arranged such service for the American Board mission among the Ojibwas and then also for the Methodists, Baptists, and Catholics on the same terms.[35] The company only refused to transport supplies when a missionary looked to competing companies, and the president of the American Fur Company expressed no grief at losing missionary trade, since it had proved unprofitable.[36]

Because a missionary occasionally dealt with competition and the large manual labor boarding school paid for services rendered in goods, it inevitably appeared in the eyes of some traders that the missionaries were in competition. Traders who feared such was the case demanded the missionaries cease all trading.[37] Other fur companies, such as Biddle and Drew, maintained policies of neutral noninterference similar to those of the American Fur Company.[38] Many missionaries felt that the rumormongering and other activities of the agents belied the companies' professed policies. One missionary reported hearing a fur company official contend that he lost five hundred dollars for each Indian who learned to read and write.[39]

Regardless of official company policy, it was the traders in the field who actually influenced Indian attitudes and conducted relations with the missionaries. Frequently these agents requested missionaries to found schools at their

[34] L. M. Warren to R. Crooks, October 16, 1834, in American Fur Company Papers, New-York Historical Society; R. Crooks to L. M. Warren, February 18, 1835, *ibid.*, Letter Book I:162-68.

[35] R. Crooks to L. M. Warren, June 7, 1836, *ibid.*, Letter Book III:276-78; R. Crooks to L. Warren, August 8, 1837, *ibid.*, Letter Book V:247; R. Crooks to Martin Bates and Sons, March 8, 1844, *ibid.*, Letter Book XXII:407.

[36] J. P. Scott to C. W. Borup, March 4, 1841, *ibid.*, Letter Book XVI:298-99; R. Crooks to C. W. Borup, September 28, 1841, *ibid.*, Letter Book XVII:220-28.

[37] G. Johnston to R. Crooks, July 17, August 10, 1841, *ibid.*

[38] J. Clark to Corresponding Secretary, October 21, 1834, in *Christian Advocate*, IX (November 28, 1834), 54.

[39] Pond, *Two Volunteer Missionaries*, iii.

headquarters to educate their children and their relatives' offspring. The American Board missions among the Chippewas and Sioux were commenced upon such applications.[40] Even French-Canadian traders who were Catholic and married to Indian women sought mission stations for this reason as well as to train their relatives in farming and housework. The first real foothold among the Sioux by the American Board was gained at the village of such a trader.[41] Similar instances occurred among the Chippewas[42] and Potawatomis.[43] At other times traders aided the missionaries because the missionaries assisted them in the fur trade.[44] Yet in these tribes as well as others the missionaries considered the majority of fur traders opposed to their object. Because of their Catholicism, many French-Canadian traders warned the Indians against Protestantism as the surest path to eternal damnation. Missionaries and traders competed to obtain the tribal annuities. A school fund gained was a trader's profit lost. Due to the easy access to the Indian mind through their native spouses, the traders were powerful rumor mills. Yet in assessing blame on these people, the missionaries were not united.[45]

Although traders other than fur agents had no reason to oppose Indian farming, they resented other aspects of missionary intervention in tribal life. Besides the competition for tribal annuities, education of the Indian destroyed the effectiveness of the charge system employed by the

[40] J. Stevens to D. Greene, June 15, 1835, ABC 18.3.7.I:6; A.B.C.F.M., *Report*, 1831, 94.

[41] Stephen R. Riggs, *Tah-koo Wah-kan; or, the Gospel among the Dakotas* (Boston, 1869), ch. x.

[42] F. Ayers to D. Greene, July, 1843, ABC 18.3.7.II:212.

[43] Isaac McCoy Journal, June 9, 1821.

[44] E.g., William Boutwell to R. Crooks, January 19, 1837, in American Fur Company Papers.

[45] Isaac McCoy Journal, April 10, 1821; W. Hamilton to W. Lowrie, January 20, 1842, AIC 8:1:77; Sioux Missionaries to S. Treat, September 12, 1849, ABC 18.3.7.III:12; T. S. Winson to S. Treat, September 18, 1849, ABC 18.3.7.III:391; S. Irvin to W. Lowrie, July 15, 1853, AIC 3:2:51.

traders, for a literate Indian could check the ledger's figures. Some of the secular activities connected with the manual labor boarding school seemed to threaten the trader's very livelihood. For example, five of the ten traders licensed by the government agent in the Choctaw country during the early 1820s were missionaries. However, their aggregate capital equaled only a third of that of the largest trading house.[46] Of all the traders, those dealing in liquor were most opposed by the missionaries, for their commodity provided the "ardent spirits" to propel the frolics with resultant license and butchery and to encourage Indians to annoy the missionaries. Missionaries condemned them as Satan's highest agents. In return for this condemnation, the liquor sellers frequently employed their influence to oppose the plans of the missionaries.[47]

If, according to the social theory of the era, white examples influenced Indian adoption of civilized life, then all whites including traders, agents, soldiers, and settlers determined Indian behavior. Therefore, the missionaries would have preferred all whites to exemplify the highest ideals of Christian civilization, but reality forced them to recognize most whites fell far short of these ideals. In fact, the missionary was forced to admit that due to the influence of bad example, "the principal vices of the Indians are emphatically *our* vices."[48] The list of these vices included whisky drinking, swearing, card playing, and Sabbath breaking—products only of white contact.

Often the missionary's own house was out of order in this

[46] "List of Licenses and to Whom Granted," November 10, 1823, to July 20, 1825, NABIA, L.R., Choctaw.

[47] E.g., J. Kerr to E. Swift, August 31, 1835, AIC 3:1:43; H. Bradley to E. Swift, June 16, 1837, AIC 3:1:89.

[48] William H. Goode, *Outposts of Zion, with Limnings of Mission Life* (Cincinnati, 1864), 58. Also, see Address by Stephen Olin to the South Carolina Missionary Society, January, 1824, in *Methodist Magazine*, VII (August 1824), 306-307.

respect. Since the manual labor boarding schools required large staffs, inevitably some whites providing bad examples would be hired, especially since the labor supply was small and the proportion of this type of person large in the small frontier population. Much of the labor in the midwestern missions was done by French-Canadians, whom the missionaries considered lazy, illiterate, and followers of a heathenism worse than that of the Indians.[49] Southern missions had to depend on slave help, since few whites could be hired, with resultant bad influence on the students. Of all the vices for which missionaries dismissed employees, drunkenness and intercourse with students predominated.[50] Occasionally missionaries themselves took sexual advantage of their students or robbed Indian property.[51]

Missionaries complained more frequently about their white neighbors than their employees. Lessees of Indian land,[52] lumber workers,[53] railroad workers,[54] and mere travelers[55] were accused of introducing vice and indolence. Occasionally charges were leveled against high government officials who had dealings with the Indians,[56] but usually the invective was directed against people "of inferior grade"

[49] W. T. Boutwell to D. Greene, December 16, 1835, ABC 18.3.7.I:89; T. S. Williamson to D. Greene, July 13, 1837, ABC 18.3.7.II:1; F. Ely to D. Greene, August 26, 1841, ABC 18.3.7.II:231.

[50] E.g., Isaac McCoy Journal, August 20, 1821; Robert Simerwell Journal, December 14, 1827; L. Slater to J. Lykins and R. Simerwell, December 14, 1827, in Isaac McCoy Papers, XIV; C. Kingsbury to J. Evarts, July 20, October 6, 1828, ABC 18.3.4.III:26, 32.

[51] F. Barker to S. Peck, January 8, 1848, in Francis Barker Papers, Kansas State Historical Society, copy; D. S. Butrick to J. Evarts, January 22, 1823, ABC 18.3.1.III:133.

[52] J. Taylor and I. Mann to Philadelphia Indian Committee, March 29, 1819, in Dept. of Records, Philadelphia Yearly Meeting, Indian Box 3.

[53] F. Ayer to D. Greene, November 2, 1840, ABC 18.3.7.II:202.

[54] S. Lukens to Philadelphia Indian Committee, October 28, 1850, in Dept. of Records, Philadelphia Yearly Meeting, Indian Box 5.

[55] C. Kingsbury to S. Worcester, July 30, 1818, ABC 18.3.4.II:5.

[56] C. Washburn to J. Evarts, September 1, 1830, ABC 18.3.1.IX:2; S. R. Riggs to S. Treat, June 22, 1853, ABC 18.3.7.III:294.

or "the lower orders."[57] Such whites were considered by most missionaries as little above the "common grade of wild Indians."[58] Because of the proximity of these lower class whites to the Indians, the Indians assimilated many lower class habits to the disgust of the missionaries, who were usually middle class. Thus missionary attacks on Indian vices frequently reduced to the condemnation of the lower class habits in their own society.

So pernicious did missionaries consider most white influence on Indian behavior that the majority of missionaries believed the less contact Indians had with the white race the more favorable the prospects of missionary success. In their opinion the opportunity to save the Indians from hell's fires passed rapidly as white settlers surrounded a tribe.[59] In actuality, the greater the contact with whites, the more likely the traditional cultural unity would crack and allow the substitution of missionary values for old values. Given the missionary train of thought, however, the logical conclusion was the removal of all Indians beyond the blighting influences of lower class white civilization. In other words, send the Indians to the wilderness in order to train them in good civilization. Such a solution posed no paradox to many missionaries, or apparently to Andrew Jackson[60] and other Americans who called for the removal of the Indians beyond the Mississippi River.

[57] For use of these terms, see Brainerd Journal, August 2, 1821, ABC 18.3.1.II:55; J. Taylor and I. Mann to Philadelphia Indian Committee, March 29, 1819, in Dept. of Records, Philadelphia Yearly Meeting, Indian Box 3; S. Lukens to E. Worth and J. Evans, April 6, 1852, *ibid.*, Box 6.

[58] Isaac McCoy Journal, September 11, 1820.

[59] A. Finney to J. Evarts, July 27, 1822, ABC 18.3.1.I:33-36; T. S. Williamson to D. Greene, December 15, 1840, ABC 18.3.7.II:16; Report of Commission on Indian Missions, in "Annual Report of American Baptist Missionary Union for 1853," *Baptist Missionary Magazine*, XXXIII (July 1853), 209-10. Cf. John R. Bodo, *The Protestant Clergy and Public Issues, 1812-1848* (Princeton, 1954), 92-93.

[60] See John William Ward, *Andrew Jackson, Symbol for an Age* (New York, 1955), 40-41, for Jackson's attitude.

Although many missionaries sincerely believed this paradox, few acted upon it with such determination as Isaac
McCoy. The idea of the detrimental influence of neighboring whites occurred to McCoy early in his missionary
career,[61] but not until mid-1823 did he think of a solution.
Itinerating among his charges, he suddenly "formed the
resolution" in that year that he would, "providence permitting, thenceforward keep steadily in view, and endeavor
to promote a plan for colonizing the natives in a country to
be made forever theirs, west of the State of Missouri."[62] He
hoped to establish a colony where Indians, civilized by the
benevolent efforts of church and government, might enjoy
the "privileges of *men,* and the prospects of a settled home,"
in which they would not be disturbed or tempted by bad
whites or heathen Indians. Under his plan the federal
government was to provide far beyond the white frontier
suitable land on which each Indian would receive a plantation. To this colony, mission societies of all denominations
were to send their finished products so that they could
encourage each other to persist on the road to Christian
civilization, for McCoy rightly believed that the graduates
of mission schools suffered under white contempt for their
race, and so "for want of a circle of friends, with whom they
may be on an equality, they often become profligate and
wretched, or to wander back into the forests, and mingle
with their barbarous kindred, to the grief of their bene-
factors, and the disparagement of the schools."[63]

Being a man of action, McCoy journeyed to Washington
in early 1824 personally to present his plan to the Baptist

[61] Isaac McCoy Journal, April 23, 1821.

[62] Isaac McCoy, *History of Baptist Indian Missions, Embracing Remarks
on the Former and Present Condition of the Aboriginal Tribes; Their Settlement within the Indian Territory, and Their Future Prospects* (Washington,
1840), 197.

[63] McCoy to L. Cass *et al.,* June 23, 1823, in Isaac McCoy Papers,
V, draft. Also see his *Remarks on the Practicability of Indian Reform, Embracing Their Colonization* (Boston, 1827).

Board of Missions and the Secretary of War. This trip marked the beginning of his career as a political lobbyist more than as a missionary. Henceforth, his subordinates managed the missions he nominally headed, while he pushed his plans before Congress and the President, before the Baptist Board of Missions, and before the public in general. Gradually McCoy's project and energies were absorbed into the general stream favoring removal.[64]

Active as McCoy but on the opposite side was Jeremiah Evarts, the corresponding secretary of the American Board of Commissioners for Foreign Missions. With the advent of Jackson, Evarts felt certain the President meant to force southern Indian removal by denying them their rights. Prior to this time Evarts had approved of experimenting with removal if it were accomplished slowly with proper safe-guards for the Indians.[65] Now he felt the American Board would not "stand acquitted before God, or posterity," unless it "bore testimony against the threatened course of proceed-ings by Jackson."[66] Anticipating the great removal debate in the next session of Congress, Evarts wrote a series of articles for the late summer and fall issues of the *National Intelligencer* under the *nom de plume* of William Penn, which were later reprinted as *Essays on the Present Crisis in the Conditions of the American Indians*.[67] Since he had studied to become a lawyer, his essays resembled a legal brief in the defense of Cherokee claims to permanent title to their lands against Georgia's assertion that the aborigines were mere possessory tenants and therefore subject to the

---

[64] The best account of his political activities on behalf of removal is his papers for the period at the Kansas State Historical Society, but see his *History* also.

[65] See Ebenezer C. Tracy, *Memoir of the Life of Jeremiah Evarts, Esq.* (Boston, 1845), 215, 268-72, 274-75, 306-307, 328-30. For background on Evarts and his efforts against removal, see J. Orin Oliphant, *Through the South and the West with Jeremiah Evarts in 1826* (Lewisburg, Pa., 1956), 1-62.

[66] Tracy, *Evarts*, 329.

[67] Boston, 1829.

state's laws which deprived them of rights essential to their remaining upon Georgian soil.[68] To make the arguments more available to the public, the corresponding secretary condensed his *Essays* into *A Brief View of the Present Relations between the Government and People of the United States and the Indians within our National Limits,* which was printed over the names of some influential citizens of New York City.[69]

At the same time, other religious men took sides in the removal question. That same spring a small group of clergymen and laymen of the Dutch Reformed Church and a few others organized to preserve the Indians in the only way possible—"the final and speedy removal of the scattered remains of the Indian tribes." For this end "the Indian Board, for the Emigration, Preservation, and Improvement of the Aborigines of America" was founded in July, 1829, to aid the administration in its aim. Behind the establishment of the society and its activities was Thomas McKenney, the Commissioner of Indian Affairs, who felt the need of religious support for Jackson's policy.[70] According to Annie H. Abel, Bishop Hobart of the Episcopal Church supported the idea of emigration.[71] The sole Episcopal missionary among the Indians declared his enthusiasm for the project to the Secretary of War.[72]

Forces far greater than Evarts and McCoy determined the

---

[68] Did John Marshall, who praised these *Essays* as "the most conclusive argument that he had ever read on any subject whatever" (Tracy, *Evarts,* 339n) utilize them as a basis for his decision in Worcester *v.* Georgia?

[69] Tracy, *Evarts,* 349.

[70] *Documents and Proceedings Relating to the Formation and Progress of a Board in the City of New York, for the Emigration, Preservation and Improvement of the Aborigines of America, July 22, 1829* (New York, 1829); Francis Paul Prucha, "Thomas L. McKenney and the New York Indian Board," *Mississippi Valley Historical Review,* XLVIII (March 1962), 635-55.

[71] A. H. Abel, "The History of Events Resulting in Indian Consolidations West of the Mississippi River," *Annual Report of the American Historical Association for 1906,* I, 377n, but see Prucha, "Indian Board," 639-41.

[72] S. Davis to J. H. Eaton, November 4, 1829, NABIA, L.R., School File.

outcome of the removal debates in Congress, and on May 28, 1830, Jackson signed the bill.[73] When the time arrived eventually for the removal of a tribe, each missionary had to decide his stand on the issue. While most subscribed to the baneful effects of corrupt white intercourse, they also felt emigration only temporarily withdrew the Indians from the contamination of the rapidly advancing frontier. They believed any such advantage was far outweighed by the harmful consequences of the agitation over emigration and the actual trip.[74] The Methodist James Finley advised the Wyandots against removal because no place in the West was safe from white settlement or liquor.[75] The Indiana Friends opposed emigration because the distrust aroused in the Indians after such harsh treatment made subsequent mission work more difficult.[76] Peter Dougherty, the Presbyterian missionary among the Chippewas, favored removal in theory but thought that missionary effort would be hindered. Agitation of the removal question in the tribe and a fear that liquor would soon flow into any settlement outweighed any theoretical consideration.[77]

That missionary opposition to removal was based more on practicality than on real principle may be seen in the American Board's switch in position during the second removal period. At that time the board approved of the transfer of both the Sioux and Ojibwas because it felt the

[73] 4 *U.S. Stat.*, 411. For background of the bill, see Abel, "Indian Consolidations," and Francis Paul Prucha, *American Indian Policy in the Formative Years: The Indian Trade and Intercourse Acts, 1790-1834* (Cambridge, Mass., 1962), 224-49.

[74] Missionaries did not worry about the loss of mission property, for they expected reimbursement from the government.

[75] Finley, *History of Wyandott Mission*, 302.

[76] Society of Friends, Indiana Yearly Meeting, *Address to the People of the United States, and to the Members of Congress in Particular, on the Civilization and Christian Instruction of the Aborigines of Our Country* (Cincinnati, 1838).

[77] P. Dougherty to D. Wells, February 6, 19, March 19, 1841, AIC 7:3:49-51.

consolidation of those tribes in the West meant easier missionization. Furthermore, the missionaries believed the rough topography of their intended home assured elimination of white settlers.[78]

Much as Evarts and McCoy represented the two sides of the removal question at the Capital, so Alexander Talley, a Methodist missionary among the Choctaws, and Samuel Worcester, an American Board worker stationed in the Cherokee Tribe, represented the two sides in the field. Talley, who had started the great Choctaw revival in 1829, favored removal so ardently that he drafted a treaty for the tribe to present to the government.[79] Worcester opposed the extension of Georgia laws over the Cherokees and went to jail for his belief along with Elizur Butler, another American Board missionary, and J. J. Trott, a Methodist missionary. His imprisonment provided a test case which reached the Supreme Court. John Marshall ruled that Indian tribes were "distinct, independent political communities" and hence Georgia laws had no force over the Cherokees.[80] As everyone knows, Georgia disregarded the decision of the Supreme Court, and eventually the Cherokees were forced to remove by the federal government. So, as in other cases, the missionaries were compelled to follow their charges westward.

That the missionaries had to bow to the dictates of federal policy points up the nature of the relationship between the missionaries and the government as well as to the rest of American society. Missionaries were only a few of the many whites in contact with the Indians. Soldiers, traders, and government agents usually preceded them. Although the missionaries were only a few among many acculturative agents, they were far more important in the contact situation

[78] S. Hall to D. Greene, February 10, 1849, ABC 18.4.1.I:75; L. H. Wheeler to S. Treat, May 7, 1850, ABC 18.4.1.I:210; A.B.C.F.M., *Report*, 1851, 156.

[79] Abel, "Indian Consolidations," 375.

[80] Worcester *v.* Georgia, 6 *Pet.*, 515.

than mere numbers would indicate. From the standpoint of physical contact, the missionaries had closer and more prolonged relations with the Indians than any other whites except the traders. Only these two groups lived constantly in the Indian villages. Even more important was the psychological concomitant of contact, for the missionaries demanded more change in the Indian way of life than any other whites. Most other Americans wanted only minor changes in Indian customs, but the missionaries sought nothing less than a revolution in social relations and basic values. The only other agency capable of demanding such a transformation was the government, and it "hired" the missionaries in most instances in which it desired such change in the period under study. Thus, of all the forces for acculturation from the Revolution to the Civil War, missionaries pushed more aggressively for change than any other whites, but while they led the drive, they still acted within the larger framework of contact: governmental coercion in the form of army and annuity and increased white contact due to advancing settlement.

Chapter Six

JEHOVAH'S STEPCHILDREN

AS the missionaries did not separate Christianity from civilization and thus presented an inextricable combination to the savages, so most Indians did not unravel the two when the blackcoat arrived in their tribe. For this reason most Indians reacted to Christian civilization as a whole. Each culture opposed the other as a totality. From an awareness of the basic cleavage between the two cultures in a given contact situation, the Indians posited a theory of cultural dualism to parry missionaries' arguments for conversion. They maintained that the Great Spirit had ordained two separate ways of life for the two races, and each race must adhere to its proper customs under penalty of divine displeasure. According to this theory, their lands, language, religion, foods, passions, and houses were all the special decree of the Great Spirit and therefore the best way of life for Indians. Afflictions visited upon them were ascribed to a neglect or violation of this rule, and only a return to the old ways and religion could bring relief.[1] Some Sioux Indians offered just such an argument to an American Board missionary: "White men were made wearing clothes to work. It is proper for them [to] plough, build houses +c. But we were made naked to dance[,] hunt and go to war. If we should abandon the customs of our ancestors the Wakan would be angry at us and we would die."[2] Sioux pagans confidently predicted the Great Spirit would destroy any of their tribesmen who dressed like white men and fully expected to see all who labored in the fields die soon after such a sacrilege.[3]

The theory of dualism served to rebut the missionaries' religion as well as their civilization. If God had wished the Indians to have the white man's religion, they pointed out, He would have given them the Bible too.[4] Some Wyandot pagan[5] leaders remarked that the Bible had not been intended for them; otherwise it would have been written in their language. Furthermore, they sagely observed, the Bible "had a great many things that did not suit a people that hunted, but those who worked the earth, as its figures [of speech] were suited to them and not us. When it speaks of plowing and sowing, and reaping, the whites understand these things, and the language suits them. But what does an Indian know of this?"[6] These Wyandots even developed two gods, and the Indian god strongly differed from that of the whites, because he "is red, paints his upper parts, and dresses with the richest trinkets, such as bells, beads, rings, bands, brooches, and buckles, and that he requires them to imitate him in that respect."[7] According to the principal chief of this tribe, the red god had vanquished the white

[1] For such a view, see P. Dougherty to C. Babcock, September 12, 1849, AIC 7:3:175.

[2] T. S. Williamson to D. Greene, May 15, 1839, ABC 18.3.7.II:12.

[3] T. S. Williamson to S. Treat, November 18, 1859, ABC 18.3.7.III:452.

[4] Robert Simerwell Journal, October 24, 1824, in Kansas State Historical Society; J. Meeker to L. Bolles, November 29, 1833, in Jotham Meeker Correspondence with Baptist Board, Kansas State Historical Society; S. Hull to D. Greene, October, 1838, ABC 18.3.7.II:122.

[5] I employ the term "pagan" to denote the non-Christian members of a tribe. The missionaries used the term to describe the Indians outside their influence regardless of the intensity of their attachment to the traditional tribal religion, and I have adopted this use for the sake of convenience. No moral judgments are rendered upon the non-Christian Indians in my use of this term.

[6] James B. Finley, *History of the Wyandott Mission at Upper Sandusky, Ohio, under the Direction of the Methodist Episcopal Church* (Cincinnati, 1840), 237-38.

[7] J. B. Finley to Editors, August 30, 1820, in *Methodist Magazine*, III (November 1820), 431-36.

god in an attempt to move a hill.[8] The Moravians among the Delawares faced another application of the theory. After hearing these missionaries relate the story of Christ's suffering, a Delaware solemnly stated: "Yes, I know who killed Him. The white people were the ones who did it, and the Indians are not to blame."[9]

As a corollary to the premise of cultural dualism, the Indians, especially in the less acculturated tribes, maintained the equal worth or superiority of their tribal culture to that of the whites.[10] From such an attitude stemmed the greatest opposition to missionary endeavors. Some tribes accepted missionaries at first in hopes of merely improving their temporal advantages. Missionaries were expected to be generous with food and provisions or to compete with traders to lower prices.[11] At other times the Indians believed the blackcoats possessed a powerful magic which could benefit (or harm) the tribe. The Sioux thought the ability to read books was a manifestation of "wakan" and were bitterly disappointed that no magic resulted after such a laborious learning process.[12] When the Indians failed to receive the expected benefits and learned the blackcoats sought the transformation of their culture, they quickly

[8] Finley, *History of the Wyandott Mission*, 165.

[9] Lawrence H. Gipson, *The Moravian Indian Mission on the White River. Diaries and Letters, May 5, 1799 to November 12, 1806* (Indianapolis, 1938), 363. Other instances of the dualism doctrine as applied to religion are, *ibid.*, 255-57; Annual Report of the New York Missionary Society Directors, March 25, 1811, ABC 23.IV; Report of the Society of the United Brethren for Propagating the Gospel among the Heathen, September 12, 1844, in *United Brethren's Missionary Intelligencer*, VIII (Second Quarter, 1845), 445-50; Extracts from Journal of Abel Bingham, August 25, 1836, in *Baptist Missionary Magazine*, XVII (July 1837), 179.

[10] For these views, see I. McCoy to W. Staughton, May 7, 1818, in Isaac McCoy Papers, Kansas State Historical Society; W. Hamilton to W. Lowrie, February 5, August 19, 1839, AIC 8:1:36, 48.

[11] E.g., S. Hall to S. Treat, October, 1838, ABC 18.3.7.II:122; T. S. Williamson to D. Greene, June 12, 1834, ABC 18.3.7.I:18(16A); S. R. Riggs to S. Treat, March 24, 1849, A.B.C. 18.3.7.III:245. Cf. the reception of H. H. Spalding among the Nez Percés.

[12] S. R. Riggs to S. Treat, March 24, 1847, ABC 18.3.7.III:245.

persecuted the missionaries.[13] The hostile tribesmen killed the mission cattle, hogs, and chickens; stole clothes, caps, knives, and forks; robbed corn; threw down or burned the mission fences; and sabotaged gristmills and sawmills.[14]

As a tribe acculturated, the dualistic attitude became less a matter of sacrosanct value and more a simple preference for the traditional way. In this stage the Indians manifested ambivalent feelings. Some Indians admitted the superiority of white culture to their tribal way of life, but felt they were too old to change their habits. However, they urged their children to become "white." An Iowa man admitted two attempts to adopt white ways and had donned a shirt and pantaloons both times, but could not keep them on because he felt so ashamed. Yet he sent his son to the Choctaw Academy and welcomed schools in his tribe for the opportunities they offered to the young.[15] Others simply admitted the superiority of white culture (for could not the blackcoats even predict eclipses?) and tried to follow their missionaries' directions. Many Oneidas at the conclusion of the American Revolution observed the difference between white and Indian lives. To them the whites appeared prosperous and the favorites of Heaven, and so they too wanted Christ and comfort.[16] Even the pagans of this tribe requested Kirkland, the Presbyterian missionary, to pray over a sick member of their party, for they believed prayer to God would "unbind" him from the evil spirits.[17] Though

13 For such an analysis by the missionaries of their reception, see T. S. Williamson to D. Greene, May 28, 1840, ABC 18.3.7.II:14; S. R. Riggs to D. Greene, May 28, 1840, ABC 18.3.7.II:59; J. Meeker to L. Bolles, February 27, 1841, in Jotham Meeker Correspondence with Baptist Board; S. Hall to Greene, February 10, 1847, ABC 18.4.1.I:66. My analysis of the history of the Sioux and Ojibwa missions of the American Board and the Kansas Baptist Ottawa mission as well as the Nez Percé mission of the American Board bear out this interpretation.

14 E.g., S. Irvin to W. Lowrie, January 8, 1847, AIC 4:3:77.

15 J. Kerr to E. Swift, May 26, 1835, AIC 3:1:36.

16 S. Kirkland to J. Bowdoin, March 10, 1784, in Samuel Kirkland Papers, Hamilton College Library.

17 Samuel Kirkland Journal, June 5, 1803.

missionaries were not without opposition in tribes such as these, it was not active persecution but rather argument and, even more so, apathy.

Since both the missionaries and the Indians viewed each other's cultures as totalities in the contact situation, the Indian convert to Christianity was also a convert to civilization. Psychologically speaking, there seemed to be no half-way point, especially among the less acculturated tribes. Evidence of this feeling existed on the simplest level. One Chippewa man upon conversion immediately commenced wearing a shirt and using a stove. The next day he was married to his wife in a Christian ceremony, was baptized, and had his children baptized.[18] Among the Sioux, some men dressed in white clothes one day to work in the fields, and the next day donned breechcloths, leggings, and blanket to conjure over the ill and attend feasts and dances. A Sioux chief told the government agent who attempted to get him to cut his hair and to accept white clothing that all who changed clothes changed religion. The agent denied such a premise, but the chief considered him stupid to think otherwise.[19] After relating these developments, a Sioux missionary wisely concluded: "It is true that a change of dress does not change their hearts, but in their estimation it does change their relations to the Dakota religion and customs. It is quite a step for an Indian to take, that is for a Dakota. It is related of the wife of one of these men at the Lower Agency, that, whenever she looked at the shorn head of her husband, she cried."[20]

Even among the more acculturated tribes, white civilization and religion were not separated. When a Brothertown woman apostatized from the Baptists, she put off her American style clothes and dressed herself and children in

---

[18] John H. Pitezel, *Lights and Shades of Missionary Life: Containing Travels, Sketches, Incidents, and Missionary Efforts, during Nine Years Spent in the Region of Lake Superior* (Cincinnati, 1857), 242-46.

[19] T. S. Williamson to S. Treat, November 18, 1859, ABC 18.3.7.III:452.

[20] S. R. Riggs to S. Treat, November 27, 1858, ABC 18.3.7.III:348.

Indian apparel.[21] A Methodist missionary noted the same
phenomenon among the southern tribes shortly after removal. "One leading sentiment I will not omit—the connection always kept in their minds between intellectual and
moral improvement. Education with them is invariably
regarded as leading to civilization, morals, and Christianity.
Hence they are received or rejected together. They have not
learned the infidel notion of the opposition of the one to the
other, or even of the existence of the one separate from the
other."[22]

Missionary after missionary reported to their patrons that
once an Indian surrendered his native religion, he commenced a garden, observed the Sabbath, attended church,
sent his children to school, took hold of the plow, cleared his
fields, signed temperance pledges, erected a house, and
married his wife in a Christian ceremony.[23] This assumption
of wholeness accounts for the confusion of one Indian who
thought he had joined the catechism class by becoming a
member of the temperance society. After an explanation, he
joined the class.[24]

Because of the nature of the switch from paganism to
Christianity, from Indian to white, those most able to negotiate it were the mixed bloods. Though the missionaries
considered these people as barbarous as the fullblooded
Indians who surrounded them, they seemed to have occu-

[21] Isaac McCoy Journal, August 10, 1821.

[22] William H. Goode, *Outposts of Zion, with Limnings of Mission Life*
(Cincinnati, 1864), 161. He refers to the less acculturated portions of these
more civilized tribes.

[23] Among many, see G. Silverheels to T. Stewardson, September 1, 1819,
in Dept. of Records, Philadelphia Yearly Meeting, Box 3; Joseph Elkinton
Diary, October 30, 1820, transcript in Friends Historical Library, Swarth-
more College; J. Elliott to J. Evarts, April 29, 1831, ABC 18.3.6.I:21;
F. Ayer to D. Greene, October 8, 1838, ABC 18.3.7.II:194; J. Meeker to L.
Bolles, February 27, 1841, in Jotham Meeker Correspondence with Baptist
Board, draft; P. Dougherty to W. Lowrie, May 16, 1842, AIC 7:3:73;
H. H. Spalding to D. Greene, October 17, 1845, ABC 18.6.3.IV:130; L. H.
Wheeler to J. Treat, July 7, 1855, ABC 18.4.1.I:248.

[24] Mary Ann Kerr to I. W. Craig, September 28, 1835, AIC 3:1:44.

pied a peculiar status in the tribe because of their ancestry. Frequently they did not think of themselves as Indian, and thus it was easier for them to embrace the missionary culture. Furthermore, many individuals of mixed descent served as a channel of communication between the two races, for they spoke the languages of the two contact cultures. Their example served as model for their fullblooded relatives to adopt the new ways. Even before missionaries arrived, such individuals desired education and agricultural training for their children.[25] A Methodist Indian preacher thought the halfbreeds were more inclined to embrace civilization and a new religion because they were less averse to manual labor.[26]

Regardless of the reason, the missionaries' first successes came from among this group. Individuals of mixed descent were the first to attend the church, to send their children to school, and to help the missionaries. In the Cherokee Nation only a few of the twenty-six students in the American Board mission school when it opened were not mixed bloods.[27] When Cyrus Kingsbury entered the Choctaw Tribe, he was greeted by the halfbreeds,[28] and Captain Folsom, a halfbreed chief in the tribe, was instrumental in aiding the missionary to establish Mayhew Station.[29] As late as 1827 Kingsbury reported that of the forty-one scholars in the tribe, only five were fullblooded.[30] The American Board missionaries among the Sioux owed their first station to a halfbreed trader, and the twelve families related to him constituted the school and church at the mission.[31] Twenty-one years later the majority

[25] For thoughts on this subject, see E. Jones to Corresponding Secretary, May 1, 1828, in *Baptist Missionary Magazine,* VIII (July 1828), 213-14; T. S. Williamson to D. Greene, June 12, 1834, ABC 18.3.7.I:18.

[26] Peter Jones, *History of the Ojebway Indians; with Especial Reference to Their Conversion to Christianity* (London, 1861), 241.

[27] C. Kingsbury to S. Worcester, June 30, 1817, ABC 18.3.1.III:9-10.

[28] C. Kingsbury to S. Worcester, June 29, 1818, ABC 18.3.4.II:4.

[29] Mayhew Journal, October 23, 1822, ABC 18.3.4.I:89.

[30] C. Kingsbury to J. Evarts, January 15, 1827, ABC 18.3.4.III:22.

[31] T. S. Williamson to D. Greene, August 3, 1835, ABC 18.3.7.I:25; S. R. Riggs to D. Greene, May 8, 1841, ABC 18.3.7.II:95.

of scholars at this station's school were still mixed breeds.[32] These events were duplicated by the board's mission to the Ojibwas.[33]

Not all halfbreeds converted, nor did all fullbloods remain loyal to the religion of their forefathers. The majority of conversions can no longer be explained, due to the lack of data from such modern devices as depth interviews and Rorschach and Thematic Apperception tests.[34] Even the few detailed accounts that remain give only superficial reasons, such as old age and fear of death,[35] or the fulfillment of a promise to embrace Christianity if a warrior escaped his enemy during battle.[36] Rather than true reasons, these seem the culminating points of long psychological struggles. Probably not a few of the converts gathered about the mission to share the "loaves and fishes" more than the blood of Christ.[37] Surely this seems to be the basis of Henry Spalding's early successes among the Nez Percés.[38]

Frequently the customs of the old way provided gateways to the new. Due to the inferior status of women in the Sioux Tribe, women found it easier to convert than men. After six years of operation, one station in this tribe had forty church members, of whom only two were men, who had joined within the last year.[39] In this tribe the males engaged in the religious rites, and these activities as well

[32] S. R. Riggs to S. Treat, September 11, 1852, ABC 18.3.7.III:284.

[33] F. Ayer to D. Greene, December 1, 1833, February 24, 1836, ABC 18.3.7.I:94, 99.

[34] For the use of these devices to determine such a question, see Robert N. Rapoport, "Changing Navaho Religious Values: A Study of Christian Missions to the Rimrock Navahos," *Papers of the Peabody Museum of Archaeology and Ethnology*, XLI (1954), no. 2.

[35] E.g., F. Ayer to D. Greene, April, 1840, ABC 18.3.7.II:200; E. Butler to D. Greene, March 27, 1831, ABC 18.3.1.VII:75.

[36] L. H. Wheeler to D. Greene, March 22, 1843, ABC 18.3.7.II:220.

[37] E.g., F. Ely to D. Greene, January 5, 1838, ABC 18.3.7.II:228.

[38] For the story of this phase of Spalding's activities, see Clifford M. Drury, *Henry Harmon Spalding* (Caxton, Idaho, 1936), 165-90.

[39] T. S. Williamson to D. Greene, May 24, 1841, ABC 18.3.7.II:17. Also see J. Potter to S. Treat, April 10, 1849, ABC 18.6.3.III:25.

as those in other areas were rigidly prescribed by custom, while the women took no part in the rites nor were their activities as clear cut.[40] Not only did this make conversion easier for a female, but her already modest dress was approved without change by the missionaries and her new religion simply meant from her husband's view a better kept house. On the other hand, a man had to cut off his hair, change his style of dress, and adopt new work patterns —in short, a whole new role.[41]

In the battle against Satan, even so small a thing as medicine played a part. To prevent the Indians from attending the conjurers and medicine men of native tradition and religion, the missionaries sought to prove the superiority of white medicines and prove cures could be effected without "the idolatrous incantations of the devil over the sick."[42] When traditional native "medicine" failed, the ill Indian called in the missionary and often promised to convert if the blackcoat's remedy was better than the old way. A rich Ottawa woman made such a bargain with Jotham Meeker,[43] and a dull-witted Sioux man made the proposition to Stephen Riggs and thus became the first fullblooded Sioux male to join the church.[44] A Potawatomi and an Ojibwa male also converted after recovery from severe illnesses.[45]

[40] Cf. Ruth Landes, *Ojibwa Woman* (New York, 1938), vii.

[41] T. S. Williamson to D. Greene, May 28, 1840, May 10, 1842, ABC 18.3.7.II:14, 21; S. R. Riggs, *Tah-koo Wah-kan; or, the Gospel among the Dakotas* (Boston, 1869), ch. XI, "Believing Women." Cf. Louise and George Spindler, "Male and Female Adaptations in Cultural Change," *American Anthropologist*, LX (April 1958), 217-33.

[42] A. Wright to D. Greene, September 13, 1834, ABC 18.3.4.V:147; P. Dougherty to D. Wells, January 18, 1843, AIC 7:3:80; T. S. Williamson to D. Greene, May 24, 1841, ABC 18.3.7.II:17. On this battle see A. Talley to Corresponding Secretary, August 21, 1834, in *Christian Advocate*, IX (October 10, 1834), 26.

[43] Jotham Meeker Journal, May 3, 1840.

[44] S. R. Riggs to D. Greene, February 24, 1841, ABC 18.3.7.II:65.

[45] I. McCoy to J. Loring, March 1, 1825, in Isaac McCoy Papers, IX, draft; F. Ayer to D. Greene, January 4, 1838, ABC 18.3.7.II:193.

Another entrance provided by native custom for conversion was through dreams. Many tribes believed revelations of the supernatural were received through dreams or visions, and it was common for individuals after hearing preaching to have dreams concerning Christianity. A young Wea man signed a temperance pledge and attended church because he dreamed of visiting Heaven, where Christ gave him a "letter." He believed the letter was the Bible.[46] Christianity was at low ebb in the Wyandot Tribe when an important pagan woman (perhaps a clan matron) suddenly became senseless and dreamed she was on the way to destruction. In her dream, God sent the Negro Stewart to teach her the "right way." She immediately exhorted those unfriendly to Christianity to repent, and her efforts revived the waning Christian party.[47]

Indians continued to dream after conversion, and these visions throw much light on the nature of Christian belief among the Indians.[48] A Wyandot woman's narrative of her dream reveals the impact of missionization and civilization on the native mind.

One night, after being at meeting, . . . I lay down to sleep, and dreamed that I saw at the council house, a high pole set in the ground, and on the top of that pole there was a white child fastened and it gave light to all around in a circle. At the foot of the pole stood the missionary, calling the Indians to come into the light, for they were all in the dark. No one went. At last, I thought if it was a good thing it would not hurt me, and I would venture. So I went; and from the foot of this pole there were two paths started: the one was a broad road, and it led down hill; the other was a narrow one, and led up a hill. These roads, he said were the only two roads that lead out of this world. The broad one leads down to hell, and the other leads up to

[46] J. Kerr to E. Swift, August 31, 1835, AIC 3:1:43.
[47] J. Finley to Editors, August 30, 1820, in *Methodist Magazine*, III (November 1820), 431-36.
[48] See Jotham Meeker Journal, July 26, 1840; S. A. Worcester to D. Greene, March 8, 1848, ABC 18.3.1.XIII:198.

heaven. I looked in the dust, and saw that all the large moccason [*sic*] tracks were on the broad road, and the small ones were on the narrow road. So I determined at once to take the narrow road. I had not traveled far until I found the way steep, and my feet often slipped, and I fell to my knees; but I held by the bushes, and got up again. So I traveled on for sometime; but the higher I got, the easier I traveled, until I got almost to the top of the hill. There I saw a great white house, and a white fence around it. There was a large gate that led to this house. At this gate stood a man, and his hair was as white as snow. He held in his right hand a long sword, and the point of it blazed like a candle. I was greatly afraid. I heard in that house the most delightful singing I ever heard before, and had a great desire to go in. When I came up to the gate, the man spoke to me and said, "You cannot go in now. You must go back and tell all your nation, that if they want to get to heaven they must take this narrow road, for there is no other that leads here." Then I started back with heavy heart; and when I got down near the council house I saw my people all in the way to ruin, and began to call on them to stop. Here I awoke.[49]

Much of the dream is a literal translation of the images used in the missionary's sermons, but the reference to a white house and fence reveals the connection of Christianity and civilization in the minds of the Indians, while syncretism is shown in the Christ child upon the traditional Indian pole employed in feasting. The impact of hymn singing on Indian ears is faithfully mirrored in her impression of the music in the house.[50]

Evidence of this sort raises the question of how "pure" a Christian was the Indian convert. Like so many answers to questions about the Indian Christian, the documents are far too few to provide entire satisfaction. A Methodist missionary wrote about the Wyandots: "I doubt whether the world produces any body of people who are more attentive

[49] Finley, *History of the Wyandott Mission*, 123-24.
[50] Apostates also had dreams in which they found the path to Heaven too difficult to negotiate. For a Seneca's "Pilgrim's Progress," see W. Hall to D. Greene, March 20, 1844, ABC 18.5.8.I:180.

to the duties of Christian religion than these Indians."[51] With less rapture but after more years of labor, Samuel Worcester, an American Board worker, concluded the Cherokee Christians evidenced the same degree of piety as whites according to their "measure of light."[52] Missionaries to the Sioux felt their church members not sufficiently impressed with a "sense of sinfulness, or to have any just and lively apprehension of the preciousness and glory of the savior, and this want of those views and emotions which are commonly considered important signs of conversion has not been supplied by that better evidence which is furnished by well-ordered lives and conversation."[53] The missionary to the Spokans never changed his opinion from his initial impression. "If any one doubts the doctrines of total + native depravity, one year's sojourn among them, I think, would remove all his doubts."[54] This spectrum of opinion reflects the missionaries' prejudices and emotions and the degree of acculturation of the tribe as much as the actual state of Indian Christianity.

The less acculturated the tribe, the more difficult a converted Indian found it to maintain a consistent Christian character. In tribes in which the native traditions were still strong and the convert a member of a small group, deviation from custom was more apparent. The red Christian in such circumstances was more apt to be torn between the two value systems and bear the brunt of majority opinion more forcibly. The difficulty of retaining church membership under such circumstances was vividly portrayed by seven fullblooded Sioux men. These men composed the total fullblooded membership in the Lacqui Parle mission church after twelve years of effort. In 1846 the discouraged mis-

---

[51] J. Gilruth to Editors, May 31, 1826, in *Methodist Magazine*, IX (August 1826), 307-309.

[52] S. A. Worcester to S. Treat, June 23, 1852, ABC 18.3.1.XIII:254.

[53] Sioux Missionaries to S. Treat, September 12, 1849, ABC 18.3.7.III:12.

[54] E. Walker to D. Greene, September 12, 1839, ABC 18.5.3.I:75.

sionary reported that three had been suspended a year before, and one more recently. Another under taunts from his fellow tribesmen commenced selling whisky and attending "idolatrous" ceremonies during the previous summer. Still another broke his promise not to drink and a few weeks before the report ran off with his brother's wife, while the remaining male never read his Bible or attended services.[55]

Religion in these tribes assumed a syncretic form. Among the Spokans, the missionary discovered his charges saw nothing inconsistent in holding both their medicine ceremonies and morning and evening prayer to God. They frankly characterized their traditional religion as devil worship, but assured him unless they appeased the devil, his anger would destroy them as surely as God's wrath.[56] A Moravian learned one of his native brethren had himself "bewitched" during an illness and promptly excluded him from communion.[57] Missionaries refused to condone the practice of Indian and white religions side by side; rather they preached the exclusiveness of Christianity.

On the other hand, the native Christian suffered persecution for his beliefs—even though they may have been far from the pure doctrine of the church. The social pressure ranged from mild derision to threats of personal violence. Among the Chippewas as among so many tribes, the missionary observed, "the Devil employs most successfully his old weapon (ridicule) to prevent any complying with our propositions. Those who settle by us and send their children to school are at once stigmatized with the name *praying Indians*."[58] The Indiana Delawares chided their few Moravian brethren for their ignorance, since they had to hear the word of God so often, while they themselves had only to hear something once in order to understand it. The pagans

55 T. S. Williamson to S. B. Treat, January 2, 1846, ABC 18.3.7.III:367.
56 E. Walker to D. Greene, February 28, 1843, ABC 18.5.3.I:81.
57 Gipson, *Moravian Indian Missions on the White River,* 259.
58 F. Ayer to D. Greene, May 15, 1834, ABC 18.3.7.I:95.

further argued that the missionaries enslaved the Christians by not permitting their attendance at "sacrifices, dances, and jollifications." This campaign gave the mission Indians "a secret inclination to heathenism," according to the Moravian missionaries, and prevented them from witnessing boldly before the heathen to the grace and salvation which the sinner enjoys through the Saviour.[59] Some of these Moravian Indians died for their beliefs, however, under the Prophet's sway of power prior to the War of 1812. Sioux "soldiers" tore the blankets off those tribesmen attending the mission churches.[60] Not a few converts' lives were threatened,[61] and sometimes these threats were carried out.[62] At times the tormented convert left his village for another more friendly to the white man's religion in order to live with his faith.[63]

The history of Simon Anáwangmane, a Sioux, illustrates the pitfalls of temptation and persecution in the path of the native Christian. He had attended the Lacqui Parle mission school in its early years, but he did not convert until 1840. He stopped feasting on Sunday and returned his "consecrated" warclub, spear, pipe, and medicine to the man who made them. Then he put on white dress, built a cabin, and fenced and cultivated a field. His wife's friends and relatives chided him, and the village children called after him, "There goes the man who made himself a woman." At the beginning of 1844, Simon and his family moved to the then new Traverse des Sioux station. There the pagans honored him, invited him to dog feasts, and offered him

59 Gipson, *Moravian Indian Missions on the White River*, 168, 219-20.

60 Riggs, *Tah-koo Wah-kan*, 198-99. For the social pressures in this tribe, see *ibid.*, ch. XII, "Persecution, 1837-1862."

61 E.g., J. Fleming to W. Lowrie, August 23, 1837, AIC 3:1:91; F. Ayer to D. Greene, June 12, 1837, ABC 18.3.7.I:103.

62 Isaac McCoy Journal, November 5, 25, 1821; R. Mettez to McCoy, August 12, 1825, McCoy Papers, X.

63 E.g., a Wea chief: J. Fleming to W. Lowrie, September 22, 1837, AIC 3:1:91; a Miami chief: Isaac McCoy Journal, April 4, 1822.

whisky. These blandishments enticed him from Christianity, and he resumed wearing Indian dress. For a while his desire to obtain horses by trading in liquor led him further astray. Finally he was suspended from the church. "Sickness in his family and other misfortunes led him to reflect upon his past back-sliding, and brought him to consecrate himself anew to the service of Christ," stated the mission records in 1847. A year later, alcohol again seduced Simon from the fold, and not until six years had passed did he return in full faith. He had frequently attempted to enter the mission church during this period, but his feet were stopped by his shame from advancing up the church steps. After the time of his second reinstatement, he was a good Christian and a prominent member of the civilized Sioux community founded at Hazelwood in 1856. During the uprising of 1862, he saved a white family from the massacre.[64]

Exemplary Christians lived among the less acculturated tribes,[65] but the white religion was more easily practiced in a tribe further advanced on the path to white civilization. Since many Indians in these tribes had accepted facets of civilization, the reception of Christianity was considered merely another aspect. In areas with a greater number of Christians, the new convert did not feel so lonely. Social pressures were milder in these tribes. Furthermore, greater social disorganization in the more acculturated tribes encouraged departures from the disintegrating code of custom. Yet even in these situations, backsliding was frequent. A Seneca woman who had been considered exemplary talked about returning to paganism because some persons said she was to marry a respectable pagan neighbor.[66] Even more

[64] S. R. Riggs to D. Greene, July 17, 1841, December 20, 1843, ABC 18.3.7.II:66, 81, September 16, 1847, August 7, 1848, ABC 18.3.7.III:234, 239; Riggs to S. Treat, March 21, 1854, January 31, April 12, 1855, ABC 18.3.7.III:306, 322, 326; Riggs, *Tah-koo Wah-kan,* 200-206.

[65] E.g., see William M. Ferry, *Notices of Chippeway Converts* (3d ed., Boston, 1833).

[66] A. Wright to D. Greene, November 11, 1840, ABC 18.5.8.I:93.

discouraging to the missionaries was the syncretism practiced by their charges in these tribes. Few Oneidas professed paganism in 1796, but Kirkland complained many were still influenced by their "old mythology."[67]

Regardless of the tribe's advance toward civilization, alcohol and adultery were the greatest causes of suspension of church members. Surely the soothing dram was a temporary solution to the effects of tribal social disorganization and the personal conflict between loyalty to Christ or medicine man for many a convert.

To become truly Christian was to become anti-Indian. The good Indian convert realized his former religion was superstition and his former habits slothful and sinful. Thus a scholar in a mission school expressed gratitude that he was not a "wild Indian."[68] An Oneida woman thanked God that He had made her different from the half-naked savages from the St. Lawrence River visiting her tribe. Her fellow church members were ashamed of the pagan activities of the unconverted Oneidas.[69]

From this shame flowed the Indian Christians' desire to proclaim the beauties of the Gospel (and civilization) to their heathen tribesmen by word and deed. The Oneida Christians beseeched the Lord to grant "that we may love one another so well, that our pagan-brethren in the wilderness, may have a good example from us, and so learn what the religion of jesus-Christ can do with Indians."[70] Sixty-eight years later, the civilized Sioux of the Hazelwood Republic issued a "Declaration of Sentiments" with the same goal and much the same tone of condescension.

[67] Jeremy Belknap and Jedidiah Morse, "The Report of a Committee of the Board of Correspondents of the Scots Society for Propagating Christian Knowledge, Who Visited the Oneida and Mohekunuh Indians in 1796," *Massachusetts Historical Society Collections*, First Series, V (1798), 15.

[68] I. McCoy to F. Wayland, Jr., November 15, 1825, in Isaac McCoy Papers, X, draft.

[69] Samuel Kirkland Journal, October 8, 1792.

[70] *Ibid.*, April 27, 1789.

We consider that we are in vastly different circumstances from those in which we were before the Word of the Great Spirit was brought into the country, and we know very well that all that is different in our present from our past life, we have learned from the Word of God. . . . We hope to make progress and teach our brethren progress. . . . It has been for the purpose of instructing according to our ability; our own relations and the whole Dakota people in regard to dress and manners, and indeed in regard to every thing that pertains to their well-being in this present life and in the life to come, that we have formed ourselves into a government.[71]

This development reached its zenith when the converts switched from example to vigorous proselyting.

No matter how pious and exemplary the Indian Christian became, the white population still considered him a savage and an inferior. In most cases, furthermore, the Indian Christian was easily differentiated from his white coreligionists by the retention of native habits or language, which only deepened white discrimination against him. On the other hand, the pagans despised him for his departure from the customs of his forefathers, no matter how slight that departure may have been. (The pagans themselves had left the path too, but not to the same degree.) Thus the Indian Christian was faced with double discrimination. No more vivid example exists of this double discrimination than the tragic story of the Moravian Delawares, who were distrusted by their fellow tribesmen and white Christians alike. After much persecution at the hands of the Indians, ninety were massacred at Gnadenhutten on March 8, 1782, by American frontiersmen.[72]

Pagan leaders used this anomalous position of the Indian

---

[71] Henok Maheyahdenapa, Secretary of the Hazelwood Republic, "Declaration of Sentiment," February 26, 1857, newspaper clipping in ABC 18.3.7.III:46.

[72] The most modern account of this story is Elma E. Gray, *Wilderness Christians: The Moravian Mission to the Delaware Indians* (Ithaca, N.Y., 1956), 37-74.

convert to persuade him back to their side. Ottawa and Ojibwa pagans spread the rumor that a "praying Indian" had died and gone to the Heaven of the whites, where he was told "praying Indians" were not admitted. Then he went to the abode of the Indian dead, but was denied entrance because he had forsaken his father's customs. According to the story, he returned to the earth to resume the form of his body and haunt his former life.[73] Such stories had a profound effect in discouraging converts and symbolized in vivid terms the plight of the Lord's stepchildren caught between two cultures.[74]

[73] W. Case to Corresponding Secretary, April 6, 1830, in *Christian Advocate*, IV (June 4, 1830), 158; S. Hall to D. Greene, October 17, 1834, ABC 18.3.7.I:52; Jotham Meeker Journal, July 26, 1840. For a general analysis of double discrimination, see Belknap and Morse, "Report," 29-30.

[74] Isaac McCoy evolved his plan for a western colony in response to this double discrimination, as described in the last chapter.

Chapter Seven

CHRISTIANS VERSUS PAGANS

CONVERSION for the Christian Indians meant not only the transformation of their values and their life ways but also the desire to impose the same ideals and behavior upon their benighted neighbors. Inevitably such attempts to reform their fellow tribesmen lead to intratribal conflict over religion. Religious differences in turn focused attention upon governmental control and even form, for government by definition, even in American Indian tribes, gives those in power legitimate coercion over others within the society. The converted Indians desired possession of their tribal government to protect themselves and to expand civilization through the allotment of annuities for schools, farm implements, and other aids. These Indians, frequently at the behest of missionaries, often favored new governmental forms which imitated white political institutions. Control of these new forms supposedly gave the Christian Indians more opportunity and power to change those aspects of their neighbors' behavior that they regarded as primitive, hence shameful. Because of the interconnectedness of all social institutions, one of the best indexes of response to missionary operations and to white culture in general, therefore, is the struggle over governmental position and structure.

Indian Christianization and tribal response to it depended upon the entire contact situation and the overall stage of acculturation in a given tribe. While for the seventy-five years under study the missionaries were a relatively homogeneous group in their ways of thinking and acting, not only were the Indians they met divided into diverse tribal cultures, but also the content of any one specific culture varied over time under the impact of white contact. Thus a tribe's reaction to missionary endeavor might be quite different in 1850 than fifty years earlier due to acculturation. From research into various tribal reactions, four basic sequences emerge depending upon the stage of acculturation and the degree of Indian autonomy. By examining the simple reactions under conditions of nondirected contact before proceeding to the more complex sequences after autonomy is lost, the clearest view can be obtained.

When the missionary entered a new field in a relatively unacculturated tribe, he settled among a local band or in a village. His efforts were not directed at the whole tribe because of the nature of social relations in a tribe. Before white contact, the tribe was composed of small communities that managed their own affairs to a very large extent. A community was characterized by face-to-face relationships among a small group of extended families. Individual rights and obligations were determined in the main by familial bonds. Such a community was highly integrated because the people shared common values and goals. In itself the societal unit, the cultural unit, and the community coincided, for the people possessing the culture were the same as those constituting the social relationships.[1]

Though such an Indian community possessed a culture and social structure similar to other communities composing

[1] In my use of the terms "culture" and "social structure" I follow Alfred L. Kroeber and Talcott Parsons, "The Concepts of Culture and of Social System," *American Sociological Review*, XXIII (October 1958), 582-83. Views similar to mine on the nature of the tribe are Alfred L. Kroeber, "Nature of the Land-Holding Group," *Ethnohistory*, II (Fall 1955), 303-14; Robert H. Lowie, "Some Aspects of Political Organization among the American Aborigines," *Journal of the Royal Anthropological Institute*, LXXVIII (1948), 17-25; Julian N. Steward, *Theory of Cultural Change: The Methodology of Multilinear Evolution* (Urbana, Ill., 1955), 43-63; George P. Murdock, *Social Structure* (New York, 1949), 79-90.

the tribe, it acted as an independent unit politically. In most actions affecting the missionary and his converts, the local chiefs or those of the neighboring villages were the only participants as government. Local autonomy was great. In the tribes under study, the authority of the chiefs was non-coercive and local. Without the support in opinion and action of his fellow Indians, the chief had no power and his decisions were lost. Such a situation did not mean the absence of law so much as there was little need for it in the community where consensus reigned and all decisions were unanimous in the sense that all capitulated to the proposed action or inaction.[2] Such was the political situation facing the entering missionary.

By the time the Protestant missionary arrived at such a village or band, much acculturation had occurred, but in most cases the change had not affected the basic social structure or cultural patterning inherited from aboriginal times. As the missionary gained adherents to his program of Christian civilization, more and more Indians accepted new values and aspired to a new way of life. As the missionary succeeded in his efforts, the Indians who retained the older customs realized their way of life was a system in opposition to his system. In fact, the very words and methods of the missionary called this idea to their attention, and they realized they must meet the challenge.

The repudiation of much of American civilization, including the missionary, forms the first sequence. Under the threat of a cultural division in the community,[3] the native-

---

[2] Little has been written about the political aspects of the tribe, but see Lowie, "Some Aspects"; Jessie Bernard, "Political Leadership among North American Indians," *American Journal of Sociology*, XXXIV (September 1928), 296-315; Fred Gearing, "The Structural Poses of 18th Century Cherokee Villages," *American Anthropologist*, LX (December 1958), 1148-57. For an idea of primitive law, see E. A. Hoebel, *The Law of Primitive Man: A Study in Comparative Legal Dynamics* (Cambridge, Mass., 1954).

[3] Or communities, if the adherents had spread to more than one band or village or more than one missionary had entered the tribe.

oriented Indians persecuted the missionary to cause his voluntary withdrawal or, in the extreme, massacred him and other whites. At this stage of contact, the Indians frequently failed to differentiate between missionary and other American contact, and so pique, whether at government agent or God, led to slaughter of mission cattle, stolen clothes, burned mission fences, and sabotaged gristmills and sawmills.[4] At the same time, the opposition employed the methods of social control normally used to correct any deviation within the community to bring them back into line with old ways.[5] Social pressure ranged from the mild derision to the threats of personal violence mentioned in the preceding chapter. After the elimination or withdrawal of the whites, the native-oriented group hoped to achieve the old cultural and social coincidence again. A simple diagram will clearly illustrate this sequence.

The massacre of the Reverend Marcus Whitman and a few other Americans in Oregon during 1847 seems to be the most dramatic and straightforward example of this sequence. The increasing number of Americans entering Indian territory as well as the disruption threatened by the success of the mission caused the massacre.[6] This possibility was open only to a tribe when American society was weak in the

[4] For example, S. Irvin to W. Lowrie, January 8, 1847, AIC 4:3:77.

[5] George P. Murdock has described these methods very succinctly: "Since its members are experienced in face-to-face cooperation, a community is ordinarily able to achieve concerted action, at least in emergencies, whether it do so under informal leaders or under chiefs and deliberative bodies with culturally defined authority and functions. Moreover, as a fundamental locus of social control, it maintains internal order and conformity to traditional norms of behavior if not through formal judicial organs and procedures, at least through the collective application of sanctions when public opinion is aroused by serious deviations. Basically, then the community is a political group, as well as a localized face-to-face culture-bearing in-group." *Social Structure*, 84.

[6] A balanced appraisal of the massacre and its causes is Frances Haines, *The Nez Percés, Tribesmen of the Columbia Plateau* (Norman, Okla., 1955), ch. xi. The story of the mission has been written by Clifford Drury, *Marcus Whitman, M.D., Pioneer and Martyr* (Caldwell, Idaho, 1937), but see the manuscript letters of the Oregon mission in American Board papers.

area of contact and the tribe's political autonomy was accordingly great.

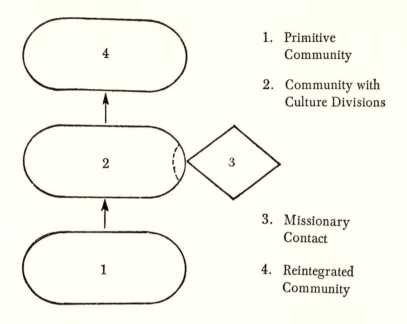

1. Primitive Community

2. Community with Culture Divisions

3. Missionary Contact

4. Reintegrated Community

Somewhat more complicated is the second possible sequence, which involved a social as well as a cultural division. Societal disruption naturally followed from missionization, for the acceptance of new values as well as pagan persecution demanded new social relationships. Sometimes conversion merely meant the end of polygamy. At other times couples separated because one spouse had converted.[7] In still other instances, people left their villages to settle in places more favorable to Indian Christianity.[8] In extreme cases new villages or bands were formed entirely of white-

[7] Isaac McCoy Journal, May 18, 1822, in Kansas State Historical Society; L. Williams to D. Greene, April 24, 1834, ABC 18.3.4.V:113; H. H. Spalding to D. Greene, September 20, 1835 (?), ABC 18.3.1.IX:203.

[8] For example, Isaac McCoy Journal, April 4, 1822; J. Fleming to W. Lowrie, August 22, 1837, AIC 3:1:91.

oriented Indians.[9] Thus in this sequence, after the initial cultural divisions, the cleavage worsened, and instead of reuniting as in the first sequence, the community broke into two physically separate groups which enabled each one to live in its own community in which culture and social structure coincided. The process might repeat itself several times within the same original population. To continue the use of diagrams, this sequence may be represented under ideal conditions thusly:

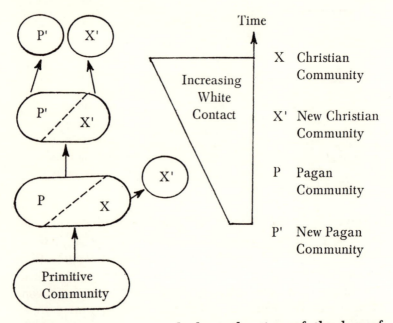

This sequence occurred about the time of the loss of political autonomy. Perhaps the most famous example of the formation of a new community was the deliberate practice of Moravian missionaries in separating their con-

[9] For example, the Hazelwood Republic among the Sioux: Riggs, *Tah-koo Wah-kan; or the Gospel among the Dakotas* (Boston, 1869), 393-94; Henok Maheyahdenapa, Secretary of the Hazelwood Republic, "Declaration of Sentiment," February 26, 1857, newspaper clipping in ABC 18.3.7.III:146.

verts from the tribe in order to practice white man's ways in white man's social relationships.[10] While the Moravians frequently operated in the period of permissive contact, Samuel Kirkland's work among the Oneidas in central New York illustrates this sequence after loss of autonomy.

Following the American Revolution, the Oneidas were confined to a reservation that rapidly dwindled as a result of land sales. By this time Kirkland's efforts, which had begun in the late 1760s, had produced the usual Pagan and Christian parties.[11] In the 1790s the main Oneida village, which contained almost the entire tribal population, was divided between the two parties: the Christians lived in the western end and the Pagans in the eastern end. The Quakers commenced work in the Pagan section of the village in 1796 to at first the delight and then the chagrin of Kirkland. The Quaker work demonstrates that the difference between the two parties was not a complete dichotomy in regard to the adoption of white civilization but rather the extent of that adoption and the specific elements.[12] After the Quakers left, the Pagans apparently revived some of their old ceremonies. They ate roasted dog and held various ceremonies

[10] A modern account of the Moravian missions is Elma E. Gray, *Wilderness Christians: The Moravian Mission to the Delaware Indians* (Ithaca, N.Y., 1956). The troubles of such a community are vividly seen in the documents gathered by Lawrence H. Gipson, *The Moravian Indian Mission on the White River. Diaries and Letters, May 5, 1799, to November 12, 1806* (Indianapolis, 1938).

[11] The best account of the mission is found in his papers at Hamilton College. For a biography, see Willard Thorp, "Samuel Kirkland, Missionary to the Six Nations; Founder of Hamilton College," in Willard Thorp, ed., *Lives of Eighteen from Princeton* (Princeton, 1946), 24-50; Herbert S. Lennox, "Samuel Kirkland's Mission to the Iroquois," (unpublished Ph.D. dissertation, University of Chicago, 1932). For evidence of the division, see his Journal, April 27, 1789.

[12] Jeremy Belknap and Jedidiah Morse, "The Report of a Committee of the Board of Correspondents of the Scots Society for Propagating Christian Knowledge, Who Visited the Oneida and Mohekunuh Indians in 1796," *Massachusetts Historical Society Collections*, First Series, V (1798), 13-14; Samuel Kirkland Journal, January 11, 1800; S. Kirkland To A. Miller, May 24, 1800, in Kirkland Papers.

in the fall of 1799. Visions were frequent, and the Pagans gained some adherents from the Christian party.[13] In mid-1800 both parties after a six-day council agreed religion should no longer interfere with political affairs.[14]

The agreement was short-lived, and finally in 1805, the two parties divided the reservation between them in order to "preserve the peace of the greater part of the nation."[15] This was the first of many divisions of the reservation. In 1816 and 1817 Eleazar Williams, the famous Indian Episcopalian who was later presumed the lost dauphin, converted many of the Pagan party, which became known as the Second Christian party, and won the Christian party from Presbyterianism to Episcopalianism.[16] Under the leadership of Williams, the Oneidas began to move to Wisconsin during the 1820s. Thereafter, blocs of First and Second Christian party Indians sold their lands separately in order to emigrate. In 1826 a Methodist missionary converted some of the remaining Pagans, who assumed the name of the Orchard party. The next year some of this party sold their land in order to go to Wisconsin.[17] This fragmentation process continued well into the 1840s.[18]

The Oneidas' attempt in 1805 to separate religious and political concerns points to the third possible sequence. As more and more missionaries arrived and more whites settled around the reservation, the coincidence between culture, social structure, and community broke down not only in one

[13] Kirkland Journal, February 25, March 31, 1800.

[14] Kirkland to A. Miller, June 7, 1800, in Kirkland Papers.

[15] Kirkland Journal, January 21, 1805; J. Skenandon *et al.* to Governor of New York State, January 24, 1805, in Kirkland Papers; Treaty of 1805, in *New York Assembly Doc.* no. 51 (1889), 259-63.

[16] Eleazar Williams, *The Salvation of Sinners through the Riches of Divine Grace* (Green Bay, Wisconsin Territory, 1842), 19-20; Morgan Dix, ed., *A History of the Parish of Trinity Church in the City of New York* (New York, 1905), III, 128-33.

[17] Wade C. Barclay, *History of Methodist Missions, Part One, Early American Methodism, 1769-1844* (New York, 1950), II, 146.

[18] See treaties in *New York Assembly Doc.* no. 51 (1889), 287-366.

village as in the preceding sequence but in many towns in
the tribe. To heal the divisions, attempts were made at
political organization on the tribal level. Such attempts
were reinforced by the activities of government agents and
missionaries. Since the Indians bordered on rapidly expanding white settlements, the governmental authorities constantly bargained for tribal lands. The peculiar ethical
views of the dominant society necessitated the signing of a
contract by the tribe as a whole through some legal representatives[19] and thus fostered the notion of a more elaborate
tribal government. At the same time the ever-diminishing
reservation impressed the concept of territoriality, which is
so essential to the modern idea of the state, upon Christian
and Pagan alike. Further, the idea of more formal government was assisted by the missionaries, who not only trained
Indians in governance through church and voluntary associations organized by this time along tribal lines,[20] but who had
always strongly advocated better Indian government, that
is, white law and organization.[21] With missionary encouragement and the experience gathered in church societies,
the members of the Christian party naturally attempted to
form a tribal government in order to force their new culture
and social relations upon their fellow tribesmen. In order
to counter this move, the Pagans were compelled to expand
the traditional political system in functions and authority,
if not in offices. The dynamics of this sequence may be seen
in the diagram on the next page. The new government was
an attempt at societal integration without the cultural integration of the whole population.

In the ideal development of this sequence, the form of
government presented by the Christians for tribal use was

[19] An illuminating discussion of this practice and its implications is Mary
E. Young, "Indian Removal and Land Allotment: The Civilized Tribes and
Jacksonian Justice," *American Historical Review*, LXIV (October 1958),
31-45.
[20] See above, pp. 63-67.   [21] See above, pp. 83-87.

modeled after that of the dominant society: a written
constitution provided for elective officers to fill positions in
a government of divided powers.[22] Though the Pagans

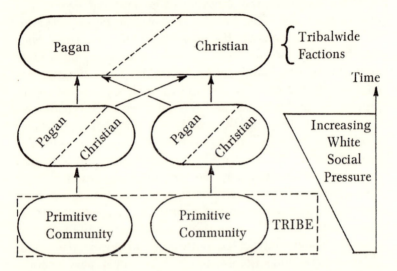

opposed the aims and even the mechanism of the Christians'
political system, they would be forced at this stage to gain
power through elections and capture the new government
established by the Christians. If all had gone well, genuine
political parties would have arisen. Yet a smoothly func-
tioning political party system was never realized, for neither
Christians nor Pagans consented to the other faction con-
trolling the government in this period. The Pagans, when
they won an election, dedicated themselves to destroying
the government—or they paid no attention to the new government at all!

The classic example of this sequence and its attendant
troubles is seen in Seneca history between the Revolution

---

[22] A convenient guide to documents on Indian political systems is Lester
Hargrett, *A Bibliography of the Constitutions and Laws of the American
Indians* (Cambridge, Mass., 1947).

and the Civil War. Until 1790 the tribe was still trying to play off British and American officials to gain favors, as had been Iroquois custom. With the decisive defeat of the Western Confederates at Fallen Timbers and the British evacuation of the frontier forts in 1796, the Senecas soon found themselves on reservations formed around their villages in scattered locations in western New York State.[23] As soon as all had quieted, the Philadelphia Friends, who had always been interested in Cornplanter on his visits to the young United States Capital, established a mission on his reservation.[24] Not long after, Cornplanter's stepbrother, Handsome Lake, awoke from a two-hour trance, uttered the first of the "good words," and founded the synchretized pagan religion which soon spread to the other reservations.[25] Although Presbyterian missionaries attempted to enter other reserves as early as the Quakers, none successfully overcame opposition until 1811.[26] Community divisions were prevalent on the four major reserves by the eve of the War of 1812. The full development of a tribewide split along Pagan and Christian lines is marked by a council in 1819, which was called to consider other questions but actually debated whether the tribe should adopt white customs and

[23] There is no recent history of the Senecas, but see Arthur C. Parker, *An Analytical History of the Seneca Indians* (Rochester, 1926).

[24] Quaker work is well covered in Aborigines' Committee of the Meeting for the Sufferings of the London Yearly Meeting of Friends, *Some Account of the Conduct of the Religious Society of Friends towards the Indian Tribes . . . to the Year 1843* (London, 1844); Halliday Jackson, *Civilization of the Indian Natives; . . . since the Year 1795 in Promoting Their Improvement and Gradual Civilization* (Philadelphia, 1830); Rayner W. Kelsey, *Friends and Indians, 1655-1917* (Philadelphia, 1917), 89-106.

[25] The best account is Merle C. Deardorff, "The Religion of Handsome Lake: Its Origin and Development," in William N. Fenton, ed., *Symposium on Local Diversity in Iroquois Culture*, Bulletin no. 149 of Bureau of American Ethnology (Washington, D.C., 1951), 79-107.

[26] The only account of this mission is found in the MS minutes of the New York Missionary Society, which are among the papers deposited by the American Board of Commissioners for Foreign Missions at Houghton Library, Harvard.

institutions.[27] This intratribal bickering was exacerbated by the Ogden Land Company's attempt to purchase the Seneca reservations in the 1820s and the federal government's efforts to remove the tribe in the following decade, which culminated in the Buffalo Creek Treaty of 1838. Many members claimed this treaty, by which the tribe ceded all their lands, was fraudulent, and they and the Quakers only obtained its repudiation after a four-year struggle.[28] Dissatisfaction with the chiefs' role in this affair brought forth experiments in tribal government, again with the help of the Quakers.[29] Finally in the famous year of revolution, 1848, dissatisfied Senecas declared in solemn constitutional convention: "We, the people of the Seneca nation of Indians . . . do hereby *abolish, abrogate* and annul our form of government by chiefs, because it has failed to answer the purposes for which all governments should be created." These failures were listed as lack of security for property, no laws for the institution of marriage, no provision for the poor, no provision for education, and no judiciary or executive departments—all Christian and white-oriented demands. This declaration served as the preamble to a constitution which provided for a government of three branches: a legislature composed of eighteen members elected annually, an executive, and a judiciary of three peacemakers for each

27 T. L. Ogden to J. Taylor, July 10, 1819, in Dept. of Records, Philadelphia Yearly Meeting, Box 3; Report of Morris S. Miller to John C. Calhoun, July 25, 1819, in NABIA, L.R., Secretary of War; "Historical and Personal Narrative of Jabez Backus Hyde Who Came to the Buffalo Creek Mission in 1811," *Publications of the Buffalo Historical Society* (1903), VI, 263-67; Jedidiah Morse, *A Report to the Secretary of War of the United States, on Indian Affairs, Comprising a Narrative of a Tour Performed in the Summer of 1820* (New Haven, 1822), 83-84.

28 For a summary of Quaker efforts, see Kelsey, *Friends and Indians,* 119-25.

29 The result of one such effort is "An Act for the Protection and Improvement of the Seneca Indians, Residing in the Cattaraugus and Alleghany Reservations in This State," May 8, 1845, in *New York State Laws,* 68 Sess., ch. 150.

reservation. Other tribal officers elected annually by all males over twenty-one were the clerk, treasurer, superintendent of schools, overseers of the poor, assessors, and overseers of the highway, as well as a marshal and two deputies for each reserve.[30] This revolution was no more successful (although less bloody) than its more important counterparts overseas, for the "Old Chiefs" party fought this government till the end of the period under discussion and secured modifications.

Certainly it is evident, even in this brief analysis, that the missionaries were only a partial cause of the Seneca Revolution and that governmental pressures and other acculturative forces played a large part. After 1819, the difference between Pagan and Christian no longer revolved about the acceptance of white ways so much as the speed and degree of adoption. Some of the Pagan party, in fact, allied with the Quakers in the 1820s after the Christian party had turned to the Presbyterians.[31] Surely as time went on, Christian civilization which had formed the focus of the conflict between divisions of the tribe in the earlier period was superseded by political divisions concerned with many other issues. In other words, the missionaries were thrown into both sides of the political division, depending upon whom they befriended. The Indian culture and social relations had become so fragmented under white contact that the natives could perceive the subtle differences in the views and behavior of the whites and classify them accordingly.

This points up the last possible sequence of missionization. Given conditions of advanced acculturation and tribal division, missionaries entering a tribe were thrown into an

[30] Declaration and Constitution are in *New York Assembly Doc.* no. 108 (1849), 8-13. A Quaker account of this affair is *Documents and Official Reports Illustrating the Causes Which Led to the Revolution in the Government of the Seneca Indians in the Year 1848* (Baltimore, 1857).

[31] This story can be found only in the manuscript letters of the period.

already existing faction rather than aiding in the creation of one. Such a possibility is seen in Cherokee and Choctaw history, where missionaries were automatically involved in factional politics revolving about removal and later slavery, in spite of their efforts at dissociation. Under these circumstances, Indian church members switched religious affiliation according to politics.

By the time the American Board missionaries entered the Cherokee Nation in 1817, that tribe had adopted a written law code with enforcement by the "Light Horse Guard" and eliminated blood revenge (perhaps with Gideon Blackburn's aid). Shortly after their arrival, the Cherokees established a bicameral legislature. Further centralization of government, the establishment of a court system, and a written constitution providing for the division of powers among the executive, legislature, and judiciary rapidly followed in the succeeding decade.[32] Opposition to these developments came from the fullbloods, who led an abortive attempt against the progressive halfbreeds to eliminate these innovations.[33]

In these circumstances the missionaries of all denominations were thrown into already existing factions rather than creating them. Here unlike in most other tribes, the missionaries could deal with the entire tribe or large districts for prompt action. In return for this convenience they were dealt with by the larger political units and so brought more directly under the control of the Indians than was the usual case. When removal sharpened the political divisions in the tribe and when these divisions evolved into factions seeking control of the governmental structure in the West, the

[32] The best description of these events is Henry T. Malone, *Cherokees of the Old South: A People in Transition* (Athens, Ga., 1956), ch. vi.

[33] Samuel Worcester's Journal, August 11, 1824, ABC 18.3.1.IV:37; S. A. Worcester to J. Evarts, March 29, 1827, ABC 18.3.1.V:235; I. Procter to J. Evarts, May 10, 1827, ABC 18.3.1.IV:185; Malone, *Cherokees of the Old South,* 87.

missionaries were automatically placed in factional politics in spite of their protests.[34] These factions were no longer based upon the acceptance of civilization, but other issues. For instance, the missionaries of northern societies were denied privileges on the basis of their abolitionist views. Some Indian church members switched membership from the northern to southern branches of churches over the question of slavery. The Cherokees received encouragement from white proslavery sympathizers in surrounding states. In other words, religious affiliation became a matter of political expediency.[35]

When Kingsbury founded the American Board mission in the Choctaw Nation, the tribe was divided into three districts. Each district was headed by a chief called a "Mingo." Clan leaders under him were called captains since their service with the United States Army against the Creeks during the War of 1812.[36] Soon after the missionaries arrived, a young Choctaw, who became a prominent chief later, expressed the conviction that only by the overthrow of the present chiefs could the tribe advance in civilization.[37] Incipient factionalism seemed present. The division was over the degree of acceptance of civilization rather than any acceptance, for even the old chiefs favored schools. In late 1822 a captain in the Southeastern District, which was closest to white settlement, promulgated the first code of written laws, which provided punishment for theft, in-

[34] Among many letters see W. Chamberlain to D. Greene, January 29, 1834, ABC 18.3.1.VII:59, July 30, 1838, ABC 18.3.1.X:38; S. Foreman to D. Greene, May 31, 1838, ABC 18.3.1.X:205; E. Butler to Greene, August 10, 1838, ABC 18.3.1.X:70; D. S. Butrick to D. Greene, June 10, 1839, ABC 18.3.1.X:9.

[35] See C. Washburn *et al.* to D. Greene, May 26, 1836, ABC 18.3.1.IX:27; S. A. Worcester to S. Treat, August 8, 1853, October 16, 1854, ABC 18.3.1.XIII:274, 298; Morris L. Wardell, *A Political History of the Cherokee Nation, 1838-1907* (Norman, Okla., 1938), 3-141, for general story.

[36] Mayhew Journal, October 5, 1822, ABC 18.3.4.I:89.

[37] David Folsom to Israel Folsom, March 29, 1822, ABC 18.3.4.IV:213.

fanticide, adultery, and lack of industry. The halfbreeds were active in obtaining these laws.[38] By mid-1826 the many halfbreeds and Christians in the General Council of the Choctaw Nation pushed a constitution through which regularized the existing government of principal chiefs and captains and the enforcement agency, the Light Horse Guard.[39] Ardent factionalism did not break out until the great revival sparked by Alexander Talley in 1828. As thousands converted, the conservatives became alarmed and those in the Southeastern District attempted to rally around the old chief, who was subsequently deposed and replaced by a Christian. Immediately the successor called a council to adopt the laws and regulations already passed in the other two districts, headed by progressives.[40]

To complicate the results of the revival, the removal question, injected in 1830, fanned the flames of factionalism higher. Greenwood LaFlore, an ardent Methodist chief who was anxious for political advancement, got the other two district chiefs to accept him as the chief of the entire tribe. Then at a council during which LaFlore and Talley played leading roles, a treaty was drafted in favor of removal. The opposition to emigration immediately crystallized around the former chiefs, Mushulatubbee and Nitakechi, and identified the Gospel with the loss of their homeland. Mushulatubbee and Nitakechi immediately replaced all the Christian captains by Pagans in their respective districts. Schools became unpopular and books were destroyed. At annuity time, civil war almost broke out. When the removal treaty was finally signed, leaders of both factions received presents

[38] Red Fort's Laws, October 18, 1822, ABC 18.3.4.II:241; Mayhew Journal, October 5, 1822, ABC 18.3.4.I:89; Horatio B. Cushman, *History of the Choctaw, Chickasaw, and Natchez Indians* (Greenville, Texas, 1899), 149-51.

[39] A.B.C.F.M., *Report*, 1826, app. no. IV, xxvi-xxvii.

[40] C. Kingsbury to J. Evarts, July 23, 1829, ABC 18.3.4.III:39; A. Wright to J. Evarts, January 1, June 26, 1829, ABC 18.3.4.III:106-107.

for their acquiescence, although only LaFlore, Mushulatubbee, and Nitakechi signed.[41] Resentment toward the signers caused the election of opposition chiefs in each of the districts.[42] After emigration, party feeling continued strong until at least the end of the decade, and the missionaries encountered much opposition, for Christianity was linked with removal after Talley's efforts.[43]

Among the Choctaws as among the Cherokees the slavery issue interfered with missionary labors. In 1848 Choctaws owned a thousand to twelve hundred slaves. Most of the owners were halfbreeds.[44] A prominent Choctaw left an American Board mission church because of that society's view on slavery and established a Cumberland Presbyterian church in his neighborhood.[45] He gathered a group of leading Choctaws about him who opposed the efforts of northernbased societies till the Civil War.[46] This group pushed a law through the National Council in 1853 to prevent slaves' children from receiving an education and to remove all missionaries who preached abolitionism.[47] Allied with but not caused by the slavery issue was the conflict over governmental structure in the late 1850s. Here the fullbloods opposed a new constitution that would have provided for the extension of territorial or state government over the

[41] C. Kingsbury to J. Evarts, May 9, June 23, 1830, ABC 18.3.4.III:47-48; A. Wright to Evarts, May 13, 1830, ABC 18.3.4.III:108; Mushulatubbee *et al.* to J. H. Eaton, June 2, 1830, in *Senate Doc.* no. 512, 23 Cong., 1 Sess. (1833-1834), II, 58-60; Grant Foreman, *Indian Removal: The Emigration of the Five Civilized Tribes of Indians* (Norman, Okla., 1932), 22-28.

[42] C. Kingsbury to D. Greene, August, 1831, ABC 18.3.4.V:159; Foreman, *Indian Removal,* 29-30.

[43] L. Williams to D. Greene, January 1, 1834, ABC 18.3.4.V:109; R. Wright to D. Greene, May 14, 1834, ABC 18.3.4.V:146; C. Kingsbury to D. Greene, November 22, 1839, ABC 18.5.1.I:49.

[44] Clipping from *The Republic,* n.d., ABC 18.3.4.VI:145.

[45] Israel Folsom to C. Kingsbury, December 20, 1847, ABC 18.3.4.VIII: 49; Kingsbury to Folsom, January 3, 1848, ABC 18.3.4.VIII:49; O. P. Stark to S. Treat, February 6, 1854, ABC 18.3.4.VIII:262.

[46] Kingsbury to S. Treat, April 5, 1859, ABC 18.3.4.VIII:150.

[47] O. P. Stark to S. Treat, February 6, 1854, ABC 18.3.4.VIII:262.

tribe. Again civil war seemed to threaten, but compromise averted the clash.[48] The agitation over slavery and politics hindered the spread of Christianity and forced the mission-aries to take sides they did not want.[49]

In both of these tribes by the 1850s the missionaries observed a widening cleavage between the English-speaking and native-speaking Indians.[50] This tendency had gone so far in the Cherokee Nation that the two language groups were settling in different areas. The English-speaking Cher-okees eagerly adopted white civilization, owned most of the slaves, and dominated the government and the school system. The other Indians resisted white innovations and opposed changes in the government that looked to a more modern state. Actually then, most of the political struggles recorded in the documents reflected the divisions in the elite rather than the cleavage between the more basic lan-guage groupings. In some ways this society is similar to Redfield's concept of the peasant society in which there is "a relatively stable and very roughly typical adjustment between local and national . . . life, a developed larger social system in which there are two cultures of upper and lower halves."[51] Intermediate between the national Ameri-can culture and the modified native culture is the elite which possesses its own distinct way of life which is the life of the peasant carried to another level of development.[52] Further comparative work must be done before Cherokee

[48] C. Kingsbury to S. Treat, March 1, 1858, ABC 18.3.4.VIII:132.

[49] For brief surveys of Choctaw history after removal, see Grant Foreman, *The Five Civilized Tribes* (Norman, Okla., 1934), 17-94; Angie Debo, *The Rise and Fall of the Choctaw Republic* (Norman, Okla., 1934), 58-79.

[50] C. Kingsbury to S. Treat, February 21, 1854, ABC 18.3.4.VIII:104; M. Palmer to Treat, April 19, 1854, ABC 18.3.1.XII:140; S. A. Worcester to S. Treat, June 5, 1854, ABC 18.3.1.XIII:286; clipping from *The Re-public*, n.d., ABC 18.3.4.VI:145.

[51] Robert Redfield, *Peasant Society and Culture: An Anthropological Ap-proach to Civilization* (Chicago, 1956), 65.

[52] *Ibid.*, ch. II.

and Choctaw society at the midcentury may safely be characterized as peasant. If it was, was it due to size and/or factions? One definite conclusion, however, is that as factionalism continued, religious affiliation frequently became a matter of mere political expediency. In other words, the Indians had acculturated to the point where they could not only differentiate the various elements of American civilization, but were themselves divided according to their perceptions of the various elements.

The mission history of most tribes was generally too complex to be an example of any one of these sequences; rather, several sequences were involved. In the period under study, the possible combination seems limited to the four sequences outlined in this chapter. A good example of several theoretical sequences in combination as well as the close relationship between governmental coercion and missionary success is the story of missionary work among the Eastern Sioux in Minnesota.

Four large divisions, the Sisseton, the Wahpekute, the Midewankton, and the Wahpeton, composed the Eastern Sioux.[53] Missionaries considered the Midewankton particularly ready for missionization because they were located closest to the white settlement and possessed an educational annuity. Beginning in the 1830s, the American Board, the Methodists, and a Swiss society founded stations in this band. The hopeful signs soon proved untrustworthy, and the stations were abandoned and restarted elsewhere in the band in rapid succession until the treaty of 1851 ended all these efforts by removing the band to a reservation in the West. Of the nine different stations opened during these years in the band, seldom did one remain in the same

---

[53] For the locations of the various divisions, see Report of Lawrence Taliafero, September 30, 1839, in *House Doc.* no. 2, 26 Cong., 1 Sess. (1839-1840), 493-98; Report of Alexander Ramsay, October 17, 1849, in *House Exec. Doc.* no. 5, pt. II, 31 Cong., 1 Sess. (1849-1850), 1014-21.

place for as long as a decade, and all demonstrated the first missionary contact sequence rather well.[54]

Illustrative of the second sequence was the most successful mission in this tribe. At the request of a halfbreed trader who wished his family educated, the American Board established a station at Lacqui Parle in 1835 among the Wahpeton. Trader Renville helped the missionary to locate and in translation work.[55] His wife was the first fullblooded Sioux to join the church, and most of the early church members and scholars in the mission school were his relatives. But even here as the Indians began to understand the implications of the religious and civil doctrines preached by the missionary and as the church slowly gained members, opposition arose. Whereas formerly the non-Christians had concealed their religious practices from the blackcoat, they made them as public as possible by 1840. Then in 1842 famine struck the Eastern Sioux, and the plight acted as catalyst for more violent opposition. The Indians believed the spirits had sent the drought as punishment for the departure from their forefathers' customs. While prior to this year the Sioux had occasionally killed mission cattle in revenge, they now began to slaughter three to ten a year. In 1845 the "soldiers" prevented the children from attending school, and the Indians broke the school windows, stole vegetables, and damaged the mill. Opposition even halted the church's growth. In the years immediately preceding the drought, the church usually gained ten members annually; after the drought, only two Indians joined the church during the next four years. To make it even worse, the

[54] Sioux Missionaries to S. Treat, September 12, 1849, ABC 18.3.7.III:12; T. S. Williamson and S. R. Riggs to R. Anderson, June 20, 1857, ABC 18.3.7.III:40; A.B.C.F.M., *Annual Reports* for the period; Stephen R. Riggs, "Protestant Missions in the Northwest," *Minnesota Historical Society Collections*, VI (1894), 117-88.

[55] For a brief biography of Renville, see Stephen R. Riggs, *Tah-koo Wah-kan*, 153-71.

famine dispersed one-half of the older members, and of the remainder, one-half had been suspended by mid-1846.

After the drought, even Renville lost some of his influence. In the opinion of one missionary, only the trader's presence protected the station. So important did this man seem to the resident missionary, that Renville's death in 1846 caused him to leave in discouragement. When the Indians realized the missionary was not obliged to stay, they appreciated his replacement, Stephen R. Riggs, slightly more. The congregation increased by a few listeners, but opposition continued without abatement. Feasts were held simultaneously with Sunday services to attract men from the church. In 1848 an old chief wanted the "soldiers" to drive Riggs out, but the local band did not sustain him. Though the church had gained members in recent years, still in 1850 the membership was only half of what it had been at the time of the famine.[56] Treaties were negotiated with this and the other bands of the Eastern Sioux in 1851, and Lacqui Parle was the only mission of the American Board included within the bounds of the new reservation.[57]

These treaties were a recognition of the increasing pressure from white settlers and the growing authority of the federal government over the tribe. The events of the next decade well illustrated the relation between government policy and Indian civilization. The treaties provided for a

[56] Twenty against thirty-seven.

[57] A general history of the mission may be found in A.B.C.F.M., *Annual Reports* for the period; Riggs, *Tah-koo Wah-kan;* Stephen R. Riggs, *Mary and I, or Forty Years with the Sioux* (Boston, 1880). These need to be supplemented by T. S. Williamson to D. Greene, May 28, 1840, May 5, 1843 ABC 18.3.7.II:14, 24; S. R. Riggs to Greene, May 8, 1841, ABC 18.3.7.II:95, December 29, 1846, June 3, 1847, ABC 18.3.7.III:230, 233; T. S. Williamson, "State and Prospects of the Mission Station at Lacqui Parle in September 1846," ABC 18.3.7.III:374; [S. R. Riggs] to S. Treat, March 7, 1848, ABC 18.3.7.III:244; Sioux Missionaries to S. Treat, September 12, 1849, ABC 18.3.7.III:12; T. S. Winson and S. R. Riggs to R. Anderson, June 20, 1857, ABC 18.3.7.III:40.

reservation along the Minnesota River, an education fund, and annuities. Henceforth the Eastern Sioux were referred to as Annuity Sioux, an appropriate recognition of their new status.[58] Though the Senate in ratifying the treaties struck out the definite reservation and substituted the laying off of a tract sometime in the future, the Indians were removed to the area specified in the treaty. Only the idea of permanence was in effect eliminated by the Senate's action. Up to 1854 the government did nothing to provide a permanent tract to quiet the Indians' anxieties. Then in that year the Commissioner of Indian Affairs designated two reservations as a "permanent home" until the President directed otherwise. After Congress confirmed the Commissioner's action, both the Indian agents and the Sioux presumed the reservations were the latter's home "forever." In recognition of this assumption, Congress appropriated funds for the survey of the reservations. However, with the continued onrush of settlers demanding land, the government took advantage of the legal imperfections of the earlier treaties to renegotiate two more treaties in 1858 whereby half of each of the "permanent" reserves was ceded. Under these treaties, specific sections provided for surveying the land in severalty and aiding all the Indians who farmed their eighty acres.[59]

Directly paralleling the governmental actions were the successes and failures of mission effort and Indian civilization. In 1851 one of the missionaries, Thomas Williamson, who had earlier served at Lacqui Parle, was invited to open a station among a local band living about thirty miles southeast of his former mission. Many of the Indians who had

[58] Charles J. Kappler, *Indian Affairs: Laws and Treaties* (Washington, 1903), II, 437-40. The negotiations are in L. Lea and A. Ramsay to A. H. Stuart, August 6, 1851, in *House Exec. Doc.* no. 2, 32 Cong., 1 Sess. (1851-1852), 278-84.

[59] Kappler, *Treaties*, II, 590-97. A brief history of the treaties is J. R. Brown to W. J. Cullen, September 10, 1859, in *Senate Exec. Doc.* no. 2, 36 Cong., 1 Sess. (1859-1860), 451-52.

removed from near the Mississippi and who favored the adoption of white dress, customs, schools, churches, and farms had moved there. Williamson settled at Yellow Medicine, or as he named it, Pejutaze, in the fall of 1852. The other American Board missions that were located in the ceded country were abandoned, and the missionaries turned to work among the white settlers. When the Lacqui Parle mission burned in 1854, the American Board secretary decided the two remaining missionaries should consolidate their efforts more. For this reason Riggs moved to an Indian village about three miles from Williamson. Here too were Indians who desired to become white men. Many Lacqui Parle Indians who adhered to Christian civilization ideals willingly moved to the new station, called Hazelwood. As the two missionaries gathered more and more Indians about them, opposition to their activities increased, and the Christian Indians were persecuted. The Indians about the missions wanted houses, and so the missionaries sawed lumber for them in the mission's mill. The non-Christians quickly used this activity as a focus for their protests. Sometimes they accused the missionaries of speculating in wood; other times they wrecked the machinery. During this period of persecution some of the Christians wavered in allegiance, including even the ruling elder at Yellow Medicine. As late as the summer of 1855, only three male church members wore white clothing, and three others thought of wearing pants. The church rolls listed only forty-three members for the two missions in 1856.[60]

The cultural and social divisions had proceeded far enough by mid-1856 for the civilized Indians in the two local bands

[60] T. S. Williamson to S. Treat, October 15, 1851, June 8, 1852, ABC 18.3.7.III:403, 407; Henok Marpiyohdinape *et al.* to Treat, June 3, 1854, ABC 18.3.1.III:2; Riggs to Treat, January 11, 31, February 19, May 23, 1855, ABC 18.3.7.III:320, 322, 324, 327; "Report of the Church at Pazhehootaze and New Hope Stations, for the Year Ending June 30, 1856," ABC 18.3.7.III:438.

to found a new band based "on the principle of labor and the adoption of the customs and habits of white people." Eighteen Sioux men signed the constitution of the Hazelwood Republic. The first article declared the existence of a "great Spirit" and His claims to men's homage. All who joined the republic promised to drop Sioux customs, to adopt white dress, and to improve their "condition." Education was declared important, and all signers pledged to erect a schoolhouse and hire a teacher. All, furthermore, intended to build houses for themselves, cultivate large fields, and maintain cattle. The signers asserted "their wish to have any one who trespasses on the rights of private property, properly punished." The men promised obedience to the United States government and requested all officials to treat them as white people. Furthermore, they desired a separate division of the annuities for their band. The new republicans elected a governor, secretary, and three councilmen annually. On July 30 the Sioux agent recognized these officers as equal to any other chiefs in the tribe and ordered a portion of the annuities be assigned the new band, which had formed according to the second sequence.[61]

At the same time the Superintendent for Indian Affairs for the Northern Superintendency applied greater pressure to prevent the interminable warfare between the Sioux and the Ojibwas, which upset civilization efforts in both tribes.[62] The authority of the agent to promote pacific agrarian practices was lost by his successor in the handling of the Spirit Lake Massacre in 1857. Inkapadoota and his renegade band killed a few whites in the vicinity of the lake of that name. The Superintendent withheld the Eastern Sioux annuities until they captured Inkapadoota. The Indians

[61] R. G. Murphy to F. Huebschmann, July 31, 1856, Copies of Northern Superintendents' letters sent to Washington, NABIA, ff. 168-70; S. R. Riggs to S. Treat, July 31, 1856, ABC 18.3.7.III:237.

[62] S. R. Riggs to S. Treat, July 11, 1856, ABC 18.3.7.III:336.

showed little enthusiasm for the task and lost their respect for the power of the United States government. In the ransoming of the captives and the subsequent expeditions against this small band, the Christian Indians played a leading part.[63]

Governmental authority was reasserted with the further loss of lands under the treaties of 1858. Many officials viewed the subsequent social change as a "revolution." Even before the treaties, twelve families on the lower reservation banded together in the fall of 1857, threw off tribal relations, drew up articles of association pledging to discard Indian clothing and customs, and elected a judge and council.[64] Around this farmer band and the Hazelwood Republic, the Sioux agent hoped to gather more civilized bands. In order to persuade the Annuity Sioux into such social groups, the agent paid agricultural and educational funds only to those Indians willing to change their lives. During 1858 the Indians who adopted the new ways received a yoke of oxen, a cow, and a house. As a sign of their new status, the Superintendent cut their hair and dressed them as whites. Some of the short-haired Indians felt that white dress necessitated conversion to white religion. When they converted, several of them were assaulted, shot, or poisoned by the other Indians. The seeming revolution of 1858 was small compared to the change during the next year. At annuity time in 1859, over two hundred men and boys had their hair cut. Men built houses and labored in the fields. Many no doubt switched to the new way to gain the farming gifts, but the new way also reflected increased pressure from the whites. While the church gained a few

[63] The most modern account of this affair is Louis H. Roddis, *The Indian Wars of Minnesota* (Cedar Rapids, Iowa, 1956), 21-48. For many documents relating to the affair, see *Senate Doc.* no. 11, 35 Cong., 1 Sess. (1857-1858), 335-403.

[64] J. R. Brown to W. J. Cullen, September 30, 1858, in *House Exec. Doc.* no. 2, 35 Cong., 2 Sess. (1858-1859), 402.

converts, it did not reap the harvest the missionaries had hoped.[65]

As Indian farmers multiplied, so did the opposition. One-sixth of the 2,550 Lower Sioux and three hundred of the Upper Sioux had declared in favor of civilization. But the bands which had less intercourse with the whites united in opposing any modification of their culture.[66] The Blanket Indians felt the Pantaloons men strengthened their white enemies as well as diminished the power of the medicine men. Only the march of Sherman's army prevented conflict between the two parties in early 1859. Soon after the march, the Blanket Indians began to murder the Pantaloons men and even fired upon some Christians about to enter Riggs' church. The agent averred that only the presence of troops prevented the destruction of the civilized Indian settlement.[67]

The culmination of the conflict over civilization came in the Sioux Massacre of 1862. The immediate causes were many, but the overriding cause seemed to be that of sequence number one.[68] Interestingly enough, the outbreak was precipitated under the leadership of Little Crow, who had always argued there was no intermediate point between

[65] T. S. Williamson to Treat, June 23, November 18, 1859, ABC 18.3.7. III:451-452; S. R. Riggs to Treat, August 24, 1859, ABC 18.3.7.III:355; J. R. Brown to W. J. Cullen, September 30, 1858, in *House Exec.* Doc. no. 2, 35 Cong., 2 Sess. (1858-1859), 401-409; J. R. Brown to W. J. Cullen, September 10, 1859, *ibid.*, no. 2, 36 Cong., 1 Sess. (1859-1860), 447-61.

[66] That the degree of intercourse is significant may be seen in the respective figures for the two Sioux reserves. The Upper Sioux, who were farther from white settlements, had fewer farmers.

[67] "Annual Return of the Population, Wealth, and Educational Progress of the Sioux of Minnesota for the Year 1859," NABIA, Northern Superintendency, L.R., Sioux Agency; J. R. Brown to W. J. Cullen, August 21, 1859, *ibid.*; J. R. Brown to W. J. Cullen, October 25, 1860, in *Senate Exec. Doc.* no. 1, 36 Cong., 2 Sess. (1860-1861), 278-87.

[68] For a summary of causes, see Roddis, *Indian Wars of Minnesota,* 51-60. For the cultural conflict as cause, see "A Sioux Story of the War . . . Chief Big Eagle's Story of the Sioux Outbreak of 1862," *Minnesota Historical Society Collections,* VI (1894), 382-400. A modern account is Kenneth Carley, *The Sioux Uprising of 1862* (St. Paul, Minn., 1961).

Indian and white ways.[69] During the uprising the Pantaloons party and especially the Christians acquitted themselves well in the eyes of the whites they so loved to imitate. They led white parties to safety and rescued whites from the camps of hostile Sioux. Almost all the members of American Board missions among the Upper Sioux and the recently founded missions of that and the Episcopalian societies at the Lower Agency refused to join the hostile Indians.[70] The connection between coercive power, conversion, and civilization is most dramatically demonstrated in the mass baptisms and huge reading classes conducted by the missionaries in the prison and camp of the captive Indians after the victorious white expedition in late 1862.[71]

Although the loss of Sioux autonomy in particular and the third and fourth sequences in general point to the eventual and complete assimilation of the American Indian, such was not to happen after the Civil War. Rather, greater fragmentation followed acculturation, and Americans always have refused final acceptance of the Indian because of racial prejudice. Furthermore, as the government took over work in the field, the missionary became less significant as the major acculturative force. The missionary had spearheaded acculturation in the seventy-five years under study only in the absence of government activity, though he was always within federal control. Yet, when the missionary was the chief force, he and the response to him provide many clues to understanding the nature of cultural change as well as the Indian history of the period.

[69] See his views in T. S. Williamson to S. Treat, November 18, 1859, ABC 13.3.7.III:452.
[70] Riggs, "Protestant Missions in the Northwest," 175-76.
[71] For this work, see Riggs, *Tah-koo Wah-kan,* 341-83.

Epilogue

THE HARVEST UNREAPED

THE "white fields," according to the religious magazines of the period, beckoned the Lord's workers to reap the bountiful harvest of converts. Nineteenth-century faithful were certain Christ's second coming was imminent, and in preparation for this glorious event, the Lord commanded the rapid mass conversion of heathen all over the world—for nothing less would satisfy the Lord or his optimistic nineteenth-century agents. Yet this optimism was not borne out by the statistics reported from the field. After thousands of dollars and hundreds of missionaries, the managers and patrons of the missionary societies had to account their eight decades of effort among the American Indians as unsuccessful. Although the modern analyst can see only the inevitable failure of the missionary enterprise given the participants' cultural assumptions in the contact situation, the religious observers of the time never saw clearly the extent of their failure or the reasons why the Lord's promise remained unfulfilled.

From the very beginning, missionary groups reached opposite conclusions, based upon the same facts, about the success or failure of their efforts. The preacher who delivered the annual discourse in 1808 to the Boston Society for Propagating the Gospel considered the colonial efforts to Christianize the aborigines successful and pointed to John Eliot, the Mayhews, Bournes, and Sergeants, as well as Wheelock, Brainerd, Hawley, and Kirkland as proof that "other men before us have labored in this work with success."[1] His colleague who presented the first address to the society viewed the efforts of these men in quite another light but hoped for better results in the future: "Although the attempts to Christianize the Indians of North America, hitherto have been attended with little effect, it is the wish of the pious and benevolent that attempts may be still continued. If experience has pointed out defects and errors, in former attempts, new experiments, and conducted on different principles, may hereafter succeed."[2]

The rush to new methods and new experiments reached its zenith in the years following the War of 1812.[3] In the first flush of enthusiasm and under the millennial hopes of mass conversion, society after society eagerly reported their experiments to be crowned with success. The United Foreign Missionary Society happily proclaimed in 1823: "that the American Savage is capable of being both civilized and Christianized, can no longer be questioned. The problem is already solved. Successful experiment has placed the subject beyond doubt."[4]

Yet the very continuance of protests that the Indians could embrace Christian civilization revealed it as doubtful in the minds of many. In 1852 both the American Baptist Missionary Union and the American Board of Commissioners

[1] Abiel Holmes, *A Discourse before the Society for Propagating the Gospel among the Indians and Others in North America, Delivered November 3, 1808* (Boston, 1808), 29-33.

[2] John Lathrop, *A Discourse before the Society for Propagating the Gospel among the Indians and Others in North America, Delivered on the 19th of January, 1804* (Boston, 1804), 19.

[3] For the use of the term "experiment" in this connection, see, for example, S. Worcester to C. Kingsbury, July 15, 1816, ABC 101.I:69-72; Annual Report, U.F.M.S. Board of Managers Records, May 5, 1823, ABC 24.III:192-93.

[4] Annual Report, U.F.M.S. Board of Managers Records, May 5, 1823, ABC 24.III:192-93. For statements to similar effect, see James B. Finley, *History of the Wyandott Mission at Upper Sandusky, Ohio, under the Direction of the Methodist Episcopal Church* (Cincinnati, 1864), 204; Quarterly Report of the Choctaw Academy, October 31, 1826, in *Baptist Missionary Magazine*, VII (February 1827), 49.

for Foreign Missions assured its supporters that the practicability of Indian work was demonstrated by the progress of their missions. The Baptist Committee declared how under missionary exertions "thousands of these tribes, who once roamed through the forests in quest of a precarious subsistence, have been reduced and won over to habits of sober and regular industry; cultivating the soil with the skill of Christian civilization, and depending on its products for a more sure support. And what is of infinitely greater account, many of these have been brought to know, to love, and to obey the Savior, and to enjoy the hope of the regenerate child of God."[5] The American Board took inventory of its missionary operations after thirty-five years and pointed with pride to its Cherokee, Seneca, and Tuscarora missions, but singled out for special praise the Choctaw mission. Its missionaries in that tribe ministered to 1,300 church members, which added to the same number cared for by other denominations equaled about one-eighth of the total population. The Choctaws had renounced drunkenness and adopted and followed a law of total abstinence. They had abandoned the chase to pursue farming. In addition they boasted of a good educational system, a written constitution, and decent government. So like their white neighbors were these Indians, asserted an aged missionary, that "the man who marries and does not provide a house and farm for his family, is in as poor repute among the Choctaws, as he would be among the whites."[6]

In spite of such optimistic reports, however, only one society ever voluntarily closed any of its missions with the claim that its work was legitimately accomplished. The

[5] Annual Report of American Baptist Missionary Union, in *Baptist Missionary Magazine*, XXXII (July 1852), 209.

[6] A.B.C.F.M., *Report*, 1852, 26-35. Cf. C. Byington to H. Newcomb, June 20, 1854, in Harvey Newcomb, ed., *A Cyclopedia of Missions; Containing a Comprehensive View of Missionary Operations throughout the World* (rev. ed., New York, 1855), 783-84.

American Board discontinued its Tuscarora and Cherokee missions in 1860.[7] For well over sixty years various societies had labored among the Tuscaroras. As early as 1804 the New York Missionary Society had concluded that the tribe was well on its way to civilization and Christianity. Yet efforts were continued, and a half century later the missionary to the tribe maintained that his charges could be counted among the civilized and Christian nations of the earth and, in fact, were more temperate, more proper in Sabbath observance, less profane, and more respectful of religion than their white New York neighbors. He boasted that a third of the Tuscaroras were church members.[8]

Before deciding to close the Cherokee mission, the American Board sought detailed statements on the religious condition of the tribe from its three missionaries stationed there. These letters report not only on the board's activities but also those of other societies, and so form the most complete analysis available of the possibilities of Christianizing a tribe. After sixty years of exposure to the Gospel, the missionaries agreed that the tribe was nominally Christian, that is, if understood to mean: "Christianity is recognized among them, as much as in any portion of the United States." In 1860 sixteen white and forty-four native preachers of all denominations toiled to bring the Cherokees to Christ. Approximately two-fifths of the whole adult population was listed as church members, subject to inaccurate rolls. The missionaries claimed few people did not hear the Gospel occasionally and almost all at least knew the main doctrines. In spite of these conclusions, the missionaries expressed grave doubts about the future of self-propagating Christianity in the tribe. They questioned whether the congregations would be capable of governing themselves without white supervision, and they were convinced the

---

[7] A.B.C.F.M., *Report*, 1860, 137-45, 151-53; *ibid.*, 1861, 128.
[8] G. Rockwood to S. B. Treat, July 12, 1853, ABC 18.6.3.III:164.

tribe would furnish few native ministers to assume the present obligations of the churches. This attitude probably reflected the Presbyterian situation more than the Methodist or Baptist, for the latter two denominations had long depended almost exclusively upon a native pastorate in their extensive operations. From the financial view, the missionaries questioned whether the Cherokees could or would support their own ministers.[9]

This ambivalence in judging even the most successful efforts is typical of the missionary mind. In reality, the American Board probably closed these two missions more for financial reasons than from any deep conviction about the success of their labors.[10] No other society followed the board's example among the Cherokee Tribe or any other tribe. Why after all their praying, preaching, and plowing did the missionaries and their patrons not consider their efforts in achieving their goal of self-propagating Christianity fruitful enough to warrant discontinuing their missions?

To the missionary mind of the period, the experiment to civilize and Christianize the American aborigines was bound to be interpreted as a failure. The criteria for judging the experiment's success were part of the basic value system of the culture in which the judges lived. Yet the very social assumptions that determined the goals hindered their realization, for these assumptions failed to correspond with the cultural reality of the contact situation. Hopes were raised of a quick success impossible in light of the cultural theory of today and unobtainable with the methods available to the missionary of that period. To complicate the judging further, the evaluation of the Indians' achievements was

---

[9] C. C. Torrey to R. Anderson, April 10, T. Ranney to R. Anderson, June 16, W. Willey to R. Anderson, July 28, 1860, ABC 18.3.1.XIV:5.

[10] Report on the Cherokee Missions, September 4, 1860, Report on Tuscaroras, n.d., in Sub-Committee Reports of the Prudential Committee of the A.B.C.F.M., Congregational House, 14½ Beacon Street, Boston, II:109, 111.

always in comparison with a variety of American culture that differed from observer to observer according to class, religion, and other subcultural variation, so that no general agreement ever resulted. From these difficulties stem the various contemporary opinions upon the outcome of missionary work in the period between the Revolution and the Civil War—and even after.

Thus the advance of Indian Christianity was both hailed and depreciated. Even so simple a thing as whether the observer preferred a religion stressing strong doctrinal knowledge or more emphasis upon emotional fervor determined the outcome of the analysis, for it was easier for the Indians to display the latter than to learn the former. Or, the more exclusive a religion the observer considered Christianity, the more he searched for and condemned syncretistic practices, and the fewer Christians he could find. Baptists, for example, judged success in quite different terms than did Congregationalists. Even if the Indians achieved the religious conditions of the white population—as the missionaries reported the Tuscaroras and Cherokees had—many observers did not concede success, for they condemned the American nation as merely nominally Christian and not fully converted. Therefore, these men actually demanded more of the Indian tribes but recently missionized than was found in their own society which was a part of the Christian heritage. Most tribes never reached this level, but missionization was slowly proceeding. However, missionaries and their patrons desired and expected rapid mass conversion because of their assumptions of a universal human nature and the attendant lack of a concept of culture. For that reason they accounted this slow success a failure.

Since the observers favored a self-propagating Christianity among the aborigines which depended upon their assuming *implicitly* an inextricable linkage between religion and civilization, the tribes had to develop the same social institutions as the whites in order to sustain sufficiently religion in the eyes of the missionaries and their patrons. Yet the more time consumed in teaching the Indians to plow and wash, the less time for prayer and catechism. By trying to provide a civilized foundation for Christ's Church, the missionaries lost the goal in the attempt to gain it. On the other hand, not to teach civilization meant the Indians would never achieve a basis for a self-sustaining religion and so the mission could never be closed. This dilemma only existed because the missionary mind *explicitly* divorced the elements of culture, unlike the theorists of today. In reality, civilization and Christianity had to go hand-in-hand, and this explains the slow progress of missionization. Furthermore, at the same time the missionaries were bringing a variety of American civilization into the forests, that civilization at home was rapidly changing in technological aspects. While this did not alter the missionary approach to the transformation of Indian character and life, it could not help but widen in white minds the gap between white and Indian ways. Even if the Indians had achieved the material condition the whites possessed at the commencement of missionization, the Indians would still have been considered backward in light of the subsequent change in American civilization. Here success turned bitter because the goal had actually changed.

The failure to see success was not the only cause for the lack of success in the missionaries' eyes. True, the missionaries could not account their work fully fruitful because of the peculiar framework of social assumptions that sustained their efforts, but objective cultural reality contributed to the failure to achieve their goals. Certainly as significant as the missionary outlook in making success difficult was the unanticipated consequences of success—factionalism. Whether the missionary created a division in the tribe or was thrust onto an existing side upon entrance, the presence of factionalism removed a significant part of the village or tribe from his influence. The greater the success of the missionary, the sharper the division and the less his influence over the other side. If the factions adopted different denominations, then the missionization succeeded, but in such a case religion was duly subordinated to other interests against the missionaries' hopes and protests.

Even the faction favoring Christian civilization could not reach the ideal envisaged by the missionaries and their supporters, not because of the Indians' desire to retain old customs but because of American racial attitudes. To realize the ideal fully, the Indians should have become integrated into the larger white society. In many cases the failure of the aborigines to achieve this goal of Christian civilization was due to civilized Christians not accepting them on equal terms, for American society traditionally discriminated against non-Caucasian peoples. By discriminating against the aborigine upon the basis of a belief of white cultural superiority, Americans forced the Indian to remain savage and guaranteed the failure of the missionary program. American citizenship, which symbolized this aim, was withheld not only because of Indian unwillingness but because of white intolerance. In some ways this discrimination caused the Indian to attempt to revive his demoralized traditional culture.

On the other hand, the anticivilization faction deliberately clung to the old ways. Even under the strong impact of American civilization, the old patterns persisted though externals and material objects had changed. This faction stubbornly resisted the missionaries even though to fight them and the other forces of the dominant society, they borrowed elements from the culture they fought in order to resist it more effectively.

The laborers in the Lord's vineyard were doomed not to reap the harvest they hoped because of their own cultural assumptions, the racial attitudes of their compatriots, and the persistence of aboriginal culture. For these reasons the missionaries could both praise their efforts in light of the growth of church rolls and yet condemn them in light of their hopes. The increasing discouragement of the missionary directors and their public with Indian work in spite of the agonizingly slow growth of Indian Christianity during the period was reflected in the annual reports of the various societies. Less and less space was devoted to American Indian missions, and mention of them was shifted further back in the report as missionary directors and patrons saw millennial hopes dashed upon the stubborn reality of culture conflict and misunderstanding.

BIBLIOGRAPHICAL ESSAY

THE READER seriously interested in Indian missionary history from the Revolution to the Civil War must soon go to the original sources. The books and pamphlets published in the period were primarily promotional literature of one or another society or denomination; many recent works are still in this tradition, and others are mere chronicles that offer the reader little insight into the complexities of the subject. Far more rewarding are the annual reports and periodicals issued by the missionary societies. These, too, were promotional but offer an account of history in the making through printed missionary letters from the field and reports on headquarters' actions. In the end, though, only the manuscript sources are so accurate or, in some cases, so surprisingly full as the researcher wishes. Many letters have been destroyed but huge numbers still exist, particularly Congregationalist and Presbyterian. A small part of this material has been published, but the far greater portion remains as it was written many years ago.

Rather than duplicate the topical arrangement of these chapters, where the reader is guided to additional material by the footnotes, this essay is organized by denominations and societies according to historical formation. Such an organization reveals the denominational basis of the literature at the same time as it provides a clue to the provenance of archival deposits. This arrangement also offers an insight into the complex history of societal origins, mergers, and schisms in the period. No general history exists of foreign missionary work similar to Colin B. Goodykoontz' *Home Missions on the American Frontier, with Particular Reference to the American Home Missionary Society* (Caldwell, Idaho, 1939), but see the 150-page appendix to the author's dissertation, "Protestant Missionaries and American Indians, 1787-1862" (Cornell University, 1960).

MORAVIAN

Moravian work was divided into Northern and Southern branches, at first unofficially and after 1821 officially, depending upon whether it was directed from Bethlehem, Pennsylvania, or Salem, North Carolina. The Bethlehem leaders organized the first missionary society in the newly independent nation, The Society of the United Brethren for Propagating the Gospel among the Heathen, in 1787. Kenneth G. Hamilton's *John Ettwein and the Moravian Church during the Revolutionary Period* (Bethlehem, 1940) is the biography of the founding bishop. In the *Stated Rules of the Society of the United Brethren, for Propagating the Gospel among the Heathen* (Philadelphia, 1788) are the outlines of policy as laid down by the Elders Conference, but one should also consult August G. Spangenberg, *An Account of the Manner in Which the Protestant Church of the Unitas Fratrum, or United Brethren, Preach the Gospel and Carry on Their Missions among the Heathen* (London, 1788). To commemorate the society's centennial, the standard history was published, *The Society for Propagating the Gospel among the Heathen, 1787 to 1887* (Bethlehem, 1888).

In reality, the post-Revolutionary work of the Northern branch was but an extension of the efforts begun in 1740, and so the history of efforts in this period is contained in the story of earlier work. Old, but still useful, is George H. Loskiel, *History of the Moravian Mission among the Indians in North America from Its Commencement to the Present Time* (London, 1838). A recent book is Elma Gray, *Wilderness Christians: The Moravian Mission to the Delaware Indians* (Ithaca, 1956). Because it is written by a famous missionary, John G. E. Heckewelder's *A Narrative of the Mission of the United Brethren among the Delaware and Mohegan Indians from Its Commencement in the Year 1740 to the Close of the Year 1808* (Philadelphia, 1820) offers the reader both a history and the mentality that operated among the Indians; for further insight, see the journals edited by Paul A. W. Wallace, *Thirty Thousand Miles with John Heckewelder* (Pittsburgh, 1958). The diaries of another famous missionary are edited by Eugene F. Bliss, *Diary of David Zeisberger, a Moravian Missionary among the Indians of Ohio* (Cincinnati, 1885), 2 vols.; his biography has been written by Edmund A. de Schweinitz, *The Life and Times of David Zeisberger, the West-*

ern Pioneer and Apostle of the Indians (Philadelphia, 1871).
The brief effort on the White River is described by Henry E.
Stocker, "History of the Moravian Mission among the Indians
on White River in Indiana," *Transactions of the Moravian Historical Society*, X (1917), part IV, but the reader should go back
to the sources edited by Lawrence H. Gipson, *The Moravian
Indian Mission on the White River. Diaries and Letters, May 5,
1799, to November 12, 1806* (Indianapolis, 1938). The even
shorter lived mission on the Sandusky may be seen through the
missionary's eyes in "Autobiography of Abraham Luckenbach,"
ed. Henry E. Stocker, *Transactions of the Moravian Historical
Society*, X (1917), 359-408. There was a hiatus in United States
Indian work by the Bethlehem group from the War of 1812 until
the return of some of the converted Delawares from Canada in
the late 1830s. The story is followed best in the *United Brethren
Missionary Intelligencer* (Philadelphia, 1822-1849) and *Periodical
Accounts Relating to the Missions of the Church of the United
Brethren, Established among the Heathen* (London, 1790 *et
seq.*). Salem's attention was almost entirely concentrated upon
the Cherokee Tribe, first in the East and then after removal in
the West. Edmund Schwarze, *History of the Moravian Missions
among the Southern Indian Tribes of the United States* (Bethlehem, 1923), is very complete.

In the end, the person interested in the missionary work of this
denomination should read the voluminous manuscripts available
at the Moravian Archives in Bethlehem, Pennsylvania.

QUAKER

Equally small in extent as operations of the Moravians are those
of the Friends. Their work was never formally concentrated in
one denominational society, but rather each Yearly Meeting
individually or in conjunction with a few other meetings supported a few of its members among the Indians. The best guide
to these scattered efforts is Rayner W. Kelsey, *Friends and Indians, 1655-1917* (Philadelphia, 1917).

The major part of the denomination's efforts was devoted to
the Senecas in western New York. A detailed account of this
work by a missionary to the tribe is Halliday Jackson, *Civilization
of the Indian Natives* (Philadelphia, 1830); a long chronicle
prepared for English Friends is *Some Account of the Conduct of*

the Religious Society of Friends toward the Indian Tribes (London, 1844). Both were derived from the extensive and excellent collection of manuscript "Records of the Indian Committee of the Philadelphia Yearly Meeting" deposited at the Department of Records, Third and Arch streets, Philadelphia. Some indication of the nature of these manuscripts as well as those in the Friends Historical Library at Swarthmore College and the Quaker Collection at Haverford College may be obtained from George S. Snyderman, "A Preliminary Survey of American Indian Manuscripts in Repositories of the Philadelphia Area," *Proceedings of the American Philosophical Society*, XCVII (October 1953), 596-610. The labors of the New York Yearly Meeting among the same Indians are recorded in the manuscript minutes preserved at the Committee on Records, 221 East Fifteenth Street, New York City.

CONGREGATIONALIST AND PRESBYTERIAN
POST-REVOLUTIONARY PERIOD

Twenty-one Congregationalist clergy and laymen founded the second society to Christianize Indians in the new United States. Its centennial also produced a history: James Hunnewell, *The Society for Propagating the Gospel among the Indians and Others in North America, 1787-1887* (Boston, 1887). Its feeble efforts to support missionaries are studied best in its records deposited at the Massachusetts Historical Society. Frederic L. Weiss, *The Society for Propagating the Gospel among the Indians and Others in North America* (Dublin, New Hampshire, 1953) contains a checklist of its many published sermons and reports as well as a complete list of missionaries.

This society, plus Harvard College, aided some of the half dozen non-Moravian missionaries that still served among the Indians at the end of the Revolution. The two corporations supported the work of Zachariah Mayhew, the fifth and last member of the famous family that ministered to the praying Indians of Martha's Vineyard; Gideon Hawley and Stephen Badger among the remnant Indians of Massachusetts; John Sargent, who followed in the footsteps of his father and Jonathan Edwards among the Stockbridges; and Samuel Kirkland, the missionary to the Oneidas, who also received additional funds from the Scots Society for Propagating Christian Knowledge. References to these missionaries may be found in the Harvard

College Records, Second Set, vols. 2 and 3, and Harvard College Papers, First Series, Box 4, in addition to the S.P.G. records at the Massachusetts Historical Society. The mission of Samuel Kirkland can be reconstructed best because his manuscript letters and journals are preserved at the Hamilton College Library, Clinton, New York. Several biographies exist: Samuel K. Lothrop, *Life of Samuel Kirkland* (Boston, 1847); Herbert S. Lennox, "Samuel Kirkland's Mission to the Iroquois" (unpublished Ph.D. dissertation, University of Chicago, 1932); Willard Thorp, "Samuel Kirkland, Missionary to the Six Nations; Founder of Hamilton College," in W. Thorp, ed., *Lives of Eighteen from Princeton* (Princeton, 1946). Brief mention of the others is contained in William A. Hallock, *The Venerable Mayhews and the Aboriginal Indians of Martha's Vineyard* (New York, 1814); "Gideon Hawley," in the *Dictionary of American Biography* (New York, 1932), VIII, 418; "A Letter from Gideon Hawley of Marshpee Containing an Account of His Services among the Indians of Massachusetts and New York and a Narrative of His Journey to Onohoghnaga," *Massachusetts Historical Collections,* First Series, IV (1795), 50-67; "Historical and Characteristic Traits of the American Indians in General and Those of Natick in Particular; in a letter by Stephen Badger" *ibid.*, First Series, V (1798), 22-45. A native minister supported by a generous Englishman is the subject of two biographies: William de Loss Love, *Samson Occom and the Christian Indians of New England* (Boston, 1899); Harold W. Blodgett, *Samson Occum* (Hanover, New Hampshire, 1935). Occum was probably the most successful product of Moor's Charity School founded by Eleazar Wheelock. The story of the sister institution of Dartmouth, after its founder's death, can be traced in Frederick Chase, *A History of Dartmouth College and the Town of Hanover, New Hampshire* (Cambridge, 1891, 1913), 2 vols. Its Indian graduates are treated in Eric P. Kelly, "The Dartmouth Indians," *Dartmouth Alumni Magazine*, XXII (December 1929), 122-25; Leon B. Richardson, "The Dartmouth Indians," *ibid.*, XXII (June 1930), 524-27.

THE SECOND GREAT AWAKENING

The standard work upon the formation of societies by these and other denominations during this period is Oliver W. Elsbree, *Rise of Missionary Spirit in America, 1790-1815* (Williamsport, Pennsylvania, 1928). The New York Missionary Society, founded by New York City ministers of Calvinist persuasion in 1796, attempted work among the Chickasaws at first but soon decided the Tuscaroras, Senecas, and Shinnecocks of their own state offered a better chance of success. The manuscript records are found among the American Board papers at Houghton Library, Harvard. Some of the letters are printed in the *New-York Missionary Magazine* (New York, 1800-1803). The printed reports of the society are rare now, but a complete set is in the manuscript Directors' Records at Houghton. The minutes end abruptly in mid-June, 1820, when the society was absorbed by the United Foreign Missionary Society.

Other societies supporting itinerant missionaries among Indians as well as frontier whites were the Northern Missionary Society (1796), whose printed *Annual Reports of the Board of Directors* (1806-1820) are even rarer than those of its sister society in New York City; the Missionary Society of Connecticut (1797), whose founding and history are well treated in Charles Keller, *Second Great Awakening in Connecticut* (New Haven, 1942); and the Massachusetts Missionary Society (1798), whose activities may be partially gleaned from the *Massachusetts Missionary Magazine* (Salem and Boston, 1803-1808) and the *Panoplist* (Boston, 1805-1817).

In name only did the Standing Committee on Missions of the General Assembly of the Presbyterian Church (1802) represent the whole church; its work was in reality regional and itinerant. Brief attention is given to its founding in Clifford Drury, *Presbyterian Panorama—One Hundred and Fifty Years of National Missions History* (Philadelphia, 1952), but see the manuscript minutes now at the Board of [Presbyterian] National Missions, 156 Fifth Avenue, New York City. Its chief Indian missionary, Gideon Blackburn, served among the Cherokees in the first decade of the nineteenth century. Unfortunately, no manuscript letters exist for him, but some letters may be located in the *Panoplist, the General Assembly's Missionary Magazine* (Philadelphia, 1805-1807), and the *Evangelical Intelligencer* (Philadelphia, 1807-1809). The standard references to these and other relevant materials about him are mentioned in Verner M. Queener, "Gideon Blackburn," *East Tennessee Historical Society Publications*, No. 6 (1934), 12-28.

The Pittsburgh Synod created a missionary society in the same year as the General Assembly. Its history is briefly told in Clifford Drury, "Western Missionary Society, 1802-1836," *Journal of Presbyterian Historical Society*, XXVIII (December 1950), 233-48. The synod's proceedings are published in *Records of the Synod of Pittsburgh, from Its First Organization, September 29, 1802, to October, 1832, Inclusive* (Pittsburgh, 1852), extracts of which pertinent to Indian work have been republished in William W. Sweet, *Religion on the American Frontier: The Presbyterians, 1783-1840* (Chicago, 1936), 605-35. The missionary society records have been copied by Thomas C. Pears, Jr., and are deposited at the Presbyterian Historical Society, Philadelphia. Its most famous missionary wrote his autobiography, *A Memoir of Rev. Joseph Badger* (Hudson, Ohio, 1851). The society also published the *Western Missionary Magazine* (Washington, Pennsylvania, 1803-1805) for a short time.

AMERICAN BOARD

Though the American Board of Commissioners for Foreign Missions was founded in 1810 and resembled for a short time the other societies of that period, it ushered in the new era of large treasuries, numerous workers, and extensive operations. Although it started as a broadly interdenominational society, it soon became the agency of Congregationalists and New School Presbyterians. The numerous histories of the board, in order of publication, are: Joseph Tracy, "History of the American Board of Commissioners for Foreign Missions," in J. Tracy, ed., *History of American Missions to the Heathen, from Their Commencement to the Present Time* (Worcester, Massachusetts, 1840); Rufus Anderson, *Memorial Volume of the First Fifty Years of the American Board of Commissioners for Foreign Missions* (Boston, 1861); William Strong, *The Story of the American Board: An Account of the First Hundred Years of the American Board of Commissioners for Foreign Missions* (Boston, 1910); Clifford J. Phillips, "Protestant America and the Pagan World: The First Half Century of the American Board of Commissioners for Foreign Missions, 1810-1860" (unpublished Ph.D. dissertation, Harvard University, 1954). Not only did the board support more Indian missionaries in the period between the War of 1812 and the Civil War than any other society, but its records are the most complete for the period. Except for the Records of the Prudential Committee and Subcommittee Reports at Congregational House, 14½ Beacon Street, Boston, the huge collection of many volumes is deposited at Houghton Library, Harvard. Although there are no substitutes for the actual letters to and from headquarters, the *Annual Reports* (1810-1862+) are good on the activities of the missions and many of the letters from the field were published in the *Missionary Herald* (Boston, 1818-1862+), although these were heavily edited at times. A small sampling of these letters is found in William W. Sweet, *Religion on the American Frontier, 1783-1850: The Congregationalists* (Chicago, 1939), 340-67.

Certain of the American Board's Indian missions are well covered by books, articles, and even, at times, published letters, while other stations are entirely neglected. The first Indian station, founded in 1817, is the subject of Robert S. Walker, *Torchlights to the Cherokees: The Brainerd Mission* (New York, 1931). A biography of one of the Cherokee missionaries is Althea Bass, *Cherokee Messenger* (Norman, 1936), and the life of one of the most illustrious products of the mission schools is told in Ralph H. Gabriel, *Elias Boudinot, Cherokee, and His America* (Norman, 1941). No really satisfactory account exists for the Choctaw missions, but see Dawson A. Phelps, "The Choctaw Mission: An Experiment in Civilization," *Journal of Mississippi History*, XIV (January 1952), 35-62; William L. Hiemstra, "Early Presbyterian Missions among the Choctaw and Chicasaw Indians in Mississippi," *ibid.*, X (January 1948), 8-16; William A. Love, "The Mayhew Mission to the Choctaws," *Mississippi Historical Society Publications*, XI (1910), 363-402. The Arkansas Cherokee mission history is found in the memoirs of one of its leading missionaries, Cepheas Washburn, *Reminiscences of the Indians* (Richmond, 1869). Paralleling the founding of these missions was an attempt to instruct heathen young people from all parts of the world at a school in a small Connecticut town. The rise and fall of this enterprise is traced in Edward C. Starr, *A History of Cornwall, Connecticut, a Typical New England Town* (New Haven, 1926), 136-57; Carolyn T. Foreman, "The Foreign Mission School at Cornwall, Connecticut," *Chronicles of Oklahoma*, VII (September 1929), 242-59.

The board expanded its Indian work beyond the southern tribes through absorption of other societies in the latter half of the 1820s. The United Foreign Missionary Society, which had been founded in 1817, transferred its stations to the American

Board in 1826. Thus its manuscript records are with those of the board at Houghton; it printed its *Annual Reports* and published many of its missionaries' letters in the *American Missionary Register* (New York, 1820-1825). Some accounts of its work among the Osages include Morris Wardell, "Protestant Missions among the Osages, 1820-1838," *Chronicles of Oklahoma,* II (September 1924), 285-97; Carolyn T. Foreman, "Hopefield Mission in Osage Nation, 1823-1837," *ibid.,* XXVIII (Summer 1950), 193-205; T. F. Morison, "Mission Neosho: The First Kansas Mission," *Kansas Historical Quarterly,* IV (August 1935), 227-34; William W. Graves, *The First Protestant Osage Missions, 1820-1837* (Oswego, Kansas, 1949). Letters from its Mackinaw station are edited by Charles Anderson in "Frontier Mackinac Island, 1823-1834: Letters of William Montague and Amanda Ferry," *Journal of the Presbyterian Historical Society,* XXV (December 1947), 192-222, XXVI (June, September 1948), 101-27, 182-91. The mission, received by the board from the Missionary Society of the Synod of South Carolina and Georgia, is treated briefly by Dawson A. Phelps, "The Chickasaw Mission," *Journal of Mississippi History,* XIII (October 1951), 226-35. To inspect these new acquisitions as well as the older stations, the board sent one of its secretaries southward, and J. Orin Oliphant has edited the journal and provided an interpretative introduction in *Through the South and the West with Jeremiah Evarts in 1826* (Lewisburg, Pennsylvania, 1956).

The board also received stations among the Tuscaroras and Senecas through an earlier merger of the New York and United Foreign Missionary Societies. Narratives of missionaries at these stations are printed in the *Buffalo Historical Society Publications,* VI (1903), and Harriet S. Caswell, *Our Life among the Iroquois Indians* (Boston, 1892). A brief article about one of the leading missionaries is William N. Fenton, "Toward the Gradual Civilization of the Indian Natives: The Missionary and Linguistic Work of Asher Wright (1803-1875) among the Senecas of Western New York," *Proceedings of the American Philosophical Society,* C (December 1956), 567-81.

Indian removal westward in the 1830s forced the reestablishment of missions among tribes formerly served and encouraged expansion among other tribes now neighbors to their charges. For chronicles of relocated work, see Carolyn T. Foreman, "The Cherokee Gospel Tidings of Dwight Mission," *Chronicles of*

Oklahoma, XII (December 1934), 454-69; and among the Choc-taws, Lona E. Millor, "Wheelock Mission," *ibid.,* XXIX (Autumn 1951), 314-23. New work among the Ojibwas can be approached through Edward D. Neill, "Memoir of William T. Boutwell, the First Christian Minister Resident among the Indians of Min-nesota," in Macalester College Department of History, Literature, and Political Science, *Contributions* (1892), Second Series, 1-59. Much excellent material exists upon work among the Sioux of Minnesota. Two books by Stephen R. Riggs, the chief missionary, give an excellent idea of the history: *Tah-koo Wah-kan; or the Gospel among the Dakotas* (Boston, 1869), and *Mary and I; or Forty Years with the Sioux* (Boston, 1880). The biography of the two Pond brothers, written by a son and nephew, is Samuel W. Pond, Jr., *Two Volunteer Missionaries among the Sioux; or the Story of the Labors of Samuel W. and Gideon H. Pond* (Boston, 1893). Theodore Blegen has written about them in "The Pond Brothers," *Minnesota History,* XV (September 1934), 273-81, and edited, "Two Missionaries in the Sioux Country: The Narrative of Samuel W. Pond," *ibid.,* XXI (1940), 15-32, 158-75, 272-83. Lastly, one should read Charles M. Gates, "The Lacqui Parle Indian Mission," *ibid.,* XVI (June 1935), 133-51. Much of the correspondence of the short-lived Pawnee mission is in "Letters Concerning the Presbyterian Mission in the Pawnee Country, near Bellevue, Neb., 1831-1849," *Kansas Historical Col-lections,* XIV (1915-1918), 570-84; the mission's story is told briefly by John Dunbar, "The Presbyterian Mission among the Pawnee Indians in Nebraska, 1834-1836," *ibid.,* XII (1909-1910), 314-22.

Probably more books exist upon the board's Oregon mission than any other. On the tours to the West, see the report by Samuel Parker, *Journal of an Exploring Tour beyond the Rocky Mountains, under the Direction of the American Board of Com-missioners for Foreign Missions . . ., in the Years 1835, 1836, and 1837* (Ithaca, 1838); F. G. Young, ed., "Journal and Report by Dr. Marcus Whitman of His Tour of Exploration with Rev. Samuel Parker in 1835 beyond the Rocky Mountains," *Oregon Historical Quarterly,* XXVIII (September 1928), 239-57. Good bibliographical references to the extensive literature can be found in the biographies of the major missionaries by Clifford M. Drury: *Henry Harmon Spalding* (Caldwell, Idaho, 1936); *Marcus Whitman, M.D., Pioneer and Martyr* (Caldwell, 1937), *Elkanah and Mary Walker, Pioneers among the Spokanes* (Caldwell, 1940). This same author has edited *The Diaries and Letters of Henry H. Spalding and Asa Bowen Smith Relating to the Nez Perce Mission, 1838-1842* (Glendale, Calif., 1958).

How slavery disrupted the southern Indian missions in the two decades prior to the Civil War is the theme of Robert T. Lewit, "Indian Missions and Antislavery Sentiment: A Conflict of Evangelical and Humanitarian Ideals," *Mississippi Valley Historical Review,* L (June 1963), 39-55.

OLD SCHOOL PRESBYTERIAN

Old School Presbyterians disapproved of the American Board, and the absorption of the United Foreign Missionary Society stimulated them to revive the Western Missionary Society, which had earlier turned over its work to the U.F.M.S. The organizational letters of the new society with its new title are in Guy S. Klett, ed., "The Correspondence of the Western Foreign Missionary Society," *Journal of the Presbyterian Historical Society,* XXXVI (June 1958), 89-113, XXXVII (March 1959), 31-43. The manuscript Minutes of the Executive Committee are in the Presbyterian Board of Foreign Missions Library, 165 Fifth Avenue, New York City. After the schism of 1837, the Old School Presbyterians established their own Board of Foreign Missions by absorbing the missionaries and the assets of the Pittsburgh organization. For the views of a leading opponent of the American Board as well as a history, see Ashbel Green, *Historical Sketch; or Compendious View of the Domestic and Foreign Missions of the Presbyterian Church of the United States* (Philadelphia, 1838). Drury in his *Presbyterian Panorama* also treats the subject briefly. The best history of this society's Indian missions is Harold S. Faust, "The Presbyterian Mission to the American Indian during the Period of Indian Removal, 1838-1893" (unpublished Th.D. dissertation, Temple University, 1943), condensed as "The American Indian in Tragedy and Triumph," *Journal of Presbyterian Historical Society,* XXII (1944), 88-123, 137-71. This society's missionaries' letters constitute the second most important manuscript source available for Indian work in the period between the War of 1812 and the Civil War. On deposit at the Presbyterian Historical Society, they are described in Charles A. Anderson, "Index of American Correspondence," *Journal of the Presbyterian Historical Society,* XXXI (March

1953), 63-70, although the specific references as to location of various manuscripts are unreliable. Some of the letters and diaries have been edited by Anderson in the *Journal*: "Letters of William Hamilton, 1811-1891," XXXV (September 1957), 157-70, XXXVI (March 1958), 53-65; "Diaries of Peter Dougherty," XXX (1952), 95-114, 175-92, 236-53. An associate, Guy Klett, has edited "Missionary Endeavors of the Presbyterian Church among the Blackfeet Indians in the 1850's," *ibid.*, XIX (December 1941), 327-54. The stories of some Presbyterian missions have been written: Ruth Craker, *First Protestant Mission in the Grand Traverse Region* (East Jordan, Michigan, 1932); Pryor Plank, "The Iowa Sac and Fox Mission and Its Missionaries, Rev. Samuel M. Irvin and Wife," *Kansas Historical Collections*, X (1907-1908), 312-26; Virginia E. Lauderdale, "Tullahassee Mission," *Chronicles of Oklahoma*, XXVI (Autumn 1948), 285-300; Robert M. Loughridge, "History of Presbyterian Mission Work among the Creek Indians from 1832 to 1888," unpublished manuscript deposited at Presbyterian Historical Society. Roland Hinds, "Early Creek Missions," *Chronicles of Oklahoma*, XVIII (March 1939), 48-61, not only discusses the Presbyterian stations to the Creeks but also clarifies the complicated mission history of that tribe. Letters from the field were published with the usual editing in *Foreign Missionary Chronicle* (Pittsburgh, 1833-1849), *Foreign Missionary* (New York, 1842-1862+), and *The Home and Foreign Record* (Philadelphia, 1850-1862+). *Annual Reports* commence in 1838.

OTHER EFFORTS

Missionary societies resulting from various schisms in the Congregationalist and Presbyterian denominations supported a few missionaries among the Indians. The work of the Cumberland Presbyterians receives brief treatment in Benjamin W. MacDonnold, *History of the Cumberland Presbyterian Church* (Nashville, 1888), but even these few facts should be checked against the reports of the United States Commissioner of Indian Affairs. When the Old School Presbyterians split finally in 1861, the mission society of the Presbyterian Church, C.S.A., took over southern Indian missions, as can be seen in John L. Wilson, "History of the Foreign Missions as Related to the Southern Presbyterian Church and Columbia Seminary," *Memorial Volume of the Semi-Centennial of the Theological Seminary at Columbia, South Carolina* (Columbia, 1884). The general history of an organization founded in 1846 by Congregationalists of strong antislavery persuasion is Augustus F. Beard, *A Crusade of Brotherhood: A History of the American Missionary Association* (Boston, 1909). It published the usual *Annual Reports*. The story of its chief mission is traced by Frank H. Foster, "The Oberlin Ojibway Mission," *Papers of the Ohio Church History Society*, II (1892), 1-25. The association's manuscripts at Fisk University pertain mainly to post-Civil War aid to the Negro.

BAPTIST

Baptist missionary work among the Indians began only after the War of 1812. Before that time, the denomination devoted its energies to increasing its white members, but a few scattered efforts at itineracy among the Indians are covered by the very complete research of Albert L. Vail, *The Morning Hour of American Baptist Missions* (Philadelphia, 1907). In 1814 the Baptists established the General Missionary Convention of the Baptist Denomination in the United States of America for Foreign Missions, and Other Important Objects Relating to the Redeemer's Kingdom, more popularly known as the Triennial Convention because it met every three years. The most recent account of its work is Robert G. Torbet, *Venture of Faith: The Story of the American Baptist Foreign Mission Society, 1814-1954* (Philadelphia, 1954), but the older work of William Gammell, *History of American Baptist Missions in Asia, Africa, Europe and North America* (Boston, 1840, and later editions), and Solomon Peck, "History of the Missions of the Baptist General Convention," in Tracy, ed., *History of American Missions,* are still useful for Indian work slighted by Torbet. The minutes of the Baptist Board of Foreign Missions are available in typed extracts at the Filing Department, American Baptist Foreign Missionary Society, 152 Madison Avenue, New York City. Much information is in the *Annual Reports of the Baptist Board of Foreign Missions for the United States, Combined with the Proceedings of the General Convention of the Baptist Denomination of the United States at Their Triennial Meeting* and in its magazine published in Boston under various titles: *Massachusetts Baptist Missionary Magazine* (1817-1824), *American Baptist Magazine and Missionary Intelligencer* (1825-1835), *American Baptist Magazine* (1850-1862+). *The Latter Day Luminary* (Philadelphia) was the specific organ of the mission board from 1818 to 1825.

In 1817 the board started work among the southern Indians, which is best followed in Gammell and the *Annual Reports,* but brief mention is in Walter B. Posey, *Baptist Church in the Lower Mississippi Valley, 1776-1845* (Lexington, 1957); James Moffit, "Early Baptist Missionary Work among the Cherokees," *East Tennessee Historical Society Publications,* No. 12 (1940), 16-27; Robert Fleming, *Sketch of the Life of Elder Humphrey Posey, First Baptist Missionary to the Cherokee Indians* (Philadelphia, 1852); H.F.S., ed., *Memorial of Thomas Roberts* (Newark, N. J., 1867). In the same year the famous Isaac McCoy commenced a mission in Indiana. The best published source on McCoy's work is his own *History of Baptist Indian Missions Embracing Remarks on the Former and Present Condition of the Aboriginal Tribes; Their Settlement within the Indian Territory, and Their Future Prospects* (Washington, 1840). However, no one interested in Baptist work should fail to read the Isaac McCoy Papers at the Kansas State Historical Society in Topeka. Deposited there also are the papers of his colleagues Robert Simerwell, Francis Barker, John G. Pratt, Jotham Meeker, and Johnson Lykins. Since no letters were apparently preserved at the central headquarters of the mission society, these collections are invaluable as the only extensive documents about Baptist field practices. Some of McCoy's publicity efforts, besides his *History,* are *Periodical Account of Baptist Missions within the Indian Territory, for the Year Ending December 21, 1836* (Shawanoe Baptist Mission, Indian Territory, 1837), and *The Annual Register of Indian Affairs within the Indian (or Western) Territory* (1835-1838).

Because McCoy had been employed more as a removal agent in the 1830s by the federal government than as a missionary, the Baptist Board finally dismissed him. Shortly thereafter in 1842 he founded the American Indian Mission Association. The usual constitution and address is in *The Baptist Banner and Western Pioneer* (Cincinnati) extra, June 18, 1842, and the initial meeting is reported in the same periodical for November 17, 1842. The new organization published the usual *Proceedings of the Annual Meeting* (1843-1852), and the usual magazine, *Indian Advocate* (Louisville, 1846-1855), but the association never flourished, and it transferred its few stations to the Domestic Mission Board of the Southern Baptist Convention. This latter group had been organized in 1845 as a result of the split in the denomination over the issue of slavery, and had naturally received the southern Indian missions in the division. For the history of the group, see William W. Barnes, *The Southern Baptist Convention, 1845-1953* (Nashville, 1954). Books about the Indian missions are Carl C. Rister, *Baptist Missions among the American Indians* (Atlanta, 1944), and Robert Hamilton, *The Gospel among the Red Man: The History of the Southern Baptist Indian Missions* (Nashville, 1930), but the latter is unreliable at times. A clearer idea of its Indian activities can be obtained from the published *Proceedings*.

After the secession of the Southern Baptists from the Baptist Missionary Convention, the northern members changed the organization's name to the American Baptist Missionary Union and supported the stations among the northern aborigines. *The Baptist Missionary Magazine* remained its organ and contains its reports. After the Civil War, the union conveyed its Indian interests to the American Baptist Home Mission Society, which had opened Indian missions as early as 1853, as may be discovered in its *Annual Reports*.

METHODIST

In 1820 the General Conference established the Missionary Society of the Methodist Episcopal Church, but this association merely reported the decisions of the bishops and the Annual Conferences. Such divided responsibility not only weakened the organization, but rendered it difficult for the society, not to say for present-day researchers, to keep track of the missionary efforts of the denomination. Fortunately, Wade C. Barclay has gathered all the available material in his *History of Methodist Missions, Part One, Early American Methodism, 1769-1844* (New York, 1949), 2 vols., but the older Nathan Bangs, *History of the Missions under the Care of the Missionary Society of the Methodist Episcopal Church* (New York, 1832), offers the viewpoint of the earlier period. No manuscript sources remain except for the brief minutes of the Board of Managers in the Library of the Board of Missions of the Methodist Church, 475 Riverside Drive, New York City, and a few letters from the Oregon mission preserved at the Board of National Missions, 1701 Arch Street, Philadelphia. Due to the dispersion of authority for missionary work, the *Annual Reports of the Missionary Society of the Methodist Church* are not always complete. Letters of fieldworkers are published in the *Methodist Magazine* (New York, 1818-1840), the *Christian Advocate* (New York, 1826-1862+), and the *Monthly Missionary Notice* (New York, 1842-1845).

Material about the famous Wyandot mission can be found in William W. Sweet, *Circuit-Rider Days along the Ohio, Being the Journals of the Ohio Conference from Its Organization in 1812 to 1826* (Cincinnati, 1923); Joseph Mitchell, *The Missionary Pioneer; or a Brief Memoir of the Life, Labours, and Death of John Stewart, (Man of Colour), Founder of the Mission among the Wyandotts at Upper Sandusky* (New York, 1827); Emil Schlup, "The Wyandot Mission," *Ohio Archaeological and Historical Society Quarterly*, XV (April 1906), 163-81. One of this mission's leading missionaries, James B. Finley, has many books under his name, but the basis for all of them is *History of the Wyandott Mission at Upper Sandusky, Ohio, under the Direction of the Methodist Episcopal Church* (Cincinnati, 1840).

Mission labors among the Oneidas of Wisconsin and the Indians of that area can be followed in the biography of the founder of these stations, Barnes Hall, *The Life of Rev. John Clark* (New York, 1857), and the autobiography of one of his successors, John H. Pitezel, *Lights and Shades of Missionary Life; Containing Travels, Sketches, Incidents, and Missionary Efforts, during Nine Years Spent in the Region of Lake Superior* (Cincinnati, 1857). Of additional interest, but to be used carefully, are the autobiographies of native missionaries: George Copway, *The Life, History, and Travels of Kah-ge-ga-gah-bowh, (George Copway), a Young Indian Chief of the Ojebwa Nation, a Convert to the Christian Faith, and a Missionary to His People for Twelve Years* (1st ed., Albany, 1847); Peter Jones, *History of the Ojebway Indians; with Especial Reference to Their Conversion to Christianity* (London, 1861). Methodist missionary history among the Indians of Minnesota is told in the autobiography of one of the leaders, Alfred Brunson, *The Western Pioneer; or, Incidents of the Life and Times of Rev. Alfred Brunson* (Cincinnati, 1872, 1879), 2 vols.

The most written-about Methodist endeavor was Jason Lee's Oregon mission, which was as dramatic as it was insignificant from the viewpoint of Indian missionary history. The best guides to the lengthy bibliography are Barclay, *Methodist Missions*, II, 200-62, and Cornelius J. Brosnan, *Jason Lee: Prophet of New Oregon* (New York, 1932). Many of the missionaries' letters have been printed in various issues of the *Oregon Historical*

Society Quarterly, as can be seen from references in the preceding. The best story of Methodist labors among the removed eastern tribes and others in the Indian Territory is J. J. Lutz, "The Methodist Missions among the Indian Tribes in Kansas," *Kansas State Historical Transactions,* IX (1905-1906), 160-230. For first-hand accounts, see Jerome C. Berryman, "A Circuit Rider's Frontier Experiences," *Kansas State Historical Collections,* XVI (1923-1925), 211-19; "Letters from the Indian Missions in Kansas," *ibid.,* 227-71, both of which are reprinted in William W. Sweet, *Religion on the American Frontier, 1783-1840: The Methodists* (Chicago, 1946), IV, 499-551. Of interest in regard to the Indian Mission Conference is William H. Goode, *Outposts of Zion, with Limnings of Mission Life* (Cincinnati, 1864). The best account of the Central Manual Labor School for these Indians is the compilation by Martha B. Caldwell, *Annals of Shawnee Methodist Mission and Indian Manual Labor School* (Topeka, 1939).

The separation of Methodists into northern and southern branches in 1845 meant, of course, the division of Indian work. The southern work is chronicled in the *Annual Report of the Missionary Society of the Methodist Episcopal Church South* (1846-1862+) and the southern edition of the *Christian Advocate;* the northern church continued the early *Annual Reports* and its version of the *Christian Advocate.* Wade Barclay has treated the northern mission story in briefer scope than his two earlier volumes in *History of Methodist Missions, Part Two, the Methodist Church, 1845-1939* (New York, 1957).

EPISCOPALIAN

In the same year as the Methodists, the Episcopalians organized the Domestic and Foreign Missionary Society of the Protestant Episcopal Church in the United States. Information about the founding is in the *Report of a Committee . . . on the Subject of a General Missionary Society* (Philadelphia, 1820), and in William W. Manross, *The Episcopal Church in the United States, 1800-1840* (New York, 1938). The standard history is Julia C. Emory, *A Century of Endeavor, 1821-1921: A Record of the First Hundred Years of the Domestic and Foreign Missionary Society of the Protestant Episcopal Church in the U.S.A.* (New York, 1921). The best guide to the actual history remains the annual *Proceedings of the Board of Missions* (1823-1862+), and its magazines, the *Missionary Record of the Domestic and Foreign Missionary Society of the Protestant Episcopal Church in the U.S.A.* (Philadelphia, 1833-1835), and after the division into a Foreign and a Domestic Committee in 1835 to handle the increased business, *The Spirit of Missions* (New York, 1836-1862+).

Although there is little available about early Episcopalian work among the Oneidas, the chief interest of the society for most of the period prior to the Civil War, the Wisconsin phase of missions to this tribe is discussed by an actual observer, Albert G. Ellis, in "Some Account of the Advent of the New York Indians into Wisconsin," *Wisconsin Historical Collections*, II (1855), 415-49; and "Fifty-four Years' Recollections of Men and Events in Wisconsin," *ibid.*, VII (1873-1876), 210-39. A biography of one of the missionaries in this period is Howard Greene, *The Reverend Richard Fish Cadle, a Missionary of the Protestant Episcopal Church in the Territories of Michigan and Wisconsin in the Early Nineteenth Century* (Waukesha, Wisconsin, 1936), and J. K. Bloomfield, *The Oneidas* (New York, 1907), is mainly the story of Episcopalian efforts among this tribe while in Wisconsin.

Shortly before the Civil War, James Breck started his mission among the Indians of Minnesota. His letters are edited by Charles Breck, *Life of the Reverend James Lloyd Breck, D.D., Chiefly from Letters Written by Himself* (New York, 1883), and his biography is by Theodore I. Holcombe, *An Apostle of the Wilderness, James Lloyd Breck, D.D., His Missions and His Schools* (New York, 1903). The later story of these Indians was the life concern of Henry B. Whipple, *Lights and Shadows of a Long Episcopate; Being the Reminiscences and Recollections of . . . Henry B. Whipple, Bishop of Minnesota* (New York, 1899).

LUTHERAN

The late start and small extent of Lutheran missionary work among the American Indians is well covered in Albert Keiser, *Lutheran Mission Work among the American Indians* (Minneapolis, 1922), and Charles F. Luckhard, *Faith in the Forest: A True Story of Pioneer Lutheran Missionaries Laboring among the Chippewa Indians in Michigan, 1833-1868* (Sebewaing, Michigan, 1952). Both books contain good bibliographies.

LITERATURE IN THE INDIAN LANGUAGES

Even without reading the missionary transliteration of native languages, a reader can determine the contents of most pamphlets and newspapers produced for Indian eyes from line-by-line translations, convenient English summaries, or even from the titles. Periodicals produced for Indian readers by the American Board were *Cherokee Almanac* (Park Hill, Indian Territory, 1836-1861); *Choctaw Almanac* (Union and Park Hill, Indian Territory, 1836-1844); *Ne Jaguhnigoagesqwathah; or, the Mental Elevator* (Buffalo Creek Reservation, New York, 1841-1850 irregularly); *Dakota Friend* (American Board Mission, Minnesota Territory, 1850-1852). Baptist newspapers were *Cherokee Messenger* (Cherokee Indian Territory, 1844-1846), and *Shawanoe Sun* (Shawnee Mission, Indian Territory [Kansas], 1835-1844). From these presses in the field as well as those near society headquarters came a small flood of native language Bibles, school texts, religious tracts, and other literature for the Indian. For lists of these publications, see the references in footnote 26 of Chapter Three (page 49). A list of publications printed in the Indian Territory by and for Indians may be found in Carolyn T. Foreman, *Oklahoma Imprints, 1835-1907: A History of Printing in Oklahoma before Statehood* (Norman, 1936); and Lester Hargrett, *Oklahoma Imprints, 1835-1890* (New York, 1951). The latter author has also compiled a list of formal Indian law codes, *A Bibliography of the Constitution and Laws of the American Indians* (Cambridge, 1947).

FOR GENERAL CONTEXT

To place Indian missionary work in perspective, the reader needs four types of material: general American religious histories, tribal histories, the story of governmental policy, and a knowledge of anthropological theory. The first is taken care of splendidly in Nelson Burr's bibliographical volumes in James W. Smith and A. L. Jamieson, ed., *Religion in American Life* (Princeton, 1961). Tribal histories are among the items compiled in George P. Murdock's extensive *Ethnographic Bibliography of North America* (3d ed., New Haven, 1960). Some tribal histories that are particularly relevant for their inclusion of missionary work are: Marion Starkey, *The Cherokee Nation* (New York,

1946); Henry T. Malone, *Cherokees of the Old South: A People in Transition* (Athens, Georgia, 1956); Morris Wardell, *A Political History of the Cherokee Nation, 1838-1907* (Norman, 1938); Angie Debo, *Rise and Fall of the Choctaw Republic* (Norman, 1934); Horatio B. Cushman, *History of the Choctaw, Chickasaw, and Natchez Indians* (Greenville, Texas, 1899); Henry Harvey, *History of the Shawnee Indians, from the Year 1681 to 1854, Inclusive* (Cincinnati, 1855); Francis Haines, *The Nez Percés, Tribesmen of the Columbia Plateau* (Norman, 1955); and the encyclopedic histories by Grant Foreman: *Indian Removal: The Emigration of the Five Civilized Tribes of Indians* (Norman, 1932); *Advancing the Frontier, 1830-1860* (Norman, 1933); *The Last Trek* (Chicago, 1946). The only state historical journal that consistently publishes articles about Indian history, including mission life, in issue after issue is the *Chronicles of Oklahoma*, but, unfortunately, many articles lack in scholarship.

A brief general introduction to American Indian history is William T. Hagan, *American Indians* (Chicago, 1961). On governmental policy, see the older George D. Harmon, *Sixty Years of Indian Affairs, Political, Economic, and Diplomatic, 1789-1850* (Chapel Hill, 1941), which is superseded in part by Francis Paul Prucha, *American Indian Policy in the Formative Years: The Indian Trade and Intercourse Acts, 1790-1834* (Cambridge, 1962). The actual reports by government agents in the field are in the Bureau of Indian Affairs, National Archives; particularly valuable are the School Files.

This is not the place to repeat the bibliography found in any good introductory text on cultural anthropology, but the reader should consult two articles of particular relevance to missionaries and acculturation: G. Gordon Brown, "Missions and Cultural Diffusion," *American Journal of Sociology*, L (November 1944), 214-19; Evon Z. Vogt, "The Acculturation of American Indians," *Annals of the American Academy of Political and Social Science*, CCCXI (May 1957), 137-46. The most recent general book upon acculturation is Edward H. Spicer, Edward P. Dozier, Edmund M. Bruner, Evon Z. Vogt, David French, and Helen Codere, *Perspectives in American Indian Culture Change* (Chicago, 1961). Appearing too late to influence the writing of this book was the important volume by Edward H. Spicer, *Cycles of Conquest: The Impact of Spain, Mexico, and the United States on the Southwest, 1533-1960* (Tucson, 1962).

INDEX

Abel, Annie H., 103
Academies, Indian, 27-31
Acculturation theory, x-xi
Agriculture: reasons for promotion of, 70-72; settlement patterns, 72-73; and selection of mission site, 73; methods used to promote, 73-82 *passim;* and white male role, 74-80 *passim;* and white female role, 74-80 *passim;* problems of promotion, 78-81; and severalty, 81-82
Alcohol. *See* Liquor
Alienation, Indian from own society, 42, 122-23
American Baptist Missionary Union, 67, 153-54
American Board of Commissioners for Foreign Missions: goal of, 3; favored civilization first, 6n; knew missions spread civilization, 10; founded Foreign Missionary School, 28; native language publications, 32, 35, 49n; and use of native languages, 34, 49; list of social and moral virtues, 35; used camp meetings, 47; and religious doctrine, 51; attitude toward native church members, 54, 55, 62; interdenominational relations, 59, 63, 94, 97; encouraged temperance societies, 65; use of native missionaries, 67-68; encouraged white male role, 78, 80; promotion of white government, 83-84; and American Fur Company, 96; founding of Sioux mission, 97, 113, 143; and removal, 102-103, 104, 105;

American Board (*continued*): and Cherokee factionalism, 138-43 *passim;* and Choctaw factionalism, 139-42 *passim;* estimates of missionary success, 153-54; successful missions of, 154-56. *See also* Brainerd mission; Butler, Elizur; Butrick, Daniel; Dwight mission; Evarts, Jeremiah; Kingsbury, Cyrus; Mackinaw station; Riggs, Stephen R.; Worcester, Samuel
American Fur Company, 95-96
American Society for the Promotion of Temperance, 65
Anáwángmane, Simon, 120-21
Apostasy, 111-12, 121
Arch, John, 43
Army, U.S.: relations with missionaries, 91

Baptist Board of Foreign Missions: goal of, 3; fusing of Protestantism and civilization, 7-8; preferred native to white missionaries, 67; appropriations for home building, 74; removal policy, 101-102
Baptists: varied on civilization-first argument, 6n; native language publications, 49n; approach to native conversion, 52; evidence of native conversion, 54; church admission requirements, 57-58; interdenominational relations, 59, 63, 93-94; church government, 63; use of voluntary associations, 66-67; and American Fur Company, 96; view of Cherokee mission, 156. *See also* American Baptist